Marx's Interpretation of History

Marx's Interpretation of History

Melvin Rader

New York
Oxford University Press
1979

Copyright © 1979 by Oxford University Press, Inc.

Library of Congress Cataloging in Publication Data
Rader, Melvin Miller, 1903–
Marx's interpretation of history.
Includes index.
1. Marx, Karl, 1818–1883. 2. History—Philosophy. I. Title.
B3305.M74R32   901   78-14851   ISBN 0-19-502475-5
ISBN 0-19-502475-3 pbk.

Preface

The purpose of the present book is mainly to clarify rather than to criticize Marx's interpretation of history. To write an adequate criticism would be a far-ranging and formidable task. It would be necessary to criticize his holistic method and use of heuristic models, his attempt to find laws of historical development, his predictions on the basis of these laws, his concept of man as an historical agent, and the relation of his theory of history to human values. Before undertaking such a criticism, one would need to understand what Marx says. There has been so much misunderstanding that the preliminary task of clarification is as difficult as it is essential. This task has been sufficient to undertake in the present book.

The book is addressed to Marxist scholars in philosophy, history, and the social sciences, and to students, teachers, and other readers who, without being scholars in Marxism, may want to understand what Marx said and meant. Because I am addressing a wide audience I try to write lucidly in ordinary language.

My intent is to examine what Marx said and not to rely on secondary sources. I have been wary even in citing Engels, his close friend and occasional collaborator. Aware that their opinions were not identical, Marx objected to lumping the ideas of Engels with his. "What is so very strange," he remarked about a contemporary reviewer, "is how he treats the two of us as one: 'Marx and Engels *says*' etc."[1] This "strange" lumping together, with Lenin's ideas

---

[1]Letter to Engels, August 1, 1856, in Marx/Engels, *Werke* (Berlin: Dietz Verlag, 1953–1968), Vol. 29, p. 68. For detailed comment on the differences between Marx and Engels see Norman Levine, *The Tragic Deception: Marx Contra Engels* (Oxford, Santa Barbara: Clio Press, 1975).

later dumped into the pot, has persisted down to the present day. The safest procedure is to allow Marx to speak for himself and not to put the words of others in his mouth.

My impetus in writing this book springs from contradictions in the various interpretations and in the apparent contradictions in the writings of Marx. I have tried to find an underlying consistency in his complex vision of history, but not at the cost of glossing over real contradictions.

Although I have tried to write without bias, I should perhaps indicate where my sympathies lie. I agree with the Marxists that a profound restructuring of our social order is necessary. I differ in a greater reliance on liberal values, not simply as ends but as means. My commitment is to the great rights of mankind that are embodied in the United States Constitution as a charter of law and in the United Nations Declaration of Human Rights as a declaratory document. But I concur with the judgment of S.S. Prawer that Marx "is too important to be left to the Marxists."[2]

[2]S.S. Prawer, *Karl Marx and World Literature* (Oxford at the Clarendon Press, 1976), p. 347.

Acknowledgments

I am especially grateful to friends who have read and criticized my manuscript: Norman Fischer of the Philosophy Department of Kent State University; Richard Fox of the Philosophy Department of Cleveland State University; Bertell Ollman of the Department of Politics of New York University; and among members of the University of Washington faculty, Ernst Behler of Germanics, Robert Coburn and Stephen Thomas of the Philosophy Department, James Herrick of the School of Social Work, and Lyman Legters of the Institute for Comparative and Foreign Area Studies. Carol Weibel, philosophy librarian at the University of Washington, has called my attention to important publications. Wayne Grytting of the University of Washington and Linda Gelbke of Cleveland State University have made helpful suggestions. Authors, colleagues, and students too numerous to mention have contributed to my understanding of Marx.

It is a pleasure to acknowledge permission to quote from the following copyrighted sources:
Karl Marx and Frederick Engels, *Collected Works*, prepared jointly by Lawrence & Wishart, London, International Publishers Company, New York, and Progress Publishers, Moscow, 1975 to date. Lawrence & Wishart and International Publishers Company have also kindly granted me permission to quote from other works by Marx.

Karl Marx, *Early Writings*, translated by Rodney Livingstone and Gregor Benton, Pelican Books in association with

New Left Review, 1975. © Rodney Livingstone, 1974. By permission of Random House and Pelican Books.

Karl Marx, *Early Writings,* translated and edited by T.B. Bottomore, 1963. © T.B. Bottomore, 1963. By permission of Pitman Publishing Ltd. for C.A. Watts & Company.

Karl Marx, *Grundrisse: Foundations of the Critique of Political Economy,* translated by Martin Nicolaus, Pelican Books in association with *New Left Review,* 1973. © Martin Nicolaus, 1973.

Karl Marx, *The Grundrisse,* edited and translated by David McLellan, Harper & Row, 1971. © David McLellan, 1971. By permission of Harold Matson Company, Inc. and Harper & Row.

Karl Marx, *Selected Writings in Sociology and Social Philosophy,* translated by T.B. Bottomore and edited by T.B. Bottomore and Maximilien Rubel, 1956. By permission of Pitman Publishing Ltd. for C.A. Watts & Company.

Miriam Glucksmann, *Structuralist Analysis in Contemporary Social Thought,* Routledge & Kegan Paul, 1974.

Quintin Hoare and Geoffrey Nowell-Smith, *Selections from the Prison Notebooks of Antonio Gramsci,* Lawrence & Wishart, 1951.

Joseph O'Malley, *Karl Marx's Critique of Hegel's "Philosophy of Right,"* Cambridge University Press, 1970.

Karl R. Popper, *The Open Society and Its Enemies,* Routledge & Kegan Paul and Princeton University Press, 5th revised edition, 1966.

Charles Taylor, *Hegel,* Cambridge University Press, 1975.

Kind permission has been granted by Holt, Rinehart and Winston, Inc. to include several brief extracts from my book *Ethics and the Human Community,* 1964.

My indebtedness to other sources is indicated in my footnotes.

Contents

Contents

Introduction

"Our criticism stands at the center of the problems of which the modern age says: *that is the question.*"[1]

These words of Marx still apply to his critique of modern civilization. Because he posed problems in terms so relevant to our age, his influence has been immense. But his complex theory of history, which is the very heart of his critique, is commonly misunderstood by both friend and foe. This misunderstanding is a main source of world conflict. Neither side in this clash can afford to misinterpret Marx.

The need for understanding is increased by the continuing spread of Marxism. Nearly half of the human race lives in China, the Soviet Union, and Eastern Europe—areas in which the Marxist tradition is officially regarded as the source of truth. In the undeveloped countries of Asia, Africa, and Latin America, the influence of Marx plays a major role. Even in such "advanced" areas as Japan, Western Europe, and the United States, there is considerable fermentation of Marxist thought. It is impossible to understand the forces shaping world history without a knowledge of Marxism.

The greatness of Marx is attested by his continuing influence. Joseph Schumpeter, who admired the very institutions that Marx detested, has said:

> We need not believe that a great achievement must necessarily be a source of light or faultless in either fundamental design or details. On the contrary, we may believe it to be a power of darkness; we may think it fundamentally wrong or

[1]*Contribution to the Critique of Hegel's Philosophy of Right—Introduction* in Karl Marx, *Early Writings*, trans. and ed. by T.B. Bottomore (London: C.A. Watts & Co. Ltd., 1963), p. 50.

disagree with it in any number of particular points. In the case of the Marxian system, such adverse judgment or even exact disproof, by its very failure to injure fatally, only serves to bring out the power of the structure.[2]

I shall attempt with as little bias as possible to examine that structure.

The question "What is Marxism?" is difficult to answer. The gulf that separates the humanistic and the antihumanistic interpretations of Marx is almost as wide as the chasm that separates antithetical interpretations of Christianity.

> The Vision of Christ that thou dost see
> Is my Vision's Greatest Enemy. . . .
> Both read the Bible day and night,
> But thou readst black where I read white.[3]

With a little change of wording these lines of William Blake could be addressed by one "Marxist" to another.

Except for such popular statements as the *Communist Manifesto*, Marx's works are hard to read and understand. He was often too ill or too harried with controversy to write with studied care. Some of his most important works, such as the Paris *Manuscripts* and the *Grundrisse*, are rough drafts. Many passages are highly technical, abstruse, or polemical. The most concise statement of his "historical materialism" is in the Preface to *A Contribution to the Critique of Political Economy*, but Michael Harrington has called it misleading. "It is so compressed," he says, "as to guarantee that most readers will miss its subtleties, or else, when it is straightforward and clear, it gives an inaccurate—and un-Marxist—description of social reality."[4] The most ex-

---

[2]Joseph A. Schumpeter, *Ten Great Economists from Marx to Keynes* (New York: Oxford University Press, 1951), pp. 3–4.

[3]William Blake, "The Everlasting Gospel." For a good discussion of conflicting interpretations of Marx and Marxism see Wolfgang Leonhard, *The Three Faces of Marxism: The Political Concepts of Soviet Ideology, Maoism, and Humanist Marxism* (New York: Holt, Rinehart and Winston, 1974).

[4]Michael Harrington, *The Twilight of Capitalism* (New York: Simon and Schuster, 1976), p. 37. I shall argue in Chapter 1 that the Preface is more internally consistent and in harmony with Marx's theory than Harrington supposes.

tended statement, Part I of *The German Ideology*, is not altogether consistent. To discover the rich content of Marx's interpretation of history we must piece together ideas gathered here and there from an immense range of works.

Even when his thought is economic, sociological, or political in its main thrust, it is also philosophical. He began as a student of Hegelian philosophy and never ceased to think in philosophical terms. As Karl Korsch has said, "The ideas contained in a philosophy can live on not only in philosophies, but equally well in positive sciences and social practice."[5] Marx's philosophy "lived on" in the form of models. This book is mainly about these models and their influence in shaping his theory of history.

The word "model" may be employed in a variety of ways. A scale model, for example, is a reproduction of an object in a different dimension—for instance, a miniature airplane that preserves the relative proportions of the original. A paradigm model is an exemplary instance—for example, a virtuous act as a pattern to emulate. A heuristic model is an imaginary construction intended to guide somebody in the pursuit of knowledge—for example, Bohr's model of the atom or Freud's model of the psyche.

In all these instances the model resembles or corresponds to certain properties or aspects of its subject matter but not all. As Max Black has said: "There is no such thing as a perfectly faithful model; only by being unfaithful in some respect can a model represent its original."[6] Most of the mistakes in the interpretation of models result from overlooking this fact. E.H. Hutton has said:

> We are forced to employ models when, for one reason or another, we cannot give a direct and complete description in the language we normally use. Ordinarily, when words fail

[5]Karl Korsch, *Marxism and Philosophy*, trans. by Fred Halliday (New York: Monthly Review Press, 1970), p. 39.
[6]Max Black, *Models and Metaphors* (Ithaca, N.Y.: Cornell University Press, 1962), p. 220.

us, we have recourse to analogy and metaphor. The model functions as a more general kind of metaphor.[7]

Theorists may fail to distinguish between a model and a literal description. When Hegel called the state an "organism," for example, he did not distinguish the respects in which the state is *like* an organism from the respects in which it is *unlike*. Attributing to the state characteristics that apply only to conscious organisms, he spoke of it as an end for itself, endowed it with will and thought, and revered it as sacred.[8]

The kind of heuristic model that we shall consider is a symbolic representation of something real. To confuse it with the reality is to make a "category mistake." This mistake is made when something is taken to belong to a different type or class ("category") than its true one. An example is the story of a Chinese painter, pursued by creditors, who painted a large goose, mounted it, and flew away. To avoid a category mistake, the metaphorical nature of models must be kept in mind.

A model may be very useful even when there are non-analogical features (as there always are). The investigator can "bracket off" the unlikeness and concentrate on the likeness. From the time of Plato and Aristotle until the present, for example, "organic unity" has been used to call attention to the similarity between an organism and a work of art. A well-composed painting or statue resembles a healthy organism with respect to adequacy, economy, and coherence. But in a real organism there is the *life* of the whole which is the end of the parts. While the coherence is analogous to the work of art, the life is not. No one is tempted literally to attribute life to a piece of sculpture. Stories of statues brought to life, as in the myths of Pygma-

[7]E.H. Hutton, "The Role of Models in Physics," *British Journal for the Philosophy of Science*, Vol. 4 (1953–1954), p. 289.
[8]See J. Macbride Sterrett, *The Ethics of Hegel* (Boston: Ginn & Company, 1893), pp. 189, 245; and J. Loewenberg, ed., *Hegel Selections* (New York: Charles Scribner's Sons, 1929), pp. 446–447.

lion and Daedalus, are obviously metaphorical. The respects in which an organism and a work of art are unlike simply do not enter the focus of attention.

My use of "model" in reference to Marx's theory is not without precedent. Alexander Erlich, Professor and member of the Russian Institute at Columbia University, speaks of models in Marx's explanation of economic growth. Among these models, he says, is base and superstructure.[9] Piotr Sztompka, Professor at the University of Krakow, compares the "systemic-functional models" of Talcott Parsons and Alvin Gouldner with the base-superstructure model of Marx. He also refers briefly to the organic model, but dismisses it because of the differences between organic and social structure.[10] Walter Buckley, Professor of Sociology at the University of California, Santa Barbara, employs a "process model" as an alternative to mechanical and organic models that have proved "inadequate." "The first names we think of in the context of such a perspective," Buckley declares, "are those of Marx and Engels, with their view of history as a dialectical process whereby new structures arise out of conditions immanent in previous ones."[11] There is nothing exceptional in my use of the term "model" in reference to Marx. Although he appears not to have used the word "model," he probably would have agreed that to speak of "the birth, life, and death of the social organism," or even to speak of the state or society as "organic" is to use an analogy.

My argument in the present book is that Marx employed three models in the interpretation of history: dialectical development, base and superstructure, and organic unity.

[9]Alexander Erlich, "Stalinism and Economic Growth Models," in Robert C. Tucker, Stalinism: Essays in Historical Interpretation (New York: W.W. Norton & Company, 1977), pp. 137–138.
[10]Piotr Sztompka, System and Function: Toward a Theory of Society (New York: Academic Press, 1974), especially Chapter 15.
[11]Walter Buckley, Sociology and Modern Systems Theory (Englewood Cliffs, N.J.: Prentice-Hall, 1965), p. 18.

(1) *Dialectical development.* The root metaphors can be found in Heraclitus:

> War is the father and king of all things. . . . Opposition is good; the fairest harmony comes out of differents; everything originates in strife. . . . We enter and do not enter the same rivers, we are and are not. . . . The way up and the way down are one and the same.[12]

These metaphors suggest that development proceeds through the strife of opposites that are interdependent and yet conflict with one another.

Another source of this model is the give and take of argument. A dispute may begin when someone advances an idea as unqualifiedly true. Advancing a counter-notion, the opponent tries to show that the original idea is false or unintelligible. The argument may continue until each disputant is made to see the weak spots in his or her own position and the strength of the opponent's. The disputants may finally agree on a synthesis that is more inclusive and well balanced than either side in isolation.

Hegel contended that this strife and resolution of partisan views is paralleled by a similar progression in human affairs. Here too antithetical tendencies jostle with one another until the clash exposes the onesidedness of each taken in isolation. Hegel tried to show that there are antitheses not only in history but all of nature. "Wherever there is movement," he declared, "wherever there is life, wherever anything is carried into effect in the actual world, there the Dialectic is at work."[13] Communist theorists have similarly generalized the dialectical model. An official manual in the Soviet Union declares: "All development, whether the evolution of the stars, the growth of a plant,

---

[12]Heraclitus, trans. by Richard Lattimore in Matthew Thomas McClure, *The Early Philosophers of Greece* (New York: D. Appleton-Century Company, 1935), pp. 123, 125.

[13]*The Logic of Hegel*, trans. by William Wallace from *The Encyclopaedia of the Philosophical Sciences* (Oxford at the Clarendon Press, 1892), p. 148.

the life of a man or the history of society, is contradictory in essence."[14]

Marx's realistic bent made him wary of such metaphysical conceptions. To find the source of the statement in the Soviet manual we would have to consult such works as Engels' *Dialectics of Nature* or Lenin's *Materialism and Empirio-Criticism*. An example of Marx's more empirical use of the model is his theory of the conflict between dynamic technology and static class structure.

I shall employ the dialectical model in characterizing revolutionary transformation and advanced communism in Chapter V (Section 10). Otherwise I shall discuss "dialectical development" only so far as it influences "base and superstructure" and "organic totality." Marx incorporates it into the structure of the other two models, and it then ceases to be an alternative. As a common ingredient it helps to bridge the apparent gap between them.

(2) *Base and superstructure*. In reaction against Hegel's idealism, Marx formulated his "materialistic interpretation of history." The model for this interpretation is a building in which the base supports the superstructure. The base, in Marx's model, is the mode of production, and the superstructure is the political state with its laws and the culture with its science, philosophy, art, religion, morality, and customs. Because a superstructure rests on its foundations and not vice versa, the implication is that the base determines the superstructure.

Marx's formulation precipitated a revolution in the interpretation of history. Most historiographers would agree with the judgment of Patrick Gardner:

> By stressing the relevance to historical explanation of technical and economic factors in the particular way he did, Marx in effect redrew the map of history. In doing so he made it difficult for historians ever to look at their subject in quite the

[14]Otto Kuusinen and others, *Fundamentals of Marxism-Leninism* (Moscow: Foreign Languages Publishing House, 1963), p. 79.

same fashion as they had done before; this is surely the mark of a considerable and original thinker.[15]

Great as its effect has been, the base-superstructure model is unsatisfactory when regarded as a literal description. It encourages the simplistic interpretation that has come to be known as "vulgar Marxism."

To counteract these simplistic tendencies, Marx and Engels tried to combine the dialectical and base-superstructure models. They maintained that there is a dialectical interaction of unequal forces in which the base is far more powerful than the superstructure. The idea of erecting something on a base, however, implies that the base is already there before the superstructure is erected. Drawing this implication would be inconsistent with the *mutual* determination of base and superstructure by dialectical interaction. The literal implications of the two models are different, but the incorporation of dialectical interaction into the base-superstructure model counteracts the reductionist interpretations.

In Chapter 1 two versions of the base-superstructure model are distinguished. One is the *fundamentalist* version which not only maintains that the "economic base" determines the political-legal and cultural superstructures, but that there is very little if any reaction of the superstructures upon the base. The second is the *dialectical* version. It admits that there is a dialectical interaction between base and superstructure, but contends that the economic base "in the last instance" always prevails. In explanations of "historical materialism" after Marx's death, Engels repeatedly advocated this version, and some passages in Marx's writings appear to favor it.

(3) *Organic totality.* When we consider the characteristics of a complex organism, we find a whole constellation of factors. The suggestiveness and fertility of the organic model make it more than a simple metaphor. A metaphor that is so rich that it can be expanded into a "world hy-

[15]Patrick Gardner, *Theories of History* (Glencoe, Ill.: The Free Press, 1959), p. 125.

pothesis" has been called by Stephen Pepper a "root metaphor"—a term almost synonymous with "model." "Root metaphors," he says, "prove more fertile than others, have greater power of expansion and adjustment. These survive in comparison with others and generate the relatively adequate world theories."[16] Pepper distinguishes four world hypotheses with a root metaphor corresponding to each. Platonic universals correspond to formism, machines to mechanism, situations to contextualism, and organisms to organicism. The philosopher that seems to Pepper the outstanding representative of organicism is Hegel.

Marx was educated as a Hegelian at the Universities of Bonn and Berlin. Although he later reacted sharply against Hegel's idealism, he found the organic model useful as a heuristic tool. One feature of a complex organism, namely hierarchical structure, enabled him to retain his emphasis on the mode of production. He also found in the organic model features that coincided with Hegelian dialectics. Dialectic as interaction and dialectic as growth are stressed by Hegel, and both are integral parts of Marx's conception of organic development. The organic model thus incorporates features of the other two models. Being more inclusive, it fits the complex totality of a social order better than either the first or second model. Base-superstructure tends to be the model used for the more reductive interpretation; organic totality combined with dialectical development is usually used for the less reductive.

The term "organic totality" may need clarification. In the present context, it does not mean "organic unity." The word "disunity" would be more consistent with Marx's intent to expose the mortal conflicts and schisms in capitalist society. "Organic totality" connotes a differentiated and dynamic structure rather than a static unity, or at the opposite extreme, a mere heap or collection. This commitment to a kind of structuralism applies both to society in cross sec-

[16]Stephen C. Pepper, *World Hypotheses* (Berkeley: University of California Press, 1942), p. 92.

tion and society in process. Although small and localized events occur, they are trivial in comparison with comprehensive structures and deep "organic" transformations. This structural principle is fundamental to Marx's interpretation of history.

While there is an obvious difference between the organic totality model and the fundamentalist version of the base-superstructure model, there may seem to be no difference between the organic model and the dialectical version. The hierarchical structure of an organism incorporates the main emphasis of base-superstructure, albeit in a transformed context and with an altered character. But when I go on to discuss other features—interdependence, organic development, concreteness, and crisis and revolution—I am relying more on the heuristic implications of the organic model than on the corresponding implications of the base-superstructure model even in its dialectical version.

Marx placed strong emphasis on the mode of production for two reasons. First, his models impelled him to search for the element that is most basic (base-superstructure model) or most vital in the hierarchy (organic model). This search was the result of his theoretical orientation—the heuristic implications of his two models. Second, he believed that empirical investigation confirmed his hypothesis that the mode of production is the key factor required to satisfy these implications. He spoke of the conflict between the forces of production and the relations of production, for example, as "a *fact*, palpable, overwhelming and not to be controverted."[17] Such "facts" disclosed by research and confirmed by observation were his ultimate justification.

Although more adequate than base-superstructure, the organic model also has its limitations. It is a heuristic device based on analogy, but the points of disanalogy should not be overlooked. So long as we bear this in mind we will not be tempted to exaggerate the similarity between an or-

[17]"Speech at the Anniversary of the 'Peoples Paper'," in Karl Marx, *On Revolution*, ed. by Saul K. Padover (New York: McGraw-Hill Book Company, 1971), p. 60. My italics.

ganism and a society. If we refer to the state or the social order as an organism, we will not regard it as "a great Leviathan, a whole related to individuals as a body to its cells. . . . We must avoid importing into our defining term the associations which belong to it in another capacity."[18]

Marx's use of the organic model is less explicit than his use of the base-superstructure model. Few writers have dealt with it in any detail. Among interpretations of Marx's theories, Georg Lukacs' idea of "totality," Agnes Heller's emphasis on "needs," Bertell Ollman's concept of "internal relations," and Michael Harrington's "image of an organic whole," fit the organic model rather than the base-superstructure model.[19] But none of these authors deals in a comprehensive way with organic totality as a model of historical explanation.

This book explores Marx's use of models in his interpretation of history. Chapter I ("Base and Superstructure") examines the base-superstructure model, its meaning, implications, scope, and defects. Chapter II ("Organic Structure") explains how internal coherence and hierarchy are combined to constitute the structural characteristics of the organic model. Chapter III ("Organic Development") considers the application of the model to historical development. Chapter IV ("The Abstract and the Concrete") discusses concreteness as an essential characteristic of the "social organism" and contrasts abstraction—in the sense of separation from the organic matrix—as disorganic. Chapter V ("Crisis and Revolution") focuses on the crisis of the social order in its late maturity and the revolutionary transformation that ensues.

[18]L.T. Hobhouse, The Metaphysical Theory of the State (New York: The Macmillan Company, 1918), pp. 132–133.
[19]See Georg Lukács, History and Class Consciousness (Cambridge, Mass.: The Massachusetts Institute of Technology Press, 1968); Agnes Heller, The Theory of Need in Marx (New York: St. Martin's Press, 1976); Bertell Ollman, Alienation: Marx's Conception of Man in Capitalist Society (Cambridge at the University Press, 1971); and Michael Harrington, The Twilight of Capitalism (New York: Simon and Schuster, 1976), Part I.

Marx's
Interpretation
of History

1

Base
and
Superstructure

1. The Fundamentalist and the Dialectical Versions of the Base-Superstructure Model

Reference was made in the Introduction to the fundamentalist and the dialectical versions of the base-superstructure model. The difference between them needs further explanation.

The fundamentalist version consists of three propositions: first, that the various strata in the social order—the economic system, the state and its laws, and the various cultural spheres (religion, custom, morality, art, science, philosophy)—are distinct and externally related; second, that changes in the economic stratum produce corresponding changes in the other strata; third, that the causal determination is entirely or almost exclusively one-way, with the economic system determining the "superstructure" and not vice versa. This set of propositions amounts to a kind of economic determinism.

The dialectical version is like the fundamentalist in maintaining that the various strata in the social order are separate and distinct, but it differs in contending that there is a "dialectical" interaction between these strata. (The word "dialectical" is here interpreted as consistent with the view that the strata are distinct. In the organic model "dialectical" no longer has this meaning because the strata are regarded as interpenetrative.) A number of the statements of Engels can be taken as illustrative. In protesting the notion that there are only one-way causal relations from base to superstructure, he wrote:

> Hanging together with this is the fatuous notion of the ide-
> ologists that because we deny an independent historical de-
> velopment to the various ideological spheres which play a
> part in history we also deny them any *effect upon history*.
> The basis of this is the common undialectical conception of
> cause and effect as rigidly opposite poles, the total disregard-
> ing of interaction. These gentlemen often almost deliberately
> forget that once a historical element has been brought into
> the world by other, ultimately economic causes, it reacts, can
> react on its environment and even on the causes that have
> given rise to it.[1]

The contention that the non-economic factors are "brought
into the world by other, ultimately economic causes" indicates that the base superstucture model is being modified
but not outrightly abandoned.

The common interpretation of Marx's "historical materialism," shared by Marxists and non-Marxists alike, tends
toward economic determinism (the fundamentalist version). Martin Seliger, a non-Marxist political scientist, has
attributed to Marx a belief in "economic mono-causality"
(one-way causal relation), declaring that "economic determination" is a "basic Marxian tenet."[2] The view of H. B.
Acton, one of the best known authorities on Marxism, is
similar: "In society taken as it is at a given time, the industrial and economic processes of life are the basis of everything else, of law and politics, of religion, philosophy and
culture generally."[3] Other non-Marxists have written in the
same vein.

The political leaders of Communist revolutions have
similarly interpreted Marx's doctrine. Lenin wrote that "the
totality of all the opposing tendencies" of the historic pro-

[1]Letter of Engels to Franz Mehring, July 14, 1893, in Robert C. Tucker, *The Marx-Engels Reader* (New York: W. W. Norton and Company, 1972), pp. 649–650. Engels on the whole appears to think of base and superstructure as interactive but not interpenetrative.

[2]Martin Seliger, *The Marxist Conception of Ideology* (London: Cambridge University Press, 1970), pp. 43, 205, 221 (index).

[3]H. B. Acton, *What Marx Really Said* (New York: Schocken Books, 1967), p. 81.

4

cess, including "all the ideas and all the various tendencies, without exception, have their roots in the condition of the material forces of production. . . . The production of the material means of life [forms] the basis of all the historical activity of man."[4] Trotsky asserted: *"All* through history mind limps after reality," and the reality "lies in economics—in class contradictions."[5] Using the term "class" in its economic connotation, Mao Tse-Tung declared: "Classes struggle, some classes triumph, others are eliminated. Such is history, such is the history of civilization for thousands of years. . . . In class society everyone lives as a member of a particular class, and *every* kind of thinking, *without exception*, is stamped with the brand of a class."[6] Stalin, who argued that "language radically differs from the superstructure," might be considered a partial exception. "Language," he wrote, "is not a product of one or another base, old or new, within the given society, but of the whole course of the history of society and the history of bases throughout centuries."[7]

The fundamentalist characterization of the base-superstructure doctrine reflects "scientific socialism," the "Marxism" formulated by theoreticians of German Social Democracy between 1875 and 1914. This "scientific" version was promulgated when less than half of what Marx had written was published. The unpublished manuscripts included *Critique of Hegel's "Philosophy of Right"* (1843), *Economic and Philosophical Manuscripts* (1844), *The German Ideology* (1846), and *Foundations of the Critique of Politi-*

[4]V. I. Lenin, *The Teachings of Karl Marx*, in Michael Oakeshott, *The Social and Political Doctrines of Contemporary Europe* (Cambridge at the University Press, 1939), p. 106. My italics. Lenin's political activism, however, constituted a break with the mechanistic determinism of Kautsky, Plekhanov, and other theorists of the Second International

[5]Leon Trotsky, *Literature and Revolution* (Ann Arbor: University of Michigan Press, 1960), pp. 18, 180. My italics.

[6]*Quotations from Chairman Mao Tse-Tung* (Peking: Foreign Language Press, 1967), p. 8. My italics.

[7]Joseph Stalin, "Marxism in Linguistics," in Berel Lang and Forrest Williams, eds., *Marxism and Art* (New York: David McKay Company, 1972), pp. 81–82.

5

cal Economy, best known by its German title, *Grundrisse der Kritik der Politischen Ökonomie* (1857–1858). These and other unpublished works did not appear in print until 1927 or later, and the *Grundrisse* as a whole was not published until 1939. Little attention was paid to these writings until the late 1940's. In the United States and England, where translations have been slow in appearing, the lag has been even greater. On the basis of the evidence now available, critics have attacked the fundamentalist interpretation.

Defenders of this version have distinguished between an early "pre-Marxist" Marx and a later "scientific" Marx. Louis Althusser, who shares some opinions of the fundamentalists, has defended this view with a sophistication uncharacteristic of most of its proponents. He believes that a radical "epistemological break" with Hegel and Feuerbach occurred in 1845 but that mature Marxism can be dated only from 1857. The break, he maintains, is represented by *Theses on Feuerbach* (1845) and *The German Ideology* (1845–1846), and he relegates all earlier works to an immature "humanist" period.[8]

Undeniably there is a transition from the more humanist emphasis of the early works to the more sociological and economic emphasis of the late. "Surplus value" and "labor power"—the economic basis of "capitalist exploitation"—emerge as the central concepts of the mature economic theory. But Althusser's contention that there was a radical break beginning in 1845 is untenable. Engels said that Marx arrived at the theory of class struggle and historical materialism in the *Critique of Hegel's "Philosophy of Right"* (1843) and his articles in the *Deutsch-Franzosische Jahr-*

[8]See Louis Althusser, *For Marx* (New York: Pantheon Books, 1969), pp. 34–38, 51–86. For a brief comment on Althusser's interpretation see David McLellan, *Karl Marx* (New York: Viking Press, 1975), pp. 90–91. Also see "The Young and the Old Marx" by Iring Fetscher and Marx W. Wartofsky in *Marx and the Western World*, ed. by Nicholas Lobkowicz (University of Notre Dame Press, 1967) for a sounder interpretation than that of Althusser.

ucher of February 1844.[9] Marx, in his Preface to *A Contribution to the Critique of Political Economy* and his Afterword to the second German edition of *Das Kapital* ascribed the emergence of the materialist conception of history to the Hegel Critique.[10] Shlomo Avineri calls attention to these statements of Marx and concludes: "Not only is there no 'caesura' between the young and the old Marx, but the guarantee of continuity has been supplied by Marx himself."[11] Even Althusser is forced to admit that the latest of Marx's works "flirt" with Hegelian expressions and contain "pre-Marxist survivals." With the exception of certain economic theories, Marx's characteristic doctrines emerged in the period 1843–1845. These include doctrines of alienation, ideology, praxis, private property as fetter, proletarian revolution as transition to a classless society, and most relevant in the present context, the model of base and superstructure. Change and development in Marx's ideas certainly occurred, but there was no radical discontinuity.

A formidable difficulty in interpretation is that the base-superstructure model is linked to Marx's entire work. We must consider its wide ramifications, especially its relation to alienation, ideology, the "human essence," and the natural world. At the same time we must not confuse our basic question, "What is Marx's model of base and superstructure?" with cognate questions. We must narrow our focus to the central question without narrowing to the point of oversimplification.

[9]Karl Marx and Friedrich Engels, *Historisch-Kritische Gesamtausgabe* (Berlin: Marx-Engels Archiv, 1929–1933), Abt. I, Bd. 2, pp. 446, 448. Subsequently referred to as *Mega*.
[10]See Shlomo Avineri, *The Social and Political Thought of Karl Marx* (Cambridge at the University Press, 1969), pp. 38–40. When Marx wrote the *Critique of Hegel's "Philosophy of Right"* he had not arrived at his theoretical communism or his full-fledged materialistic interpretation of history, but these doctrines were emerging in the course of writing it. A few weeks later, when he composed his Introduction to the *Critique*, the transition had largely occurred.
[11]*Ibid.*, p. 40. See also David McLellan, *Karl Marx: His Life and Thought* (New York: Harper & Row, 1973), pp. 303–305.

Another difficulty is that a survey of Marx's comments will disclose contradictions. Neither side in the ongoing debate suffers from a want of quotations from the original texts. Among passages that have been interpreted as fundamentalist is the following:

> In acquiring new productive forces men change their mode of production; and in changing their mode of production, in changing the way of earning their living, they change all their social relations. The hand-mill gives you society with the feudal lord, the steam-mill, society with the industrial capitalist.[12]

In a non-fundamentalist passage from the same book, The Poverty of Philosophy, Marx ridicules Proudhon for isolating a single phase of the "dialectical movement" of social forces "without having recourse to all the other relations of society.... How, indeed, could the single logical formula of movement, of sequence, of time, explain the structure of society, in which all relations co-exist simultaneously and support one another?"[13] The contradictions may be more apparent than real. When read in context the quotations often take on a different appearance. The sentence about the hand-mill and the steam-mill, for example, can be understood as a use of catchy phrases for literary and polemical, rather than scientific, purposes. As Engels wrote to a friend, he and Marx often overstated their views:

> Marx and I are ourselves partly to blame for the fact that younger writers sometimes lay more stress on the economic side than is due to it. We had to emphasize this main principle in opposition to our adversaries, who denied it, and we had not always the time, the place, or the opportunity to allow the other elements involved in the interaction to come into their rights.[14]

[12]Marx, The Poverty of Philosophy (New York: International Publishers, no date), p. 92.
[13]Ibid., pp. 93–94.
[14]Letter of Engels to Joseph Bloch, September 21, 1890, in Marx and Engels, Selected Correspondence 1846–1895 (New York: International Publishers, 1942), p. 477.

Another explanation of inconsistencies is that Marx was groping toward a theory that he had not yet entirely thought out. He said that his intellectual development was a process of "clarifying my own ideas."[15] Moreover, he was being influenced by several models; and he did not always see how they could be reconciled, if indeed he was even conscious of the contradictions. Whatever be the explanation of real or apparent contradictions, their occurrence should not obscure the fact that his doctrines, which appear to be simple, are complicated. There are enough disagreements among interpreters and enough ambiguities and complexities in the original texts to justify a careful reexamination.

Engels was aware of fundamentalist misinterpretations and he tried to correct them. After the death of Marx, he insisted upon the interaction between all three levels—the "material base," the political and legal superstructure, and the ideological and cultural superstructure. But his wording, as I have noted in the Introduction, still retained a trace of economic determinism. In his letter to Joseph Bloch of September 21–22, 1890, he said:

> According to the materialist conception of history, the *ultimately* determining element in history is the production and reproduction in real life.... The economic situation is the basis, but the various elements of the superstructure ... also exercise their influence upon the course of the historical struggles.... There is an interaction of all these elements, in which ... *the economic movement finally asserts itself as necessary*....[16]

Also in a letter to Heinz Starkenburg of January 25, 1894, Engels said:

> It is not that the economic position is the *cause and alone active*, while everything else only has a passive effect. There is, rather, interaction on the basis of the economic necessity, which *ultimately* always asserts itself.[17]

[15]See David McLellan, *Karl Marx: His Life and Thought,* p. 305.
[16]Marx and Engels, *Selected Correspondence 1846–1895,* p. 475.
[17]*Ibid.,* p. 517.

Marx did not use such expressions as "the *ultimately* determining element," "the economic movement" that "finally asserts itself as necessary," and "the economic necessity which *ultimately* always asserts itself." Although Engels must have thought that he was interpreting Marx faithfully, he found it difficult to extricate himself from the fundamentalist version. The same difficulty has been characteristic of a great many others in the Communist movement.

Marx conceived the elements in the social order as internally related. There is not only the interaction that Engels remarked but the *essential* character of the elements is modified by the interaction. In Marx's more organic formulations, there is no sharp dualism or clear-cut distinction between the productive forces and the productive relations, the polity and the economy, theory and practice, science and industry, culture and base. All of them not only interdepend but interpenetrate.

The greatest weakness of the base-superstructure model is that it fails to make this fact clear. The weakness is especially apparent in the fundamentalist version, but it applies also to the dialectical version. In the latter the various strata in the social order are still conceived to be distinct and externally related. This distinctness and externality largely disappears in the organic totality model. The term "dialectical" then no longer has the restricted meaning that it retains in the interactionist version of the base-superstructure model; it is reinterpreted so as to be consistent with the internality of relations. This less-restricted meaning will be clarified in the following chapters.

2. Summary of Marx's "Materialist Interpretation of History"

I shall begin with the classic summary in the Preface to *A Contribution to the Critique of Political Economy*. I apologize for quoting such a long and familiar passage, but we need to have the wording squarely before us. For our purposes, the most important sentences are as follows:

My investigation led to the result that legal relations as well as forms of state are to be grasped neither from themselves nor from the so-called general development of the human mind, but rather are rooted in the material conditions of life. . . . In the social production which men carry on they enter into definite relations that are indispensable and independent of their will; these relations of production correspond to a definite stage of development of their material powers of production. The sum total of these relations of production constitutes the economic structure of society—the real foundation, on which rise legal and political superstructures and to which correspond definite forms of social consciousness. The mode of production in material life conditions the general character of the social, political and spiritual processes of life. It is not the consciousness of men that determines their being, but, on the contrary, their social being determines their consciousness. At a certain stage of their development, the material forces of production in society come into conflict with the existing relations of production, or—what is but a legal expression for the same thing—with the property relations within the framework of which they have operated hitherto. From forms of development of the forces of production these relations turn into their fetters. Then comes the period of social revolution. With the change of the economic foundation the entire immense superstructure is more or less rapidly transformed. In considering such transformations the distinction should always be made between the material transformation of the economic conditions of production which can be determined with the precision of natural science, and the legal, political, religious, aesthetic or philosophic—in short ideological forms in which men become conscious of this conflict and fight it out. Just as our opinion of an individual is not based on what he thinks of himself, so can we not judge of such a period by its own consciousness; on the contrary, this consciousness must rather be explained from the contradictions of material life, from the existing conflict between the social forces of production and the relations of production.[18]

[18]Marx, Preface to *A Contribution to the Critique of Political Economy* (Chicago: Charles H. Kerr & Company, 1904), pp. 11–12. Translation modified.

11

Noteworthy in this passage is the undefined character of its key terms. John Plamenatz has charged that the vagueness is used "not to express thought but to cover up its absence."[19] Even Engels complained that the summary was "a very abstract abstract."[20]

The passage is not so vague if we define its main terms. On the basis of what Marx says elsewhere, I hazard the following definitions. "The forces of production" are the labor power, raw materials, tools, techniques, and organization of the working personnel, involved in the production of economic goods and services. "The relations of production" are the social interactions into which human beings enter at a given level of development of the productive forces. Most important are the division of labor, for example, the division between brain-workers and hand-workers, and the economic class structure, for example, the division between slave owners and slaves, feudal lords and serfs, factory owners and industrial workers. "Ideological forms of consciousness" are the ideas and doctrines that reflect class interest and that are held without an understanding of their economic basis. "The contradictions of material life" are the struggles between opposing economic classes and the conflicts and incompatibilities between the forces of production and the relations of production.

Armed with these definitions, we can restate "historical materialism"[21] in more understandable language. At the beginning of history the classless society of primitive man was disrupted by the introduction of slavery and other forms of class domination. In Western Europe slavery was

[19]John Plamenatz, German Marxism and Russian Communism (New York: Harper & Row, 1965), p. 21.

[20]Letter of Engels to Marx, April 9, 1858, in Marx and Engels, Werke (Berlin: Dietz Verlag, 1967), Vol. 19, p. 319.

[21]According to Erich Fromm, Marx himself never used the terms "historical materialism" and "dialectical materialism." See Fromm, Marx's Concept of Man (New York: Frederick Ungar Publishing Company, 1961), p. 9. Marx, of course, did speak of the "materialistic basis" of history and the "dialectical method."

followed by feudalism and feudalism by capitalism. (Development in the Orient as we shall see differed substantially.) In the early expanding phases of a class-based economy, the interacting factors in the productive system, including the forces and relations of production, are in a state of relative equilibrium and therefore develop progressively and harmoniously. The productive forces on the whole determine the productive relations, and the relations in turn facilitate the forces and condition the political and intellectual processes. But sooner or later the expanding forces of production clash with the contracting relations of production. Not only is there a difference between the forces and relations in the *tempo,* but also in the *direction* of change. Under the spur of technology, the forces develop more rapidly, and in a direction incompatible with the relations of production. The *capacity* to produce expands, the *ownership* of the means of production contracts (big companies gobble up small). As a result, the productive forces can no longer develop freely within the confines of the class structure: the old fetters the new, the relations fetter the forces, the contraction fetters the expansion. Alienation and disfunction spread, class conflicts intensify, and the polarization and fracture of social life are expressed in ideology— the largely unconscious and therefore uncontrolled reflection in thought of the schisms in the economic foundations of life. This conflict between the forces and relations of production intensifies until, in a period of revolutionary upheavals, the social relations are reorganized so as to harmonize with the productive forces. Thereby the forces are unfettered, the productivity of the economy again surges ahead, and the superstructure is radically altered. In the past, revolution has taken the form of the displacement of the dominant class by a new rising class, for example, the displacement of feudal lords and guild masters by the bourgeoisie. But thanks to the expansive forces of capitalism and the growth of technology, such enormous progress has been made in productive capacity that the whole class structure of modern society, including its ideological expressions, has become obsolete and irrational—a fetter rather than a spur to progress. Fortunately, mankind has developed the social and scientific means to guide the revolutionists in the emancipation process, so that in the future an informed proletariat can overcome alienation through the abolition of classes and the reintegration of mankind. The economic system will be reorganized on the basis, not of competitive production for profit, but of cooperatively planned production for use. No longer will men and women enter blindly into social relations that are "independent of their will"—they will establish control over the material powers of the economy and achieve a life that is proper and worthy for human beings.

Marx's theory is not free from ambiguities. The kinds of relations between the base and superstructure are not precisely defined. Marx uses such diverse terms as "determination," "correspondence," "reflection," "dependence," "condition," and "outgrowth" to indicate these relations, leaving the nature of the connections open to various interpretations. His use of other terms besides "cause" served his holistic point of view. While these terms do seem ambiguous from the standpoint of causality, they are truer to his explanatory intention than any mono-causal explanation could be.

3. A Non-Reductive Interpretation
   of the Preface

The wording in the Preface need not be interpreted reductively. By "reductive," in this context, I mean the view that the economic system is the base that causally determines the political and cultural superstructure. In its most reductive form, it is the notion that the superstructure is an epiphenomenal "reflex" that arises mechanically in response to the dynamics of a material substructure. This, in my terminology, is a fundamentalist view.

To the extent that non-economic causes are recognized, Marx's theory of history is non-fundamentalist. Although Marx occasionally exaggerates the role of economic causes, he is not a pure economic determinist. Even the Preface, so often cited as evidence of economic determinism, should not be so interpreted.

The most crucial sentence in the Preface has been implausibly translated. The original reads: "Die Produktionsweise des materiellen Lebens bedingt den sozialen, politischen und geistigen Lebensprozess überhaupt."[22] The plausible translation is as follows: "The mode of production of material life conditions (bedingt) the social, political and intellectual life processes in general (überhaupt)."[23] (My italics.) Although a number of translators have used the word "determines"[24] instead of "conditions," Marx would probably have used a stronger verb than "bedingt," such as "bestimmt," had he intended this meaning. The authoritative Muret-Sanders dictionary defines "bedingt" as "conditioned" or "to be conditioned by something." The word "determines" or "determined" does not appear in the definition of either the verb or its cognate nouns. Some translations have omitted "in general (überhaupt)." I admit that "überhaupt" can be translated "altogether" and that "bedingt" is sometimes translated "determines." One translation reads as follows: "The manner of production of material life determines altogether the social, political, and intellectual life processes."[25] In view of what Marx says elsewhere, this translation, which seems to imply economic determinism, is implausible. If we substitute the more plausible translation, the implication is far from economic determinism. The words "conditions" and "in general," which other translators have used, imply no more than partial, incomplete determination.

[22]Marx and Engels, Werke, Vol. 13 (1961), pp. 8–9.
[23]Marx and Engels, Selected Works, two volume edition (New York: International Publishers, no date), Vol. I, p. 503.
[24]Among the translators who employ the word "determines" are I. N. Stone,, in Marx, A Contribution to the Critique of Political Economy (Charles H. Kerr, 1904); T. B. Bottomore, in Marx, Selected Writings in Sociology and Social Philosophy (C. A. Watts & Company, 1956), and René Wellek, A History of Modern Criticism (Yale, 1955), Vol. III, p. 236.
[25]Peter Demetz, Marx, Engels, and the Poets, translated by Jeffrey L. Sammons (Chicago: University of Chicago Press, 1967), p. 72.

The passage as a whole uses a variety of terms to indicate the relations between the diverse elements in society. Definite forms of consciousness are said to "correspond" to the economic structure of society. The word "corresponds" leaves plenty of elbow-room for non-economic causes. The strongest term, "determines (bestimmt)," occurs in the following sentence: "It is not the consciousness of men that determines their being, but, on the contrary, their social being determines their consciousness." "Social being" is broad enough to cover family ties, political relations, and other social connections and activities. There is no implication of one-way or exclusive economic causation. The sentence, as a matter of fact, is no more than a paraphrase of Feuerbach's "transformative principle": "Being is the subject, thought the predicate." (See below, page 67.) By no stretch of the imagination could Feuerbach be called an economic determinist.

The language that refers to the relation between the economy and the legal-political system is non-reductive:

> At a certain stage of their development, the material forces of production in society come into conflict with the existing relations of production or—*what is but a legal expression for the same thing*—with the property relations within the framework of which they have operated hitherto. (My italics.)

Far from saying that the conflict between the forces and relations of production *determines* the legal system, Marx declares that the term "property relations" merely expresses in *legal* terms *the same thing* as "the existing relations of production." The clear implication is that the laws of property, which of course are enacted and enforced by the state, are logically inseparable from the relations of production. In another sentence, Marx declares that "legal relations as well as forms of state . . . are rooted [in the organic sense: *wurzeln*] in the material conditions of life." The language fits an organic rather than a mechanical analogy, and does not imply that economic causes are alone determinative. The fundamentalist interpretation that consigns the state with its laws to a superstructure wholly determined by an economic base is unsupported by Marx's language.

Marx's references in the Preface to the forms of social consciousness do not imply that they are either ineffectual or illusory. We must distinguish, he says, between social science and ideology. Social science is far from illusory and may be as precise as natural science: "The material transformation of the economic conditions of production . . . can be determined with the precision of natural science." This scientific understanding, diffused among the workers, is Marx's great aim in life: he considers it essential for the emancipation of the working class. When he distinguishes social science and the "ideological forms" of consciousness—"legal, political, religious, aesthetic, or philosophical"—he does not suggest that *ideology,* much less science, has little or no influence on class conflict. He speaks, instead, of "the ideological forms in which men become conscious of this conflict and *fight it out."* (My italics.) Ideologies are weapons and have an undeniable impact.

Marx uses the word "material" repeatedly to characterize the base. As I shall point out in the next section, the word "material" is not merely a synonym for "economic." It refers to the fundamental conditions of production, including human nature and the natural environment. Again the language, when properly understood, does not imply economic determinism.

If one reads the Preface carelessly, Marx seems to be saying that the productive forces determine the productive relations and that these in turn determine the political and cultural-ideological superstructure. However, if one reads attentively and checks the translation against the German original, this interpretation is seen to be oversimplified. Although the interdependence is among unequal forces, each sphere is conditioned by all the others. There is dominance and subordination as in any complex organic whole. The Preface, I believe, reveals nothing contradictory to the organic model. Marx articulated this model in the *Grundrisse* manuscript at about the same time that he wrote the

17

Preface. The base-superstructure and organic models must not have seemed contradictory to him. Both models were used to develop a comprehensive theory, and this theory is more coherent than most critics of Marx have realized.

4. Nature and the Human Person

I shall now try to define more precisely what is included in the base. Following the usual interpretation I have spoken of the base as "economic," but Marx almost always uses the word "material." In the long passage that I have quoted from the Preface to the *Critique of Political Economy,* he refers to "the material conditions of life," "the material forces of production," "the mode of production in material life," "the contradictions of material life," and "the material transformation of the economic conditions of existence" (implying a distinction between "material transformation" and "economic conditions"). Similar language occurs in the *Grundrisse, Capital, The German Ideology,* the *Communist Manifesto,* and other works. What does he mean by "material"? Is the word no more than a synonym for "economic"? I think he had in mind the fundamental conditions of human production both economic and noneconomic. These conditions include constant as well as transitory factors. In the Introduction to the *Grundrisse* he distinguishes between the enduring and the changing elements in the productive process:

> Some of these elements belong to all epochs, others are common to a few. Some of them are common to the most modern as well as to the most ancient epochs. No production is conceivable without them. . . . The conditions which generally govern production must be differentiated in order that the essential points of difference should not be lost sight of in view of the general uniformity which is due to the fact that the subject, mankind, and the object, nature, remain the same.[26]

[26]Marx, *The Grundrisse,* ed. by David McLellan (New York: Harper & Row, 1972), p. 18.

18

Similarly in *Capital* Marx speaks of man and nature as constant factors in production:

> Labour is . . . a process in which both man and nature participate and in which man of his own accord, regulates, and controls the material reactions between himself and nature. He opposes himself to nature as one of her own forces, setting in motion arms and legs, head and hands, the natural forces of the body, in order to appropriate nature's productions in a form adapted to his own wants.[27]

This human interchange with nature is a permanent part of the base. The base thus includes the natural environment and the human hereditary endowment.

Without reference to this human element we cannot explain the revolt against inhuman conditions. According to Marx, revolution is caused primarily by the conflict between the forces of production and the relations of production. John Plamenatz asks:

> Why should not the "relations of production," once they have become incompatible with the forces, continue so forever? Why should not economic progress come to a stop? Why should there not be economic and social stagnation?[28]

The workers finally rebel because they are the chief sufferers from this "contradiction." The dissenting devil under the human skin will not tolerate so much misery and frustration. This is the answer that is expressly stated by Marx:

> The propertied class and the class of the proletariat present the same human self-estrangement. But the former class feels at ease and strengthened in this self-estrangement; it recognizes estrangement as *its own power* and has in it the *semblance* of a human existence. The latter feels annihilated in estrangement; it sees in it its own powerlessness and the reality of an inhuman existence. It is, to use an expression of Hegel, in its abasement the *indignation* at that abasement, an indignation to which it is necessarily driven by the contradic-

[27]Marx, *Capital*, I, pp. 197–198.
[28]John Plamenatz, *German Marxism and Russian Communism*, p. 29.

tion between its human *nature* and its condition of life, which is the outright, resolute and comprehensive negation of that nature.[29]

The flagrant contradiction between the deepest human needs and the actual human condition impels revolt.

Many "Marxists" have been loathe to invoke human nature as an explanatory principle. They admit that in Marx's early writing he distinguished between the "human essence" and "human existence," but they think that this distinction was soon abandoned. In the *Communist Manifesto*, Marx ridiculed the German True Socialists, a Utopian sect, for harping on "the alienation of humanity," and for sacrificing the real "interests of the proletariat" to the imaginary "interests of human nature, of man in general, who belongs to no class, has no reality, who exists only in the misty realm of philosophical fantasy." This statement is a sharp attack upon the anti-historical ideas of a particular sect, but *not* a total repudiation of the naturalistic humanism of the early works.[30]

Marx dropped his Hegelian terminology of "essence" and "existence," probably because he wanted to make clear that "the essence of man is no *abstraction* inherent in each separate individual," and that the reality of human life is to be found in "the *ensemble* of social relations" (*Theses on Feuerbach*). There was a change from the anthropological emphasis derived from Feuerbach to the economic and sociological emphasis of the later works. Otherwise there was no great shift in point of view. Early and late he distinguished between comparatively permanent and impermanent human traits. In the Paris *Manuscripts* of 1844, he characterized the whole of human nature as dynamic and changing, but he thought that the generic core of man's being is *relatively* constant. Otherwise he could not speak

[29]Marx and Engels, *The Holy Family*, in *Collected Works*, Vol. 4 (New York: International Publishers, 1975), p. 36.
[30]For a discussion of the relation between Marx's early humanism and his later doctrines, see Adam Schaff, *Marxism and the Human Individual* (New York: McGraw-Hill Book Company, 1970), pp. 1–48.

as he does of what is essential as opposed to what is superficial and transient in human nature. In notes drafted during the writing of *The German Ideology*, he distinguishes semi-permanent human desires, which are modified by changing historical conditions, from impermanent desires which owe their origin to a specific form of society, production, or exchange.[31] There is a similar passage in *The Holy Family*, in which the distinction is drawn between the enduring human drives, such as hunger and love, and the changing appetites, which spring from "certain social structures and certain conditions of production and communication."[32] In criticizing Jeremy Bentham's theory of utility as an expression of "shopkeeper" mentality, he declares in *Capital*:

> To know what is useful for a dog, one must study dog-nature. This nature itself is not to be deduced from the principle of utility. Applying this to man, he that would criticise all human acts, movements, relations, etc., by the principle of utility, must first deal with human nature in general, and then with human nature as modified in each historical epoch. Bentham makes short work of it. With the dryest naiveté he takes the modern shopkeeper, especially the English shopkeeper, as the normal man. Whatever is useful to this queer normal man, and to his world, is absolutely useful. This yard-measure, then, he applies to past, present and future.[33]

Unlike Bentham with his middle-class view of human nature, Marx distinguishes between the more permanent traits ("human nature in general") and the traits that are limited to a particular socio-economic formation ("human

---

[31]See the quotation corresponding to note 44 in Chapter 5. For a fuller statement of this conception of human nature, see Erich Fromm, "Marx's Contribution to the Knowledge of Man," in the Unesco Symposium, *Marx and Contemporary Scientific Thought* (The Hague: Mouton, 1969), p. 456. Fromm's essay is an excellent account of Marx's dynamic psychology.

[32]Marx, *Heilege Familie*, in *Mega*, Abt. I, Bd. 5, p. 359, cited by Fromm, *Marx's Concept of Man* (New York: Frederick Ungar Publishing Co., 1961), p. 25.

[33]Marx, *Capital*, I, p. 668 n.

nature as modified in each historical epoch"). Both in the late and early works, he deplores the "dehumanization" or "loss of humanity" under capitalist exploitation, and prophesies that mankind, after its long exile in the desert of alienation, will come into its own.

We must interpret his "materialism" in the light of his theory of human nature. In a brief sketch of the history of materialism in *The Holy Family*, he attacks materialists such as Hobbes for their mechanistic doctrines. "Materialism," he says, "became one-sided" and "hostile to humanity." He rectifies this one-sidedness by emphasizing the social nature of man and the dynamic character of human needs and impulses. Even at the sub-human level, matter exhibits the inherent qualities of "*impulse, vital life-spirit, tension,*" and "the living, individualizing *forces of being.*" These qualities are more marked at the human level where man "is free . . . through the positive power to assert his true individuality." Marx rejects the "crude, uncivilized" materialism of Babeuf and his followers in favor of Owen and "the more civilized French communists," who "developed the teaching of *materialism* as the teaching of *real humanism* and the *logical* basis of *communism.*"[34]

The main point of Marx's "materialism" is that man is basically a productive agent in creative interaction with nature and society. I agree with Erich Fromm's contention that "Marx's whole psychological thinking is dynamic, and not behavioristic-descriptive."[35] The interpretation of "the material base" as involving only the objective side of economic processes and not the subjective side of human potentialities striving toward fulfillment, is open to all of Marx's criticisms of reductive materialism in the *Theses on*

[34]Marx and Engels, *The Holy Family*, pp. 128, 131. It is unnecessary to blame Marx for the naive metaphysics of Engels in *Dialectics of Nature* and Lenin in *Materialism and Empirio-Criticism*. Marx as a philosopher was profounder than either Engels or Lenin. See Alfred Schmidt, *The Concept of Nature in Marx* (London: NLB, 1971), Chapter Four.

[35]See Fromm, *Marx and Contemporary Scientific Thought*, p. 462

Feuerbach. The ultimate reason that men revolt against inhuman conditions is that they are human.

The "material reactions" between man and external nature, as Marx said, are part of the productive process. A striking example is to be found in Marx's discussion of "the Asiatic mode of production":

> Climate and territorial conditions, especially the vast tracts of desert, extending from the Sahara, through Arabia, Persia, India, and Tartary, to the most elevated Asiatic highlands, constituted artificial irrigation by canals and water-works, the basis of Oriental agriculture. . . . This prime necessity of an economical and common use of water, which, in the Occident, drove private enterprise to voluntary association, as in Flanders and Italy, necessitated, in the Orient where civilization was too low and the territorial extent too vast to call into life voluntary association, the interference of the centralizing power of government. Hence an economical function devolved upon all Asiatic governments, the function of providing public works. This artificial fertilization of the soil, dependent on a central government and immediately decaying with the neglect of irrigation and drainage, explains the otherwise strange fact that we now find whole territories barren and desert that were once brilliantly cultivated, as Palmyra, Petra, the ruins of Yemen, and large provinces of Egypt, Persia and Hindustan. . . . [36]

As a result of these conditions of soil and vast territorial expanse, centralized despotism was necessary to provide great hydraulic public works. Consequently "the Asiatic mode of production" exhibited little resemblance to the feudal and capitalist modes of European production. Clearly Marx included the interaction of man and nature among "the material forces of production." "All production," he said, "is appropriation of nature on the part of an individual within and through a specific form of society."[37]

[36]Marx, "The British Rule in India," in Marx and Engels, *Selected Works*, II, p. 652.
[37]*Grundrisse*, trans. by Martin Nicolaus (Harmondsworth: Penguin Books, 1973), p. 87.

5. The Conflict Between the Productive Forces and the Productive Relations

According to Marx, the conflict between the forces and relations of production, with all their psychological aspects and accompaniments, is the principal cause of revolution. For example, the multiplication of inventions, the expansion of trade and manufacture, and the development of urban life in the late period of feudalism could not be reconciled with the rigid, hierarchical structure of feudal society. A profound revolution—the rise of capitalism—was necessary. In the mature stages of capitalism, the forces of production outstrip and "contradict" the relations of production. A revolutionary transformation is again necessary.

Fundamental to this interpretation is the division of labor. For Marx this division has a twofold meaning. First, it refers to occupational specialization in all its forms, such as the division between skilled and unskilled crafts, mental and physical labor, and agriculture and manufacture. Second, it refers to the division between classes. Marx held that such a division has been an essential feature of human society throughout most of recorded history.

Given this broad concept of the division of labor, Marx could not draw a sharp distinction between the productive forces and the productive relations. That the division of labor falls under the category of the social relations of production is obvious. Marx so categorizes it in many passages. He also tells us that it falls under the category of the forces of production. In *Capital* he declares that "the division of labor is a necessary condition for the production of commodities," and that "cooperation based on the division of labor . . . becomes the recognized and systematic form of capitalist production."[38] In *The German Ideology* he asserts that "a certain mode of production, or industrial stage, is always combined with a certain mode of co-operation, or

[38]Marx, *Capital*, I, pp. 49, 399. See Chapters XIII and XIV for a fuller account.

social stage, and this mode of co-operation is itself a 'productive force'."[39] In *Wage-Labour and Capital* he contends:

> In production, men not only act on nature, but also one another. They produce only by co-operating in a certain way and mutually exchanging their activities. In order to produce, they enter into definite connections and relations with one another and only within these social connections and relations does their action on nature, does production, take place.[40]

These statements indicate that the social relations are to be counted among the productive forces. There is an overlap between the relations and the forces because both include the organization of the work process and the division of labor among the working personnel.

Consequently, it is difficult to understand in what sense the forces and relations can be in "contradiction." Gordon Leff has remarked:

> If there is no actual distinction between the forces of production and productive relations the contradiction between them is not the motive force of change; if a productive relation is inherent in a productive force they are no more entities to be juxtaposed than are the heart and the brain; they are each inseparable from the ensemble which they compose.[41]

Leff's criticism is plausible but unfounded. He incorrectly assumes that there must be an absolute distinction or none at all.

Marx contends, on the contrary, that the forces and relations of production are sometimes but not always pitted against each other. Under normal conditions of economic expansion the relations of production are in a sense productive forces—they facilitate rather than impede material production. Only when the forces can no longer freely de-

---

[39]Marx and Engels, *The German Ideology* in *Collected Works,* Vol. 5 (New York: International Publishers, 1976), p. 43.

[40]Marx, *Selected Works,* I, p. 264.

[41]Gordon Leff, *The Tyranny of Concepts: A Critique of Marxism* (London: Merlin Press, 1961), pp. 111–112.

velop within the confines of the existing social relations does the conflict come to a head. The social relations cease to be productive, and they are then fetters upon production. In consequence there is an intolerable waste and misdirection of productive resources. This is what Marx means when he says that the forces and relations are in "contradiction."

That Leff's criticism is invalid becomes clear if we examine what is meant by the division of labor. I have said it has a twofold meaning, namely, occupational specialization and class structure. Specialization is not only a potent productive force but also a major cause of alienation. In *Capital* Marx quotes with approval Urquhart's condemnation of detailed specialization, with its endless repetition of a routine task:

> To subdivide a man is to execute him, if he deserves the sentence; to assassinate him if he does not. . . . The sub-division of labour is the assassination of a people.[42]

Marx adds his own condemnation. These routines, he says, "mutilate the labourer into a fragment of a man, degrade him to the level of an appendage of a machine, destroy every remnant of charm in his work and turn it into a hated toil."[43] With an eye to paradox, he contends that human beings must be reduced to this absolute spiritual poverty in order to give birth to all their spiritual wealth. There must be a "poverty which is conscious of its spiritual and physical poverty, dehumanization which is conscious of its dehumanization, and therefore self-abolishing."[44] When the workers become fully conscious of dehumanization they will take revolutionary steps to end it. This revolution of the human person is the deeper import of revolution.

[42]Marx, *Capital*, I, p. 399.
[43]*Ibid.*, p. 708.
[44]Marx and Engels, *The Holy Family*, p. 36. For similar passages see *Economic and Philosophical Manuscripts*, p. 160 and Marx, *Early Writings*, trans. by Rodney Livingstone and Gregor Benton (New York: Random House, 1975), p. 419.

The second meaning of the division of labor, *class structure*, is fundamental to Marx's interpretation of historical crisis and revolution. The social core of the economy, its structure of privilege, is either contracting or relatively static, and the forces of production, especially technology, are dynamic and expanding. The conflict between the relations and the forces, moving in different tempos and in opposite directions, is the main socio-economic cause of historical crisis, and its abolition is the principal meaning of revolution. Marx defines revolution as the radical alteration of the inertial core of privilege, either by the overthrow of the ruling class by a new ascendant class, or (in the instance of communist revolution) by the total abolition of classes.

The division of labor eventually becomes an intolerable fetter. In the form of detailed specialization, "it converts the labourer into a crippled monstrosity, by forcing his detail dexterity at the expense of a world of productive capabilities and instincts: just as in the States of La Plata they butcher a whole beast for the sake of his hide or his tallow."[45] In the form of class structure, the division of labor produces a disequilibrium between the dynamic and expanding forces and the retarded and contracting relations, with the consequent misuse or curtailed use of productive capacities. In both forms, the division is a fetter upon human capacities.

Leff remarks that the productive relations and the productive forces are as inseparable as the heart and brain, but he forgets that vital organs may be in conflict. When the heart misfunctions, the brain may suffer, and vice versa. Such conflicts arise in the illness or old age of an organism. To speak of the productive forces and the productive relations as parts of an "organic unity" makes sense, but does not exclude conflict between the relations and forces.

6. The Interpenetration of "Science" and Economic Base

The base and superstructure overlap—for example, science

[45]Marx, *Capital*, I, p. 396.

may belong in the base as well as in the superstructure. This kind of multiple counting, the location of an element in more than one category, occurs frequently in Marx's interpretation. If we cannot characterize the foundation without introducing elements from the superstructure, must we conclude that the base-superstructure model is false? In seeking to answer this question, I shall begin by contrasting Engels and Marx in their characterizations of science.

In general, Marx used the German word *Wissenschaft* rather than the English word *science*. The German word covers not only the physical sciences but the human and social, such as economics, sociology, and history. Marx regarded his work in economics as, in this sense, scientific, remarking in the Introduction to *Capital* that he welcomed every opinion of his work "based on scientific criticism." Engels was less preoccupied with economics, and when he spoke of science, he generally had in mind the physical sciences. In reply to a German correspondent, he contended that science depends mainly on economic technology:

> If, as you say, technique largely depends on the state of science, science depends far more still on the *state* and the *requirements* of technique. If society has a technical need, that helps science forward more than ten universities. The whole of hydrostatics (Torricelli, etc.) was called forth by the necessity for regulating the mountain streams of Italy in the sixteenth and seventeenth centuries. We have only known anything reasonable about electricity since its technical applicability was discovered. But unfortunately it has become the custom in Germany to write the history of the sciences as if they had fallen from the skies.[46]

Engels did not deny that science and the economic "base" interact, but he thought that the interaction is of unequal forces, of which the economic are by far the most powerful. Science, he thought, springs almost entirely from material need and economic technology, not from previous scientific advance in a cumulative process of growth. To the

[46]Letter of Engels to Heinz Starkenburg, January 25, 1894, in Marx and Engels, *Selected Correspondence 1846–1895*, p. 517.

extent that he recognized the latter he would have to limit his theory.

It is difficult to estimate the extent to which Marx agreed with the interpretation of Engels. Judging from a passage in *The German Ideology*, we might conclude that the two friends were in agreement:

> Where would natural science be without industry and commerce? Even this "pure" natural science is provided with an aim, as with its material, only through trade and industry. . . . [47]

Marx and Engels collaborated in writing *The German Ideology*, and its content evidently reflected the opinions of both men. But there is reason to think that Marx's considered judgment did not wholly coincide with this statement.

I suspect that he knew from his own experience that science has a momentum of its own. Without his enormous erudition in the field of economic science he could not have written the *Grundrisse* or *Capital*. He was indebted to Hegel for the analysis of civil society, to Smith and Ricardo for the labor theory of value, to Linguet and Saint-Simon for the emphasis on class conflict, to Sismondi for the interpretation of economic crises, and to many others. He must have realized that a social science such as economics exhibits a maturation process in which later ideas derive in large part from earlier ideas, and that derivation from previous thought implies a considerable degree of independence from the economic base. The cumulative development of natural science is even more detached from "industry and commerce," because the ideas of physical science, such as the theory of quantum mechanics or relativity, are more independent of social change than are the concepts of economics.

The plausibility of the view that natural science depends mainly on economic technology rather than vice versa was much greater in the lifetime of Marx and Engels than it is today. As C. P. Snow has said, the old "industrial revolution" was almost entirely the creation of clever me-

[47]Marx and Engels, *The German Ideology*, p. 36.

chanics and inventors, with scant knowledge of science. Very different is the new "scientific revolution" of electronics, atomic energy, computers, and synthetics. The new revolution springs directly from quantum mechanics, the physics of relativity, advanced chemical research, and other developments in pure science.[48] Consider that elegant little gadget, the transistor. With all its amazing progeny of electronic devices, it is one of the great revolutionary forces of our age. Yet it is quantum-mechanical in its very essence, originating from the great scientists of quantum physics, such as Planck, Heisenberg, and Schrödinger. Similarly the technology of nuclear power, with its staggering potentials for human weal and woe, emerged from the theories of Einstein, Fermi, and other theoretical physicists. Even in Marx's lifetime science floated uncertainly between base and superstructure, being both cause and effect of industrial technology. Now it belongs at the very basis of modern society and is one of the cardinal "productive forces."

Marx anticipated this development more than Engels. One of the presuppositions of Engels' interpretation with which Marx could not agree is that the industrial-technological base is separate and distinct from the scientific "superstructure." To the extent that science, as inseparable from technology, belongs to the productive forces in the base as much as to the cultural elements in the superstructure, the interpretation of Engels collapses. Marx's doctrine of "praxis," in contrast to a dualistic theory, denies the separation of theory and practice. In the second of the *Theses on Feuerbach* he asserts:

> Man must prove the truth, that is, the reality and power, the this-worldliness of his thinking in practice. The dispute over the reality or non-reality of thinking which is isolated from practice is a purely *scholastic* question.[49]

[48]See C. P. Snow, *The Two Cultures and the Scientific Revolution* (New York: Cambridge University Press, 1959).

[49]*Theses on Feuerbach* in Marx/Engels, *Collected Works* (New York: International Publishers), Vol. 5 (1976), p. 3.

In the eighth and eleventh theses he reiterates his belief that theory and practice belong together. It would seem to follow that technology, as the *practice* of science, is inseparable from theoretical science, and that if technology is located in the base, so should science be.

This rejection of a dualistic interpretation of science and technology characterizes Marx's early and late pronouncements. In the *Economic and Philosophical Manuscripts* (1844) the young Marx contends that the natural and human-life sciences should be united and, in this form, become the foundation of nonalienated life. Just as natural science has become the basis of alienated existence, so the combined science of man and nature will become the basis of an all-human emancipation:

> Natural science has penetrated all the more *practically* into human life through industry. It has transformed human life and prepared the emancipation of humanity, even though its immediate effect was to accentuate the dehumanization of man. *Industry* is the actual historical relationship of nature, and thus of natural science, to man. . . . Natural science will . . . abandon its abstract materialist, or rather idealist, orientation, and will become the basis of a *human* science, just as it has already become—though in an alienated form—the basis of actual human life. One basis for life and another for science is *a priori* a falsehood.[50]

This interpretation of science was not just a passing fancy. It is repeated in the *Grundrisse* (1857–1858), where Marx argues that modern machine industry derives increasingly from the advanced level of science and technology:

> Nature builds no machines, no locomotives, railways, electric telegraphs, self-acting mules, etc. These are products of human industry; natural material transformed into organs of the human will over nature, or of human participation in nature. *They are organs of the human brain, created by the human hand*; the power of knowledge, objectified. The development

[50]*Economic and Philosophical Manuscripts*, in Marx, *Early Writings*, trans. and ed. by T. B. Bottomore (London: C. A. Watts & Co., Ltd., 1963), pp. 163–164.

of fixed capital[51] indicates to what degree general social knowledge has become a *direct force of production,* and to what degree, hence, the conditions of the process of social life itself have come under the control of the general intellect and been transformed in accordance with it.[52]

With prophetic insight, Marx describes the advanced stage of industry in which science has become the major productive force:

The entire production process appears as not subsumed under the direct skilfullness of the worker, but rather as the technological application of science. It is, hence, the tendency of capital to give production a scientific character; direct labour is reduced to a mere moment of this process. . . . It is . . . the analysis and application of mechanical and chemical laws, arising directly out of science, which enables the machine to perform the same labour as that previously performed by the worker.[53]

Of course Marx did not use terms of recent coinage, such as "automation" and "cybernation," but he foresaw the massive displacement of laborers by machines:

Labour does not seem any more to be an essential part of the process of production. The human factor is restricted to watching and supervising the production process.[54]

As I shall indicate in Chapter 5, Marx characterizes the technological application of science as preparing the collapse of capitalism and the transition to a communist soci-

[51]"Fixed capital," as defined by Adam Smith, is capital employed in the improvement of land, in the purchase of buildings and useful machines, or "in such like things." An increasing cost of fixed capital is the cost of machinery. The ratio between this cost and the cost of "the materials and wages of labor" ("circulating capital") is indicative of the level of industrial technology.

[52]Marx, *Grundrisse* (Nicolaus), p. 706. For other passages in which Marx characterizes science as a productive force, see *Capital,* I, pp. 397, 421, 422, 504, 684, and III, p. 124.

[53]*Grundrisse* (Nicolaus), pp. 699, 704.

[54]Marx, *The Grundrisse* (McLellan), p. 142. I quote from McLellan's translation when I prefer it to that of Nicolaus.

ety. He is far from denying its importance in shaping the course of history.

7. The Role of Education in the Productive Process

A compelling argument for rejecting the fundamentalist version of the base-superstructure model can be derived from Marx's mature economic theory. Important changes in his theory occurrred between *Wage Labour and Capital* (1847) and *A Contribution to the Critique of Political Economy* (1859). These changes prompted Engels in the 1891 reprint edition of *Wage Labour and Capital* to make alterations in the text, mainly by the substitution of the phrase "labour power" for the term "labour." In his Preface Engels explained that the revision brought the reasoning of the pamphlet into conformity with Marx's mature insights.

What is the significance of this shift in theory? Marx substitutes "labour power"—the *capacity* to perform labor—in place of "labour." The worker, lacking capital, is obliged to sell his labor power to an employer because it is about the only commodity that he has to sell. He sells, in other words, "a temporary disposition over his labouring capacity,"[55] and in return he receives wages which represent (on the average) the exchange-value of the labor power. This exchange-value (like the value of any commodity) is determined by the amount of "socially necessary" labor required to produce it. In this instance it is the amount required to maintain the worker, *to train him for the given skill,* and to rear and *educate* a certain quota of children who are to replace him on the labor market when he wears out.

Labor power, as a value-creating activity, is different from all other commodities: it produces more exchange-value than it is worth on the market. In an eight-hour work day, for example, the worker may in the course of five hours provide sufficient value to compensate the employer

[55]*Grundrisse* (Nicolaus), p. 293.

for the wages paid him. In the next three hours he will produce "surplus value"—an amount in excess of his wages. This excess is the source of profit. Marx's mature economic theory revolves around these two concepts—labor power and surplus value.

The exchange-value of the labor power is relative to the technological level of the given society. It is roughly equal to the subsistence of the worker and his family *plus the expense of education and training.*

> In order to modify the human organism, so that it may acquire skill and handiness in a given branch of industry, and become labour power of a special kind, a special education or training is requisite, and this, on its part, costs an equivalent in commodities of a greater or less amount. This amount varies according to the more or less complicated character of the labour power.[56]

If skill levels rise the inputs needed to produce the average labor power will increase proportionately. Even as late as the writing of *Capital,* Marx thought that technological advancement tends to simplify the worker's task and that consequently skill levels would tend to fall rather than rise. But in a number of remarkable passages in the *Grundrisse,* some of which I have already quoted, he laid the foundation for a different set of expectations. In these passages foretelling the development of automation, he predicted that the contribution of a very high level of technology would greatly outweigh the contribution of the ordinary unskilled worker.

> The means of labour passes through different metamorphoses, whose culmination is the *machine,* or rather, an *automatic system of machinery* ... set in motion by an automaton, a moving power that moves itself; this automaton consisting of numerous mechanical and intellectual organs, so that the workers themselves are cast merely as its conscious linkages.[57]

[56]*Capital,* I, p. 191.
[57]*Grundrisse* (Nicolaus), p. 692.

Scientific-technological "know-how" becomes the major factor in the productive process, not only in developing the means to automation, but in producing the technicians to superintend and maintain the technical apparatus.

The role of education thus becomes crucial to the growth of productivity. It is crucial in the most fundamental sense, namely, in the production of skilled labor power as a commodity. Many educators engage in teaching scientific-technological skills or in contributing through their own research to the advancement of technology. The tendency of some "Marxists" to regard academic personnel as an "ideological class" and to contrast it with the "productive class" runs counter to Marx's mature insights.

The need at the present time for education and retraining in the new technologies is obvious. Many thousands, even millions, of technicians are required to staff the productive systems throughout the world. This need will almost certainly be even greater in the future. The technologically advanced nations will be forced to train many new technicians and organize retraining programs for those who cannot interrupt their work life. The time is fast approaching when "the man who has nothing but his physical power to sell has nothing to sell which is worth anyone's money to buy."[58]

To sum up, education—not only for a minimal standard of literacy but for scientific and technical proficiency—is involved in the production of the most important of all commodities, labor power. It therefore belongs in the base and not simply in the superstructure. The sharp dualism of base and superstructure again breaks down.

8. *Property, Law, and the State*

Other concepts that do not neatly fit the model of base-superstructure are "state" and "law." In *The German Ideology*

[58]Norbert Wiener, *The Human Use of Human Beings* (Boston: Houghton Mifflin Company, 1950), p. 180.

Marx describes the state as "the form of organization which the bourgeoisie are compelled to adopt . . . for the mutual guarantee of their property and interests."[59] The implication is that the state and its legal apparatus are necessary for the maintenance of the class structure. In the Introduction to the *Grundrisse* Marx refers to "legal relations" as among "the relations of production."[60] But on the other hand, he declares in *The German Ideology*: "The material life of individuals . . . is the real basis of the state and remains so at all the stages at which division of labour and private property are still necessary. . . . These actual relations are in no way created by the state power; on the contrary, they are the power creating it."[61] In the Preface to the *Contribution to a Critique of Political Economy*, Marx characterizes "the relations of production" as "the real foundation on which rise legal and political superstructures."[62] Thus Marx in some passages locates the state, law, and property rights in the superstructure and in other passages locates them in the base. These contradictions could, in some measure, be removed if law, rights, and polity are in certain respects superstructural and in other respects basic.

Both Marx and Engels recognize that the political system may develop a degree of independence or may react in complex ways upon the economic system. According to Engels, the economic order, as the more powerful force, determines on the whole the political and legal structure, but in exceptional circumstances "the struggling classes balance each other so nearly that the public power gains a certain degree of independence by posing as a mediator between them."[63] In *The Eighteenth Brumaire of Louis Bonaparte* Marx cites as an example the French Second

[59]*The German Ideology*, p. 90.
[60]*Grundrisse* (Nicolaus), p. 109.
[61]*The German Ideology*, p. 329.
[62]Marx, Preface to *A Contribution to the Critique of Political Economy*, p. 11.
[63]Engels, *The Origin of the Family, Private Property, and the State* (Chicago: Charles H. Kerr & Company, 1902), p. 209.

Empire under Napoleon III. He also was aware that development in the economic sphere does not necessarily entail corresponding development in the political sphere. For example, he thought that England was far more advanced industrially than France, but that France was in many respects more advanced politically. He also noted that Roman law continued as a dominant influence in Europe long after the ancient Roman economy had perished. Hence the correlation between the economic and the legal-political spheres may be rather loose.[64]

I have said that economics like other branches of science develops a momentum of its own, being in large part an outgrowth of the pre-existing stock of knowledge and belief. Engels remarked that law is likewise shaped and channeled by pre-existing law:

> In a modern state, law must not only correspond to the general economic position and be its expression, but must also be an expression which is *consistent in itself*, and which does not, owing to its inner contradictions, look glaringly inconsistent. And in order to achieve this, the faithful reflection of economic conditions is more and more infringed upon. All the more so the more rarely it happens that a code of law is the blunt, unmitigated, unadulterated expression of the domination of a class—this in itself would already offend the "conception of justice."[65]

The reference to the "conception of justice" implies that law has its intrinsic norms to which it must in some measure conform. I think Marx would have agreed with this statement.

A very significant exception to the primacy of economic forces over political occurs in the revolutionary transition from one kind of class-based social order to another. In terms of the base-superstructure model, the normal order is for the forces of production to determine the relations of

[64]See David McLellan, *The Thought of Karl Marx* (New York: Harper & Row, 1974), p. 182.
[65]Engels, letter to Conrad Schmidt, October 27, 1890, in Marx and Engels, *Selected Correspondence 1846–1895*, p. 481.

production and the relations to determine the superstructure. But in a period of revolution the order is reversed. After seizing political power, the rising class uses the state to alter fundamentally the obsolete relations of production and thereby to remove the institutional fetters on the forces of production. On this basis of priority, dictatorship has been rationalized and the power of the state has been enormously enhanced in the Soviet Union and the Peoples Republic of China. *Political* determinism has here been carried to an extreme far beyond anything that Marx prophesied.

Under both socialism and fascism there is an amalgamation of the economic and the political—hence, it would be a mistake to consider the latter as a superstructure of the former. Even in a welfare state such as Sweden or in a lesser degree the United States and England, the interpenetration of economic and political power has become common. Old-fashioned *laissez faire* has virtually disappeared, and the fusion of economic and political control characterizes modern society. The governing institutions have continuously intervened in the economic system to prop it up.

A very important factor in the interpenetration of economic and political factors is the exercise of the coercive power of the state. Marx believed that police and military power is the instrument of class domination. Without it the privileges of the ruling class cannot be safeguarded. There can be no system of property without a body of laws to define, and a state to enforce, the rights of property. In the *Communist Manifesto* Marx declares:

> For many a decade past the history of industry and commerce is but the history of the revolt of modern productive forces against the modern conditions of production, against *the property relations that are the conditions for the existence of the bourgeoisie and its rule.*[66] (My italics.)

If property, so necessary to the class structure, belongs in the base, so do the laws that define and guarantee it and the

[66]Marx and Engels, *Selected Works*, I, p. 211.

juridical and police power required to enforce these laws. As Adam Smith said, private property would not exist "a single night" without government.[67]

According to Marx's mature theory, one kind of social order is distinguished from another primarily by the way in which surplus value is extracted from its workers. The extraction of surplus value in each instance requires a legal and property system based on authority. What compels the slave to obey his master? It is the legal power of the slave owner enforced by the state. (When Roman slaves under Spartacus revolted they were killed in battle or crucified.) What compels the peasant to render his due to the lord? It is the custom of the manor to impose fines upon him, or try him in court, or subdue him with military and coercive power that the lord can command. What compels the wage-laborer to work for the profit of his employer? His livelihood depends upon employment by those who own the means of production, and the ownership of the means of production is enforced by the state with its laws, police, and military force. Although the power of the capitalist is less obvious than that of the ancient despot, it is nonetheless real:

> This power of Asiatic and Egyptian kings, Etruscan theocrats, etc., has in modern society been transferred to the capitalist whether he be an isolated, or as in joint-stock companies, a collective capitalist.[68]

According to Marx's own premises, it is unrealistic to separate the economic factors from the political, and to relegate the state with its legal system wholly to the superstructure.

Contrary to the anarchists who sought to use only nonpolitical means such as the industrial strike, Marx recognized the necessity of political action. In his Inaugural Address in 1864 to the First International, for example, he spoke of the "immense physical, moral and intellectual

[67]Adam Smith, *Wealth of Nations* (New York: Modern Library, 1937), p. 670.
[68]Marx, *Capital*, I, p. 366.

benefits" of the Ten Hours Bill.[69] Such basic reform, he maintained, would never occur without political pressure from the workers. Far from decrying the need for political action, he said in the Inaugural Address: "To conquer political power has . . . become the great duty of the working classes."[70] Marx hated the political state, but his hatred did not make him underestimate its power or the importance of its laws.

For the sake of analysis it is useful to distinguish two functions of law. One is the promulgation and enforcement of compulsory laws. In his characterization of both precapitalist and capitalist economic formations in the *Grundrisse* Marx repeatedly refers to the necessity of law enforcement by the state. Property rights must be established and guaranteed by law backed by force. The second function of law, as H. L. A. Hart has argued in *The Concept of Law*, is to establish a system of rights, expectations, and obligations that allow people to carry on market exchanges and other transactions. Such laws, which are enabling rather than coercive, provide individuals with the facilities for conducting their business.

> Some rules are mandatory in the sense that they require people to behave in certain ways . . . whether they wish to or not; other rules such as those prescribing the procedures, formalities, and conditions for the making of marriages, wills, or contracts indicate what people must do to give effect to the wishes they have.[71]

Marx is less clear about the facilitating legal rules than about the mandatory legal rules, but he recognizes both. He realizes that there must be a system of expectations and rights that allow people to define things as their own and to exchange them under stipulated conditions. Far from the legal sphere being a mere reflex of the economic, the mod-

[69]Marx and Engels, *Selected Works*, II, p. 439. See also Marx's lengthy discussion of the struggle to limit by law the working time in *Capital*, I, Chapter X.

[70]*Ibid.*, p. 440.

[71]H.L.A. Hart, *The Concept of Law* (Oxford at the Clarendon Press, 1961), p. 9.

40

ern economic system could not exist without the exercise of these two functions of law.[72]

All this and more would probably have been made clear if Marx had ever written the volume on the state which, according to the Introduction to the *Grundrisse,* he planned as part of his *Economics.* The first three volumes were to be followed by a fourth volume on "the synthesis of bourgeois society in the shape of the State." The absence of this volume is one of the principal gaps in Marx's theoretical system. Lacking this extended discussion, we should be wary of such simple formulations as that of the *Communist Manifesto:* "Political power, properly so called, is merely the organized power of one class for oppressing another." Marx's mature theory is that the state with its laws, no less than science, transcends the dualism of base and superstructure. There is this difference: *science* mainly interpenetrates the *forces* of production—the *state* mainly interpenetrates the *relations* of production. Nonetheless both forces and relations belong to the base, and neither the state nor science is confined to the superstructure.

9. *Ideology*

I have maintained that neither science nor the state with its laws fits neatly into the base-superstructure model. The ideological forms of consciousness, reflecting the schisms and class interests in the social relations of production, fit the model better.

The theory of ideology is familiar to all students of Marxism. Just as Freud exposes the illusory nature of rationalization by uncovering the instinctive underpinning of human motivation, so Marx exposes the illusory nature of ideology by uncovering the material substructure:

> As in private life one differentiates between what a man thinks and says of himself and what he really is and does, so

[72]See Norman Fischer, *Economy and Self: Philosophy and Economics from the Mercantilists to Marx* (Westport, Conn.: Greenwood Press, 1979), Chap. VII, Section D.

in historical struggles one must distinguish still more the phrases and fancies of parties from their real organism and their real interests, their conception of themselves from the reality.[73]

An ideology is a misleading set of ideas with which men, more or less unconsciously, rationalize and excuse or conceal their class interests. As Engels explained:

Ideology is a process accomplished by a so-called thinker consciously, indeed, but with a false consciousness. . . . He works with mere thought material which he accepts without examination as the product of thought; he does not investigate further for a more remote process independent of thought.[74]

This passage defining ideology as "false consciousness" was written after the death of Marx. There seems to be no evidence that Marx used these precise words, but he used nouns such as "illusion," "distortion," and "self-deception" and adjectives such as "incorrect," "twisted," and "untrue" to describe ideology. I agree with Martin Seliger that he usually meant by "ideology" an illusory or distorted set of ideas.[75] Although Georges Gurvitch claims to have distinguished various meanings of ideology in Marx's writing,[76] the most common meaning is a false body of ideas used, perhaps unconsciously, to conceal or excuse vested interests. Marx thus differs from theorists who characterize *all* ideas in support of political or economic interests as "ideological" whether or not they are false. He differs even more from those who contend that ideology permeates

[73]Marx, *The Eighteenth Brumaire of Louis Bonaparte*, in Marx, *Selected Works*, II, pp. 344–345.

[74]Letter of Engels to Franz Mehring, July 14, 1893, in Marx and Engels, *Selected Correspondence 1846–1895*, p. 511.

[75]See Martin Seliger, *The Marxist Conception of Ideology*, pp. 30–31. On variant meanings of "ideology" see Raymond Williams, *Marxism and Literature* (Oxford University Press, 1977), I, 4.

[76]Georges Gurvitch, *Études sur les Classes Sociales* (Paris, 1966), pp. 55–56. Cited by Bertell Ollman, *Alienation: Marx's Conception of Man in Capitalist Society* (Cambridge at the University Press, 1971), pp. 6, 256. But see Seliger, *op. cit.*, p. 29 f.n.

every body of ideas. Although "ideology" has different connotations for different theorists, I am using the term in the original Marxist sense of false consciousness in defense of class interests. Ideology in this meaning of the word may not be false through and through but it is false on the whole.

In *The Eighteenth Brumaire of Louis Bonaparte,* Marx characterizes bourgeois ideology as follows:

> Unheroic as bourgeois society is, yet it had need of heroism, of sacrifice, of terror, of civil war and of national battles to bring it into being. And in the classically austere traditions of the Roman Republic its gladiators found the ideals and the art forms, the self-deceptions that they needed in order to conceal from themselves the bourgeois limitations of the content of their struggles and to keep their passion at the height of the great historical tragedy. Similarly, at another stage of development, a century earlier, Cromwell and the English people had borrowed speech, passions, and illusions from the Old Testament for their bourgeois revolution.[77]

The proletarian revolution, in contrast, must strip off "all superstition in regard to the past" and "let the dead bury their dead." Truth must replace ideology. Marx's prodigious labor in economic research and writing was intended to promote this very purpose.

When "scientific" Marxists stress economic determinants, they usually assume that "ideology" is simply a reflection of the base. Antonio Gramsci, along with members of the "Frankfurt School" (Horkheimer, Adorno, Habermas, Marcuse), has repudiated this crude interpretation of Marx:

> To the extent that ideologies are historically necessary they have a validity which is "psychological"; they "organize" human masses and create the terrain on which men move, acquire consciousness of their position, struggle, etc. . . . The claim presented as an essential postulate of historical materialism, that every fluctuation of politics and ideology can be presented and expounded as an immediate expression of the structure [i.e., base], must be contested in theory as primitive

[77]*The Eighteenth Brumaire of Louis Bonaparte,* pp. 316–317.

infantilism, and combatted in practice with the authentic testimony of Marx. . . . [78]

Gramsci distinguishes two ways in which the ruling class attains and prepetuates its power. On the one hand, there is the domination of the state with its police and military force. On the other hand, there is the ideological control through education, language, culture, and the mass media.

As Carl Boggs has written, this two-dimensional conception of class domination

> leads to an important strategic proposition: that any crisis of the established order which might open the way to revolutionary transformation must follow a crisis of ideological hegemony in civil society. . . . [79]

In the words of Gramsci:

> If the ruling class has lost its consensus, i.e., is no longer "leading" but only "dominant," exercising coercive force alone, this means precisely that the great masses have become detached from their traditional ideologies, and no longer believe what they used to believe previously, etc. The crisis consists precisely in the fact that the old is dying and the new cannot be born; in this interregnum a great variety of morbid symptoms appear.[80]

For the masses to escape from this malaise, new meanings and norms of everyday life must be created to take the place of the old "false consciousness."

Gramsci's claim that Marx recognized the profound impact of ideology is borne out by the following passage from *The German Ideology*:

> The ideas of the ruling class are in every epoch the ruling ideas: i.e., the class which is the ruling *material* force of

---

[78]Quintin Hoare and Geoffrey Nowell-Smith, *Selections from the Prison Notebooks of Antonio Gramsci* (London: Lawrence and Wishart, 1971), pp. 371, 407.

[79]Carl Boggs, *Gramsci's Marxism* (London: Pluto Press Ltd., 1976), p. 40. For a discussion of the present "crisis of ideological hegemony" see Jürgen Habermas, *Legitimation Crisis* (Boston: Beacon Press, 1975), especially Chapters 6 and 7 in Part II.

[80]*Selections from the Prison Notebooks of Antonio Gramsci*, p. 276.

society is at the same time its ruling *intellectual* force. The class which has the means of material production at its disposal, consequently also controls the means of mental production, so that the ideas of those who lack the means of mental production are on the whole subject to it. . . . For each new class which puts itself in the place of one ruling before it *is compelled, merely in order to carry through its aim,* to present its interest as the common interest of all the members of society, that is, expressed in ideal form: it has to give its ideas the form of universality, and present them as the only rational, universally valid ones.[81] (My italics.)

Similarly in *The Eighteenth Brumaire of Louis Bonaparte* Marx asserts that ideological hegemony is a necessity for the rise to power and domination of the ruling class.[82] As I shall point out in Chapter V, he believed that the erosion of bourgeois ideology and its replacement by a realistic mass consciousness is necessary for proletarian revolution.

10. The Relation of Art to Base and Superstructure

Art no less than science can transcend the relativities of class and the distortions of ideology. Engels remarked that Balzac rose above "his own class sympathies and political prejudices" in his faithful portrayal of French society.[83] Marx similarly admired Balzac as a superb realist who depicted the sordid realities of his own bourgeois society. Marx also praised Dickens, Thackeray, Charlotte Brontë, and Elizabeth Gaskell for their authentic representation of English middle-class life.[84] Recognizing the automony and intrinsic value of art, Marx defended Heine when he was

---

[81]*The German Ideology,* pp. 59–60.
[82]*The Eighteenth Brumaire of Louis Bonaparte* in Marx and Engels, *Selected Works,* II, pp. 315–319.
[83]Letter of Engels to Margaret Harkness, April 1888, in Marx/Engels, *On Literature and Art,* ed. by Lee Baxandall and Stefan Morawski (New York: International General, 1974), pp. 116–117.
[84]Maynard Solomon, *Marxism and Art* (New York: Alfred A. Knopf, 1973), p. 11.

attacked for not being tendentious in his poetry.[85] In *The Holy Family*, he and Engels pilloried a mediocre novelist, Eugene Sue, as a mere ideologist, implying that the greatest novelists are not so tied down by class interests. If ideology is "false consciousness," Sue's *Mysteries of Paris* is ideological, but the novels of Balzac and Dickens as characterized by Marx are *true* consciousness and hence non-ideological.

Although fictional characters and events are not true in the literal sense, they may be true on the imaginative plane. The novelist would not claim that *these* particular characters exist and *these* particular events occur, but he might justifiably claim that *such* characters exist and *such* events occur. Beings and happenings of the *kind* depicted in fiction may be real. In this sense a novel may be as revealing of the nature of things as a scientific treatise. Marx recognized and appreciated this kind of truth.

Even the symbolism of myth need not be dismissed as false. An example is Prometheus as the symbol of tragedy and hope. In the Preface of his doctoral dissertation (1841) Marx wrote that "Prometheus is the foremost saint and martyr in the philosophical calendar," and his entire dissertation was pervaded by the spirit of Promethean humanism. Also in the brief "Confession" that he wrote late in life for his daughter Laura he listed Aeschylus as a "favorite poet" along with Shakespeare and Goethe. His son-in-law, Paul Lafargue, declared that Marx "every year ... read Aeschylus in the original."[86] The figure of Prometheus in the play by Aeschylus symbolizes the humanistic arts and sciences, seeking to displace the tyrannical rule of the gods by diffusing their power among men. Thus he stands for a moral ideal of the deepest human significance—the rational control of the environment, both natural and social.

[85]Marx/Engels, *On Literature and Art*, pp. 150–151.
[86]Marx's "Confession" and Lafargue's reminiscences are reproduced in Erich Fromm, *Marx's Concept of Man, op. cit.*

The inventor I, who many a shape did show
Of science to mankind.[87]

We know from Marx's writings that he interpreted this creative role in no narrow technological sense—that he believed passionately that man the toolmaker should be also man the artist.

Chained on the mountainside with vultures gnawing at his liver, Prometheus is also the symbol of the redemption that may come from long suffering. He calls on the whole world to bear witness to the agonies that he suffers at the hands of the gods. This ordeal only strengthens his resolve to defy his persecutors ("I hate the pack of gods!"). Mankind, said Marx, must likewise suffer the pangs of alienation before it can achieve the will and the wisdom to emancipate itself, and the proletariat is the Promethean agent in this emancipation. So interpreted, *Prometheus Bound* is for Marx an example of symbolic truth and not of false consciousness.

He was keenly aware that the economic base limits the kind of art that can be created. "Is Achilles possible side by side with powder and lead?" he asked. "Or is the *Iliad* at all compatible with the printing press and steam press?"[88] Although his answer is No, he did not believe that artistic development is necessarily proportional to economic development. Progress in the one does not necessarily entail progress in the other. "It is well known," he said, "that certain periods of highest development in art stand in no direct connection with the general development of society, nor with the material basis and the skeleton structure of its organization."[89] Capitalist development, even in its progressive phases, tends to be inimical to art, because it replaces individual craftmanship with factory routine. Of medieval handicraft Marx remarked: "This work is still

---

[87]*Prometheus Bound*, translated by E.A. Havelock in *The Crucifixion of Intellectual Man* (Boston: Beacon Press, 1950), lines 469–470.
[88]Marx, *A Contribution to the Critique of Political Economy*, p. 311.
[89]*Ibid.*, pp. 309–310.

half-artistic, it has still the aim in itself."[90] The capitalist division of labor, he contended, has largely destroyed this aesthetic component in production. The effect has been "the exclusive concentration of artistic talent in certain individuals, and its consequent suppression in the broad masses of the people."[91]

When Marx turns from a consideration of the role of the creator to that of the appreciator, he rejects the theory that aesthetic value is entirely relative to the economic stage of development. He points out that Greek art and poetry "still constitute with us a source of aesthetic enjoyment and in certain respects prevail as the standard and mode beyond attainment."[92] He similarly characterizes the enduring vitality of Shakespeare. The artistic creations of long ago exert "an eternal charm" even though the ancient social orders have disappeared and will never return.

Ideally art belongs in the base among the forces of production and not merely in the superstructure. In distinguishing between human beings and lower forms of life, Marx stresses the imaginative character of human production:

> We presuppose labour in a form that stamps it as exclusively human. A spider conducts operations that resemble those of a weaver, and a bee puts to shame many an architect in the construction of her cells. But what distinguishes the worst architect from the best of bees is this, that the architect raises his structure in imagination before he erects it in reality. At the end of every labour process, we get a result that already existed in the imagination of the labourer at its commencement.[93]

Similarly in the *Economic and Philosophical Manuscripts* Marx distinguishes between human and animal productivity:

> Of course, animals also produce. They construct nests, dwellings, as in the case of bees, beavers, ants, etc. But they

[90]Marx/Engels, *On Literature and Art*, p. 16.
[91]*The German Ideology*, in *Mega*, Abt. I, Bd. 2, p. 373.
[92]*A Contribution to the Critique of Political Economy*, pp. 311–312. That similar observations can be made about other intellectual productions is pointed out by Gordon Leff, *The Tyranny of Concepts*, pp. 128–143.
[93]Marx, *Capital*, I, p. 198.

only produce what is strictly necessary for themselves or their young. They produce only in a single direction, while man produces universally. They produce only under the compulsion of direct physical needs, while man produces in freedom from such needs. Animals produce only themselves, while man reproduces the whole of nature. The products of animal production belong directly to their physical bodies, while man is free in face of his product. Animals construct only in accordance with the standards and needs of the species to which they belong, while man knows how to produce in accordance with the standards of every species and knows how to apply the appropriate standard to the object. Thus man constructs also in accordance with the laws of beauty.[94]

The aesthetic element in human nature is no veneer. It is the product of the whole socio-historical development of mankind—inseparable from the humanization of nature and the naturalization of man:

Only through the objectively unfolded richness of man's essential being is the richness of subjective *human* sensibility (a musical ear, an eye for beauty of form—in short, *senses* capable of human gratification, senses affirming themselves as essential powers of *man*) either cultivated or brought into being. For not only the five senses but also the so-called mental senses—the practical senses (will, love, etc.)—in a word, *human* sense—the human nature of the senses—comes to be by virtue of its object, by virtue of *humanized* nature. The *forming* of the five senses is a labor of the entire history of the world down to the present.[95]

Insisting on the sensory and passional nature of man, Marx conceived of aesthetic cultivation as an essential part of human self-realization. Few writers have gone so far as Marx in characterizing human nature in terms of its imaginative and artistic capacities. Except under conditions of human alienation the productive process brings these ca-

[94]Marx, *Economic and Philosophical Manuscripts*, p. 128.
[95]Marx, *The Economic and Philosophical Manuscripts of 1844*, trans. by Martin Milligan (New York: International Publishers, 1964), p. 141. I prefer Milligan's translation to Bottomore's in this instance.

pacities into play. It conforms to "the laws of beauty," and it is enjoyed by the worker because it "gives play to his bodily and mental powers."[96] In a healthy society art and aesthetic impulse occupy an important place in the base.[97]

11. Other Spheres of Culture: Religion, Morals, and Philosophy

Religion and morality form the realm of human values in their purest expression. How does Marx interpret this "spiritual" dimension of life? His answer with respect to religion is plain. Religion, as the fantasy of alienated man, is an example of false ideological consciousness. "It is the fantastic realization of the human being," he contends, "inasmuch as the human being possesses no true reality."[98] In calling it "the opium of the people," Marx implies that it diverts the masses from social reform and revolution. But both the Peasant War in Germany under the religious leadership of the Anabaptists and the English Cromwellian revolution under the leadership of the Diggers and other radical sects indicate that religion is not always an "opium" that dulls resentment to the established order. Marx, however, was inclined to deplore even positive religious leadership. "The Peasant

[96]Marx, Capital, I, p. 198. The quoted phrases are reminiscent of Schiller's Letters on the Aesthetic Education of Man, a work with which Marx was familiar.

[97]Compare Solomon, Marxism and Art, especially pp. 20–21. For an admirable summary of Marx's indebtedness to the aesthetics of Kant, Schiller, Hegel, and others see Stefan Morawski, "Introduction" to Karl Marx/Frederick Engels, On Literature and Art, ed. by Lee Baxandall and Stefan Morawski (New York: International General, 1974), pp. 40–45. See also Mikhail Lifshits, The Philosophy of Art of Karl Marx (London: Pluto Press, 1973). For a comprehensive discussion of Marx's theories of aesthetics and literary art, see S.S. Prawer, Karl Marx and World Literature (Oxford at the Clarendon Press, 1976). Prawer declares: "The present book should ... have demonstrated beyond doubt that in his actual dealings with literature Marx never makes mechanical and rigid use of the 'base-superstructure' model, and that it does not, in fact, figure at all prominently in his appreciations of existing literary works." (p. 412).

[98]A Contribution to the Critique of Hegel's Philosophy of Right: Introduction, in Marx, Early Writings, p. 43.

War, the most radical event in German history," he complained, "came to grief because of theology."[99]

The principal case study in original Marxist sources that bears on this great historical event is Engels' *The Peasant War in Germany* (1850). This book deals with Thomas Münzer, the revolutionary advocate of equalitarian communism, and the peasant rebellion of which he was the charismatic leader. Engels recognizes the strong religious character of this radical movement, but he tries to fit it into the pattern of economic base and religious superstructure. The effect of the War, he argues, was not to free the peasants, because economic conditions were not ripe for this kind of revolution, but to attack feudal institutions and thereby to promote burgher reform. More credit, however, should have been accorded to religion for the changes that occurred. Engels should have stated unequivocally that without the religious Reformation the Peasant War would have been impossible. In this instance the primary economic "contradiction" between the forces and relations of production was determinant only in fusion with "superstructural" religious factors. The religious aspects of the Reformation alone could not have caused the Peasant War, but neither could the economic malaise alone have caused it. Marx and Engels would have been more realistic if they had explicitly admitted a plurality of "contradictions" in society, the economic contradiction often being fused with others. Without this fusion the economic often would not suffice as explanation. The distinction between economic causes as necessary and economic causes as *both* necessary and sufficient to explain the given phenomenon is too seldom made.[100]

[99]*Ibid.*, p. 53. For a comprehensive discussion of the Peasant War see the special issue of the *Journal of Peasant Studies*, Vol. 3, No. 1, October 1975, on the occasion of the 450th anniversary of the German Peasant War of 1525.
[100]For an illuminating discussion of multiple causation, see "Contradiction and Overdetermination" in Louis Althusser, *For Marx*, pp. 89–128, especially the discussion of the Russian Revolution. Althusser points out that the Revolution was caused by a whole constellation of causes. See also Bertrand Russell's remarks in *Freedom Versus Organization* (New York: W. W. Norton and Company, 1934), pp. 197–200.

Many of Marx's references to morality are hostile. He calls into question bourgeois morals by depicting them as a reflection of the interests of a privileged class. This relativistic interpretation of morality is a critical weapon of great potency, but it would be a mistake to classify Marx as no more than a relativist. His theory of alienation and its overcoming and his faith in progress imply objective standards. Without some objective criteria there is no way to distinguish disalienation from alienation and progress from retrogression. In his youth he declared that "the categorical imperative" is "to overthrow all those conditions in which man is an abased, enslaved, abandoned, contemptible being."[101] Far from deserting his early ethical humanism he continued to cling to it throughout his lifetime. In *Capital* he declared that the goal is to produce "fully developed human beings" and to achieve "the full development of the human race."[102] He reminded the delegates at a meeting of the First International of the need to recognize "the simple laws of morals and justice, which ought to govern the relations of private individuals, as the rules paramount of the intercourse of nations."[103] Similarly Engels believed in a rationale of progress running within and across the centuries. He noted in *Anti-Dühring* that feudal, capitalist, and socialist morality represent progressive stages of historical development.[104]

Philosophy is akin to religion and morals in its concern for values and akin to science in its concern for truth. For Marx it should be critical and activist. In his Introduction to *The Critique of Hegel's Philosophy of Right* he concludes:

> Just as philosophy finds its *material* weapons in the proletariat, so the proletariat finds its intellectual weapons in philosophy. . . . Philosophy can only be realized by the abolition

[101]Marx, *A Contribution to the Critique of Hegel's Philosophy of Right: Introduction*, p. 52.
[102]*Capital*, I, pp. 530, 555.
[103]Marx, *Selected Works*, II, p. 442.
[104]Engels, *Herr Eugen Dühring's Revolution in Science* (New York: International Publishers, no date), pp. 108–109.

of the proletariat, and the proletariat can only be abolished by the realization of philosophy.[105]

Repudiating philosophy in its spectator role, Marx attacks idealism for its lack of realism and "all previous materialism" for its passivity. To be acceptable to Marx, philosophy must be *accurate* in depicting real life and *effective* in inciting men to action. "The philosophers," he exclaims in the *Theses on Feuerbach*, "have only *interpreted* the world in different ways; the point is to *change* it." Philosophy that inspires the masses bridges the gulf between base and superstructure. "Material force can only be overthrown by material force; but theory itself becomes a material force when it has seized the masses."[106]

The fact that an idea is determined by the base does not prove that it is false; the fact that an idea is true does not prove that it is undetermined by the base. The truth or falsity of an idea must be judged by objective logical criteria. But the genesis of ideas may be *somewhat* indicative of their truth or falsity. False ideas are more likely to be class-biased than are true ideas. If all or almost all ideas and values were relative to class interest, we would have much more reason to think that the fundamentalist version of the base-superstructure model is sound. In recognizing that philosophy, science, morality, and art often transcend the relativities of class and economic period, Marx shows that he is not entrapped by the base-superstructure model. He is aware that all these modes of culture have their intrinsic norms of truth or validity, and he recognizes that all have an important impact upon the base.

12. *Base-Superstructure and Organic Totality*

If base-superstructure is understood as a metaphor drawn from architecture, it is misleading as a model of Marx's

[105]Marx, *A Contribution to the Critique of Hegel's Philosophy of Right: Introduction*, p. 59.
[106]*Ibid.*, p. 52. For a perspicacious survey of Marx's philosophical ideas see William Leon McBride, *The Philosophy of Marx* (New York: St. Martin's Press, 1977).

interpretation of history. In a building the superstructure rests on the base; the base does not rest on the superstructure. The metaphor, implying separate levels and one-way support, is false to the reciprocal relations among the elements in the social order. The very phrase, "base and superstructure" has misleading connotations.

The interrelation between base and superstructure is stated non-reductively in *Theories of Surplus Value*. Marx clearly distinguishes between "class-ideology" and "free intellectual production" such as art and science.[107] He also distinguishes between "spiritual" and "material production" and speaks of their interplay:

> In order to examine the connection between spiritual production and material production it is above all necessary to grasp the latter itself not as a general category but in *definite historical* form. Thus for example different kinds of spiritual production correspond to the capitalist mode of production and to the mode of production of the Middle Ages. If material production itself is not conceived in its *specific historical* form, it is impossible to understand what is specific in the spiritual production corresponding to it and the reciprocal influence of one on the other.[108]

This quotation expresses the truth of the base-superstructure model without the reductionism that has been read into it. Marx is insisting on the close relation between material and spiritual production and the historical specificity of their interaction. Far from asserting a one-way causal relation he recognizes "the reciprocal influence of one on the other." While still maintaining that the economy has a predominant influence, he realizes that innumerable circumstances and influences outside of the economic base also play an important role in the dialectical interplay.

> The form of [the] relation between rulers and ruled naturally corresponds always with a definite stage in the development

---

[107]See S. S. Prawer, *Karl Marx and World Literature*, pp. 313–314.
[108]Marx, *Theories of Surplus Value* (Moscow: Foreign Languages Publishing House, no date), I, p. 276.

of the methods of labor and of its productive social power. This does not prevent the same economic basis from showing infinite variations and gradations in its appearance, even though its principal conditions are everywhere the same. This is due to innumerable outside circumstances, natural environment, race peculiarities, outside historical influences, and so forth, all of which must be ascertained by careful analysis.[109]

The historical resultant is too complex and concrete to be described by the simplifications and abstractions of economic determinism.

In conclusion, I do not deny the importance of the base-superstructure model. Until the advent of Marxism most historical interpretation was idealist, depicting events as the outcome of religious, moral or philosophical ideas. This idealist interpretation reached its apogee in Hegel. In turning Hegel's theory "right side up," Marx's model of base and superstructure marks a great change. Almost all modern treatments of economic history go back to Marx's interpretation, and even the history of culture has been enormously influenced by it. Works such as E. J. Hobsbawm's *The Age of Revolution*, J. L. and Barbara Hammond's *The Town Labourer*, George Thomson's *Aeschylus and Athens*, and Arnold Hauser's *The Social History of Art*, could not have been written without Marx's formulation.

The problem is to separate truth from exaggeration. I have argued that the reductionist implications of the model as ordinarily interpreted are contradicted by numerous passages in Marx's own writings. Even Engels' dialectical version is unsatisfactory because it resembles the fundamentalist approach. Science and technology, law, politics, religion, morality, art, and philosophy transcend the dualism of base and superstructure. The question is whether an organic theory of relations can be formulated so as to preserve the truth in the base-superstructure doctrine while eliminating its untruth. I shall maintain in the next chapter that such an organic theory is implicit in Marx's works. He is his own antidote.

[109]*Capital*, Vol. III, p. 919.

2

Organic Structure

1. The Organic Totality Model

In the preceding chapter we have noted both the strength and the weakness of the base-superstructure model. Its *strength* is its emphasis on the historical importance of the mode of production—an approach that has revolutionized the writing of history. Its *weakness* is its tendency toward reductionism. By relegating government and law to the superstructure, it misdescribes the power relations of capitalism. In likewise consigning science to the superstructure, it is just as unrealistic—modern industrial technology is inconceivable without a scientific basis. Other components of culture—philosophy, art, religion, and morality—are less decisive in their economic impact, but they are much more than ineffectual by-products of economic forces. The fundamentalist version of the model is inadequate, and even the dialectical version understates the internal relatedness of base and superstructure.

The organic totality model retains the strength and avoids the weakness of the base-superstructure model. Some parts in an organism play a more decisive role—this hierarchical structure preserves the strength of the base-superstructure model by weighting some factors more than others. The parts stand in internal relations with one another, and this web of internal relations avoids the weakness of reductionism. Of the two models, base-superstructure and organic totality, the latter is more faithful to Marx's mature insights.

To employ the fashionable terminology of "structural-ism," Marx's account of the organic nature of society comprises both a *synchronic* and a *diachronic* analysis. The synchronic is an analysis of the structure that remains fairly constant throughout history. The diachronic is the analysis of historical development into temporal stages. In the Preface to *The Critique of Political Economy* quoted in Chapter 1, these two kinds of analysis are distinguished with respect to the base-superstructure model. On the one hand, there are the more enduring structural characteristics—the *base* with its interaction of man and nature and its dialectical interplay of the forces and relations of production, and the *superstructure* with its divisions between the political-legal and the cultural components (both ideological and non-ideological). On the other hand, there are the *stages* of historical development—the primitive, "Asiatic," classical, feudal, capitalist, and communist modes. A similar distinction between the synchronic and the diachronic perspectives is applicable to the organic approach. In the next chapter I shall concentrate on the diachronic (society in process) and in this chapter I shall focus on the synchronic (society in cross section). The synchronic structure is a synthesis of internal relatedness and hierarchy. Just what this means I shall try to explain.

Marx clearly indicates the relevance of organic totality to his historical inquiry. In his Preface to the first edition of *Capital* he remarks that "the present society is no solid crystal, but an organism capable of change, and it is constantly changing"; and in his Afterword to the second edition he quotes with approval the remark of a Russian reviewer that "the scientific value of such an inquiry lies in the disclosing of the special laws that regulate the origin, existence, development, and death of a given social organism and its replacement by another and higher one." Scattered through the book are organic metaphors, such as the "cell-forms" of the economic structure, the "metabolism" of the work process in assimilating nature's raw materials, the growth of a social embroyo in the "womb" of the old social order, and the "birth pangs" in the emergence of the new social order. In the *Grundrisse* bourgeois society is characterized as an organic system:

> While in the completed bourgeois system every economic relation presupposes every other in its bourgeois economic form, and everything posited is thus also a presupposition, this is the case with every organic system. This organic system itself, as a totality, has its presuppositions, and its development to its totality consists precisely in subordinating all elements of society to itself, or in creating out of it the organs which it still lacks. This is historically how it becomes a totality.[1]

The society thus described is not a mere arithmetical sum of separate and distinct parts but a configuration of interdependent elements. There is a total functional integration in which each element is what it is because of its relations to the other elements and to the whole. Each entails and is entailed by the other elements.

Marx explains the economic interrelations of production, distribution, consumption, and exchange in terms of organic unity:

> The conclusion we reach is not that production, distribution, exchange and consumption are identical, but that they all form the members of a totality, distinctions within a unity. Production predominates ... over the other moments. ... The process always returns to production to begin anew. ... A definite production thus determines a definite consumption, distribution and exchange as well as *definite relations among these different moments*. Admittedly, however, *in its one-sided form*, production is itself determined by the other moments. For example if the market, i.e. the sphere of exchange, expands, then production grows in quantity and the divisions between its different branches become deeper. A change in distribution changes production, e.g., concentration of capital, different distribution of the population between town and country, etc. Finally, the needs of consump-

[1]*Grundrisse: Foundations of the Critique of Political Economy (Rough Draft)*, trans. by Martin Nicolaus (Harmondsworth: Penguin Books, Ltd., 1973), p. 278.

tion determine production. Mutual interaction takes place between the different moments. This is the case with every organic whole.[2]

The last two sentences in this quotation indicate that the "mutual interaction" between the internal elements ("moments") is characteristic of *all* organic wholes. The interdependence of part and part, and part and whole, is the very mark of an organism.

The preceding reference to production "in its one-sided form" is a bit puzzling. Apparently Marx means that production may be considered more or less abstractly. When abstracted from other elements with which it is internally related, it is one-sided—for example, when it is thus abstractly distinguished from distribution, consumption, and exchange. But even when the whole complex of these economic factors is included there remains a degree of abstraction because production in its organic totality is internally related to "moments" that are not usually thought of as economic. Marx declares in the *Economic and Philosophical Manuscripts*, for example, that "religion, family, state, law, morality, science, art, etc., are only particular modes of production."[3] This surprising statement is the very antithesis of the fundamentalist version of the base-superstructure model. It indicates that factors that are usually relegated to the superstructure—religion, law, science, art, etc.—contribute their share to the productive process *in its many-sidedness*. A residual degree of one-sidedness remains so long as the entire complex of economic relationships is abstracted from the other elements in the total organic structure.

We need to combine this concept of organic totality with what is said in the passage from the *Grundrisse*: "Production predominates . . . over the other elements. . . . The process always returns to production to begin anew." This weighting of elements—production being weighted most

[2]*Ibid.*, pp. 99–100.
[3]*Economic and Philosophical Manuscripts*, trans. by Martin Milligan (New York: International Publishers, 1946), p. 136.

heavily—conforms to the principle of hierarchy, which I shall discuss in a later section. The two principles, hierarchy and organic interrelatedness, go together. Although production is dominant in the organic hierarchy, it is not independent; it is part of the organic whole. This is also true of the economy in its totality. It is false to regard it as independent of the social, political, and cultural structure.

Because the Paris Manuscripts is an earlier work, it might be thought to express a point of view that was later abandoned. But the Theories of Surplus Value, representing the mature stage of Marx's thought, states just as unequivocally that production is caught up in a web of internal relations:

> All circumstances . . . which affect man, the subject of production, have a greater or lesser influence upon all his functions and activities, including his functions and activities as the creator of material wealth, of commodities. In this sense, it can truly be asserted that all human relations and functions, however and wherever they manifest themselves, influence material production and have a more or less determining effect upon it.[4]

Outside of this web of internally related parts the elements would lose their identity. Production, no more than language, can be separated from the society:

> The human being is in the most literal sense a political animal, not merely a gregarious animal, but an animal that can individuate itself only in society. Production by an isolated individual outside society . . . is as much of an absurdity as is the development of language without individuals living together and talking to each other.[5]

The only apparent exception occurs "when a civilized person in whom the social forces are already dynamically present is cast by accident into the wilderness."[6] This is no real exception because the society has been internalized in the

[4]Theorien Über den Mehwert, 3 vols. ed. by Karl Kautsky (Stuttgart: 1905–1910), Vol. I, pp. 388–389. Quoted by T.B. Bottomore and Maximilien Rubel in Marx, Selected Writings in Sociology and Social Philosophy (London: C.A. Watts & Co., 1956), p. 100.
[5]Grundrisse (Nicolaus), p. 84.
[6]Ibid., my italics.

language and data of thought. As Marx notes in the *Economic and Philosophical Manuscripts*, the solitary thinker moulds and is moulded by society:

> Even when I carry out *scientific* work, etc., an activity which I can seldom conduct in direct association with other men, I perform a *social*, because *human*, act. It is not only the material of my activity—such as the language itself which the thinker uses—which is given to me as a social product. My *own existence* is a social activity. For this reason, what I myself produce I produce for society, and with the consciousness of acting as a social being.[7]

Because man is internally related to other men, the dualism of individual and society is false: "The individual *is* the *social being.*"[8]

Marx is no less opposed to the dualism of man and nature. A human being is what he is because of his internal relations to the natural as well as the human environment. "A being which does not have its nature outside itself," Marx explains, "is not a *natural* being and does not share in the being of nature."[9] The internal relations are reciprocal: the human being is natural and nature is human. Nature shares a common essence with man.

> To say that man *lives* from nature means that nature is his *body* with which he must remain in a continuous interchange in order not to die. The statement that the physical and mental life of man, and nature, are interdependent means simply that nature is interdependent with itself, for man is part of nature.[10]

Thus Marx thinks in terms of wider and wider structures of organic wholeness. The psycho-physical individual is an organic structure, the society of which he is an organic member is a wider structure, nature of which mankind

[7]*Economic and Philosophical Manuscripts* in Karl Marx, *Early Writings*, trans. by T. B. Bottomore (London: C.A. Watts & Co., 1963), pp. 157–158.
[8]*Ibid.*, p. 158.
[9]*Ibid.*, p. 207.
[10]*Ibid.*, p. 127.

and its social formations are organic parts is a still wider structure.

In the Paris *Manuscripts,* Marx is discussing nature in a *human* context. "Nature ... taken abstractly, for itself, and rigidly separated from man, is *nothing* for man."[11] It is valuable and knowable only in relation to human beings. Hence Marx is not discussing the internal relatedness of things-in-themselves entirely apart from human perspectives. He is not saying that the *whole universe* is a single all-embracing organic unity. This organic view of the universe is frequently attributed to Hegel, but even he recognizes that *in actuality,* not in logical schematism, there are incoherences and disconnections in the structure of things.

2. How the Conception of Organic Totality Took Shape in Marx's Thought

As a student of philosophy, Marx read the works of Aristotle, Spinoza, Leibniz, Hume, Kant, and especially Hegel. It might be possible to trace the impact of all these philosophers on Marx, but I shall presently confine myself to the Hegelian influence. In a long letter to his father from Berlin dated November 1837, Marx said that he had come to know the philosophy of Hegel from beginning to end.[12] His intimate association with the Young Hegelians at the Universities of Bonn and Berlin indoctrinated him in the Hegelian tradition. Later he reacted strongly against the idealism of Hegel. There is a little verse that goes:

> Long ago in London town
> Marx turned Hegel upside down.[13]

Marx's own account of how he up-turned Hegel and still remained "the pupil of that mighty thinker" is too well known to quote. That he continued to admire Hegel and

[11]*Ibid.,* p. 217.
[12]Letter of Marx to his father in Trier, November 10–11, 1827, in Karl Marx/Frederick Engels, *Collected Works* (New York: International Publishers, 1975), Vol. 1, p. 19.
[13]*Encounter* (magazine) June 1963, p. 65.

greatly preferred him to Comte is indicated in a letter of
July 7, 1866, to Engels:

> I am also studying Comte now, as a sideline, because the
> English and French make such a fuss about the fellow. What
> takes their fancy is the encyclopaedic touch, the synthesis.
> But this is miserable compared to Hegel. (Although Comte, as
> a professional mathematician and physicist, was superior to
> him, i.e., superior in matters of detail, even here Hegel is
> infinitely greater as a whole.)[14]

I need not multiply quotations to indicate that Marx was
profoundly influenced by Hegel.

The concepts of organic unity and internal relations are
deeply imbedded in the philosophy of Hegel, but he does
not believe that the entire universe is an organic unity.[15] He
distinguishes between the inorganic and organic, and he
recognizes degrees of integration among plants, animals,
and societies. He even speaks of miscellaneous collections
and human aggregations as "heaps" rather than as articulated and coherent structures. Mere aggregations, he says,
are "untrue," but he explains that untruth does not imply
non-existence.

> We must remember . . . what "untrue" signifies. When it oc-
> curs in a philosopohical discussion, the term "untrue" does
> not signify that the thing to which it is applied is non-exis-
> tent. A bad state or a sickly body may exist all the same; but
> these things are untrue, because their notion and their reality
> are out of harmony.[16]

By "notion" Hegel means the pure definition of the entity,
the kind of thing it ideally is, what it ought to be to realize
its essential nature. In a bad state, there is a breach, a dis-

---

[14]Marx and Engels, *Selected Correspondence 1846–1895* (New York: International Publishers, 1942), p. 210. Letter of July 7, 1866.

[15]See J.N. Findlay, *Hegel: A Re-Examination* (London: George Allen &
Unwin, 1958), pp. 20–23. Findlay denies that Hegel intended such sweeping metaphysical generalization.

[16]*The Logic of Hegel Translated from the Encyclopedia of the Philosophical Sciences* by William Wallace (Oxford at the Clarendon Press, 1892), p.
150.

harmony, between the state as it *is* (existence as untrue to its essence) and the state as it *ought* to be (its notion).

Although Hegel applies the notion of organism to social formations, the paradigm example is a biological organism.

> The limbs and organs . . . of an organic body are not merely parts of it: it is only in this unity that they are what they are, and they are unquestionbly affected by that unity, as they also in turn affect it. These limbs and organs become mere parts only when they pass under the hands of the anatomist, whose occupation, be it remembered, is not with the living body but with the corpse.[17]

The whole and its parts is an inadequate category to apply to an organism because the organs are *internally* related to each other and because the total configuration and its elements reciprocally determine each other. This kind of articulated unity is the universal mark of organisms.

In calling the political state an organism, Hegel implies that it is or ought to be a unity of internally related members. Providing the widest and deepest integration of interests, the state supplies the individuals and groups that comprise its membership with the richest form of social participation. The true life of the members is found in and is identical with the life of the whole. Such is the *notion* of the state. Existing states fall short of the notion, to a greater or lesser degree. But every state, so far as it is *truly* a state, achieves this higher synthesis.

The state is an inclusive structure that encloses a hierarchy of structures. In between the family and the state is "civil society," which includes school and church and cultural association and economic group. Hegel's analysis of civil society, in which he is largely concerned with economic activities and property rights, is unsparing in its exposure of anarchic tendencies. In the clash of acquisitive individuals, the conflict of private interests, the welter of competing institutions, he discerns an inherent drive toward dissolution. The increasing division of labor intensi-

---

[17]*Ibid.*, pp. 145–146.

fies the narrowness and monotony of jobs, and wealth piles up among the few while poverty spreads among the many. Anomie and alienation run rampant.

> When the standard of living of a large mass of people falls below a certain subsistence level . . . and when there is a consequent loss of the sense of right and wrong, of honesty and the self-respect which makes a man insist on maintaining himself by his own work and effort, the result is the creation of a rabble of paupers. At the same time this brings with it, at the other end of the social scale, conditions which greatly facilitate the concentration of disproportionate wealth in a few hands.[18]

The result is underproduction in relation to need and overproduction in relation to effective demand. If the attempt were made to alleviate these conditions by public doles to the needy, this would contradict the principle of the free-enterprise system and undermine the independence and self-respect of the recipients. The needy could be provided with employment by the state, but this might simply aggravate the crisis of overproduction and overpopulation in relation to resources. Finally "the inner dialectic of civil society" might drive it to seek markets and colonization abroad. The history of the English and Spanish colonies indicates that such imperialism is no solution—it results in war, revolt, and ultimate independence of the colonial peoples.[19] It is not difficult to see that Hegel's argument finds powerful reverberations in Marx.

Because of the anarchic and centrifugal tendencies within civil society, Hegel believes that it is necessary to achieve a binding synthesis that will integrate all divergent individuals and institutions within a supreme social organism. This cohesion is achieved in and through the state. In the ideal state, Hegel explains, "the private interest of its citizens is one with the common interest of the state," and "the one finds its gratification and realization in the

[18]*Hegel's Philosophy of Right*, trans. by T.M. Knox (London, Oxford, New York: Oxford University Press, 1967), p. 150.
[19]*Ibid.*, pp. 150–151, 277–278.

other."[20] Although the ideal has not been attained, the state provides the living force that pervades and enlivens the whole social organism.

> On some principle or other, any state may be shown to be bad, this or that defect may be found in it; and yet, at any rate if one of the mature states of our epoch is in question, it has in it the moments essential to the existence of the state. But since it is easier to find defects than to understand the affirmative, we may readily fall into the mistake of looking at isolated aspects of the state and so forgetting its inward organic life. The state is no ideal work of art; it stands on earth and so in the sphere of caprice, chance, and error, and bad behavior may disfigure it in many respects. But the ugliest of men, or a criminal, or an invalid, or a cripple, is still a living man. The affirmative, life, subsists despite his defects, and it is this affirmative factor which is our theme here.[21]

The organism of the state is articulated in subordinate "estates"—the landed aristocracy, the business community, the governmental bureaucracy. To achieve the cohesion necessary to constitute a state, the citizens should not enter the political sphere as "atomistic" individuals, but through their associations, corporations, and estates. Finally the unity of the whole is embodied in the Constitution and is symbolized by the Crown. The state in toto must be strong enough to curb the antagonisms of civil society and synthesize its multifarious interests. This in brief sketch is the argument of The Philosophy of Right.

In view of Marx's Hegelian background, it is not surprising that his first major work was the Critique of Hegel's "Philosophy of Right," which he wrote in 1843 at the age of twenty-five. It was a time of hope and awakening which culminated in marriage to his childhood sweetheart, Jenny von Westphalen. In this period when Jenny and Karl dwelt for three months in her mother's house and in the period soon after (from October 1843 to February 1845) when they

[20]Hegel, The Philosophy of History, trans. by J. Sibree, (New York: P.F. Collier, Inc., 1900), p. 70.
[21]Hegel's Philosophy of Right, op. cit., p. 279.

lived in Paris, his ideas rapidly crystallized. During this time, Ludwig Feuerbach was enjoying great popularity in German leftwing circles. Two of his works, *The Essence of Christianity* (1841) and *Preliminary Theses for the Reform of Philosophy* (1843), excited Marx's enthusiasm. *The Essence of Christianity* maintained that the divine is the imaginative projection of human needs and ideals. The predicates of God (love, wisdom, power, etc.) are human— they are the attributes of humanity purified and reified. The *Preliminary Theses*, which came into Marx's hands just before he started work on the Hegel-Critique, advocated the subject-predicate conversion as a general method of criticizing Hegel's philosophy. According to Feuerbach, "The true relationship of thought to being is this only: Being [the human and material world] is the subject, thought the predicate."[22] But Hegel inverts this relation: *thought* is the subject, *being* the predicate. He reifies thought in the form of a cosmic Spirit or Absolute and regards man as a vehicle of this cosmic reality. To restore the truth, we must recognize that human life in the natural world is the "subject," and that thought is no more than an activity ("predicate") of real, concrete human beings.[23] God, Spirit, the Absolute, the System of the Categories—call it what you will—is an unreal abstraction. Marx accepts this argument.[24]

His *Critique*, left in manuscript and not published until 1927, is an analysis of sections 261 to 313 of Hegel's text (pages 161 to 204 of the standard English edition of the *Philosophy of Right* edited and translated by T. M. Knox). Marx comments on the sections that deal directly with the state, but he also has in mind sections depicting the weaknesses and antagonisms of civil society. He concurs with

[22]*Preliminary Theses on the Reform of Philosophy*, in *The Fiery Brook: Selected Writings of Ludwig Feuerbach* (Garden City, N.Y.: Doubleday & Company, 1972), p. 168.

[23]*Ibid.*, p. 154.

[24]In a letter to Arnold Ruge in March 1843, Marx expressed his hearty agreement with the *Preliminary Theses*. His sole regret expressed in the letter was that Feuerbach had not extended his transformative criticism— the subject-object conversion—to the sphere of politics.

Hegel's main concept that the state is an "organism." "It is a great advance," he says, "to consider the political state as an organism, and hence no longer to consider the diversity of powers as inorganic, but rather as living and rational differences."[25] But there is a fundamental contrast between Hegel and Marx. The former regards the state-molded society (at least in pure concept) as healthy, the latter regards it as diseased. This at once distinguishes Marx from all who extol the state as an organic unity. Both in this period and later Marx is concerned with organic disunity—the schisms and "contradictions" that fatally impair the unity of the whole.

Far from overlooking Hegel's characterization of civil society as the arena of conflict, he contends that not only the economy but the state is rent by the antagonisms of civil society. He quotes a remark of Hegel that virtually concedes that this is the case:

> Just as civil society is the battlefield where everyone's individual private interest meets everyone else's, so here (in the political sphere) we have the struggle (a) of private interests against particular matters of common concern and (b) of both of these together against the organization of the state and its higher outlook.

"This is especially worth noting," Marx comments, "because of the definition of civil society as the *bellum omnium contra omnes*," and "because private egoism is revealed to be the secret of the patriotism of the citizens."[26]

Thus Marx and Hegel agree to a great extent about the defects of bourgeois society; they disagree about the remedy. Hegel clings to the hope that a strong authoritarian state will be able to overcome these schisms and achieve a

[25]Marx, *Critique of Hegel's "Philosophy of Right,"* trans. by Annette Jolin and Joseph O'Malley and ed. by Joseph O'Malley (Cambridge at the University Press, 1970), pp. 11–12. In place of the word "inorganic" Marx had written "organic," but as O'Malley points out this is "an obvious writing error."

[26]*Ibid.*, pp. 41–42. The phrase *"bellum omnium contra omnes"* (war of all against all) originates in Hobbes' *Leviathan* (1651), Part I, Chapter 4.

healthy organic unity. Marx regards this hope as an illusion, because he believes that the state inevitably reflects the defective character of the economy. He accuses Hegel of inverting the true relation between the state and civil society. Anticipating his later base-superstructure model, he contends that the economy is the fundamental social reality and the state is largely shaped and determined by economic forces. The stance of Hegel, with his pan-logical "mysticism," is the opposite: in the world of logical abstraction, the "notion" of the state is ultimately determinative, and the tragic divisions in society are destined to be transcended (*aufgehoben*) in the inevitable march of history.

Marx's critique takes the form of a polemic against abstractions. Hegel is charged with subsuming all organisms under a single abstract category (the Idea or Notion) and with neglecting the specific characteristics of the *political* organism.

> The sole interest here is that of recovering the Idea simply, the logical Idea in each element, be it that of the state or of nature; and the real subjects, as in this case the political constitution, become mere names. Consequently, there is only the appearance of a real understanding, while in fact these determinate things are and remain uncomprehended because they are not understood in their specific essence. . . . At least what he says applies to every organism, and there is no predicate which justifies the subject, "*this* organism." What Hegel really wants to achieve is the determination of the organism as the constitution of the state. But there is no bridge by which one can pass from the universal idea of the organism to the particular idea of the organism of the state or the constitution of the state, nor will there ever be.[27]

The lack of specificity applies not only to the political organism as a whole but also to its powers, for example, the executive and the legislature.

> The various powers each have a different principle, although at the same time they are equally real. To take refuge from

[27]*Ibid.*, pp. 12, 14.

their real conflict in an imaginary organic unity, instead of developing the various powers as moments of an organic unity, is therefore an empty, mystical evasion.[28]

Hegel's general definition of organism, Marx concludes, does not advance our understanding to the extent of distinguishing between the executive and the legislature, or even between animal and political organisms.

3. *Internal and External Relations*

The nature of an organism is described by Hegel in the *Logic* and his other works. There is an inner design—an interdependence and interpenetration of elements—in which each element cannot exist without the other elements, and in which each exists in and for the others. The elements are the means of the life of the "whole," and the "whole" has no existence apart from the members in which it is manifested. A mere heap has distinct parts, but even an imperfect organic unity is more than a heap. It is a structure of internally related members. Hegel believes that there is a kind of logical nisus (a dialectical movement) toward greater and richer integration, but he does not believe that the goal of perfect integration has been reached.

According to the common interpretation of Hegel's philosophy of internal relations, everything is internally related to everything else. What is meant by internal relations? A. C. Ewing, in a chapter on "The Theory of Internal Relations," discloses an almost impenetrable thicket of philosophical disagreements and ambiguities. Without trying to penetrate this thicket, we can accept Ewing's definition that in a matrix of internal relations "the nature of any one thing taken by itself is incomplete ... without the whole system on which it depends. Things by their very essence belong together."[29] This statement can be understood in either or both of two meanings. One meaning is that everything is linked to the rest of the system in terms

[28]*Ibid.*, p. 59.
[29]A.C. Ewing, *Idealism: A Critical Survey* (London: Methuen & Co. Ltd., 1961), p. 187.

of entailment. The other meaning is that it is linked by *causal* connection. Hegel is generally understood to believe in both kinds of linkage: the whole of reality is a system in which each thing, including its every aspect and attribute, is causally and logically (in Hegel's peculiar sense of dialectical entailment) related to everything else.

I doubt that this is a correct interpretation. It attributes to Hegel a more inclusive theory of internal relations than he asserts. I have already ventured the opinion that he does not believe that the entire universe in all its levels and aspects is an organic unity. He speaks of heaps and loose collections and recognizes various kinds of integration. His conception of the universe seems to me akin to that stated by Plato in the *Timaeus*. According to the Pythagorean speaker in this dialogue, God contemplates the eternal forms in their static perfection, and he is inspired to try to copy them in the fluctuant stuff of space-time. He does not succeed in reproducing them (since nothing sensible can be eternal), but he makes the sensible world as nearly eternal as he can. He thus produces "the moving image of eternity"—an unsteady and distorted image. If I am correct in my interpretation, Hegel likewise distinguishes between the logical harmony of the Absolute and the imperfection of space and time. In the human and natural world, there is dialectical nisus toward the Absolute but the actuality falls short.

The interpretation of Bartell Ollman is somewhat different from mine. In his very important book *Alienation: Marx's Conception of Man in Capitalist Society,* he contends that Marx was a firm believer in an all-inclusive theory of internal relations derived from Hegel and his predecessors. According to this theory, the basic unit of reality is not a separable being but a cluster of relations that radiate out in all directions in space and time. Since every concept, as well as every entity, is internally related to every other, the meanings are extraordinarily complex and interdependent. "Marx," declares Ollman, "could not keep a definition of one factor from spilling over into everything."[30]

[30]Bertell Ollman, *Alienation: Marx's Conception of Man in Capitalist Society* (Cambridge at the University Press, 1971), p. 25.

Ollman cites Vilfredo Pareto's remark "that Marx's words are like bats: one can see in them both birds and mice."[31] It is impossible to pin down each of his key words to a single unequivocal meaning because it refers to more than one category. I took note of this fact in Chapter 1 when I spoke of "multiple counting." (See p. 28.) For example, the division of labor belongs among both the forces and relations of production in the base and shows up again in political bureaucracy and intellectual specialization in the superstructure. Science, law, and property belong in both the base and the superstructure. In attaching different meanings to the same expression, Marx is reflecting the interpenetration of categories. But this does not prove that he accepted an *extreme* theory of internal relations. I do not agree that Marx's definitions spill over into *everything.*

The theory of internal relations may be more or less extreme. The extreme theory is that *all* relations are internal. It holds that every entity and every object of thought is what it is in virtue of its relations to whatever else exists or is thought. Its intrinsic nature is affected not by some of its relations only but by all relations whatsoever, no matter how external they may seem. Everything is internally related to everything else, and to know a thing completely is to know its relations to everything in the universe. According to Ollman, Hegel's theory of the Absolute entails this extreme theory.

I see no reason to think that Marx agreed with this extreme. The evidence marshalled by Ollman shows that Marx naturally thought in terms of relations, and that the relations that fascinated him were not those of mere adjacency, external association, or mechanical coordination, to the neglect or exclusion of closer ties. But I can find no evidence that he conceived *all* relations as internal. The fact that he was influenced by Hegel proves nothing, since he rejected many Hegelian doctrines.

To suppose that there can be no middle ground or com-

[31]*Ibid.,* p. 3.

promise between internality and externality is a mistake. This assumption overlooks such middle positions as William James' concatenism.[32] In a long concatenation of relations the connections become increasingly remote or nonexistent as the links are farther and farther apart. The coughing of someone sitting near me in the theater is annoying, but the coughing of someone in an ancient Greek theater, far removed in space and time, has no discernible effect upon me. Still more tenuous is the connection between a minute atomic event millions of light-years away in a stellar galaxy and the flicking of an eyelash here and now. Even when relations are indubitably present, the internality or externality of the relations is of many different degrees. The organs in a human body, for example, are more closely related than the things in a pile of miscellaneous junk. The notion that there is no middle ground between the extremes has resulted in absurd doctrines, such as the concept of society as a superorganism of which individuals are but cells, or at the opposite pole, the concept of society as a mere arithmetical sum of self-enclosed egoists. Marx probably held the common sense view that some relations are of the loose, strung-along type, and that some things are either unrelated or very tenuously related.

Marx never advocated a cosmic theory of internal relations in any published work. Instead he focused on the socio-economic realm and left speculations about the whole cosmos to Engels. In one passage in his early *Manuscripts*, however, he speaks of a kind of reciprocal relation between the sun and a plant: "The sun is the object of the plant—an indispensable object to it confirming its life—just as the plant is an object of the sun, of the sun's objective essential power."[33] But this merely says that the life of the plant depends on the light of the sun, and the radiating power of

[32]See William James, "The One and the Many," *Pragmatism* (New York: Longmans, Green and Company, 1907) for his statement of the concatenistic theory of relations.

[33]*Economic and Philosophical Manuscripts*, trans. by Martin Milligan (Moscow, 1959), p. 157. Cited by Ollman, *op. cit.*, p. 28.

the sun is exhibited in the growth of the plant—facts that no one would deny. A number of other passages in the early manuscripts imply that human beings must live in interchange and symbiotic harmony with nature to fulfill their species-potentialities. There is no implication in any of these statements of a cosmic web of internal relations.

Because Hegel differed temperamentally from Marx, it is reasonable to think that they differed in their beliefs about internal relations. Bertrand Russell has suggested that Hegel's cosmic vision "must have come to him first as mystic 'insight'; its intellectual elaboration . . . must have come later."[34] There is a striking similarity between Hegel's metaphysics and mystical monism. The familiar lines of William Blake may be cited as an example of the latter:

> To see a World in a Grain of Sand
> And a Heaven in a Wild Flower,
> Hold Infinity in the Palm of your hand
> And Eternity in an hour.

Less familiar are the lines of Francis Thompson:

> All things by immortal power
> Near or far
> Hiddenly
> To each other linkéd are
> That thou canst not stir a flower
> Without troubling a star.

There is a deep affinity between this mystical vision and Hegel's theory of internal relations. But no one is inclined to claim this kind of affinity between the naturalism of Marx and the mysticism of Blake and Thompson. The words "mystical" and "mysticism" appear occasionally in Marx's writings, but always it seems with a disparaging connotation. Marx is much less of a religious believer and more of a social scientist than Hegel.

The two also differ in their analysis of organisms. Marx is more intent than Hegel on exposing *disorganic* character-

[34]Bertrand Russell, *A History of Western Philosophy* (New York: Simon and Schuster, 1945), p. 731.

istics. In a plant, animal, or human being there may be useless or harmful organs, such as the vermiform appendix in the human body. In every organism, death finally results from the impairment of organic unity. As I shall maintain in Chapter 5, Marx is mainly bent on disclosing the *pathological* elements in the "social organism"— the ways in which its organic unity is impaired and "bourgeois society," in consequence, doomed.

The interpretation of organic unity that I present in this book is akin to that of Ollman, but it differs in being less sweeping in its generalization of internal relatedness. Even if I am mistaken and Ollman is correct, the difference scarcely affects the subject matter of this book. My subject is Marx's interpretation of history, not his interpretation of the universe. Speculations about what lies beyond the human sphere are irrelevant.

4. Hierarchy

As both Hegel and Marx recognize, the members of an organic totality are related in superordination or subordination, some being more important than others. In a human organism, for example, the clipping of hair is not serious, the loss of an arm is serious, total damage to the heart is fatal. Similarly in a society some parts or functions are of greater consequence than others. Hegel in the *Philosophy of Right* sketches in detail the hierarchical structure of the state, with its citizens, estates, police, legislature, executive, judiciary, and monarch, each with its status and functions defined in an authoritarian constitution. Marx denounces this hierarchy as based on exploitation, but he does not deny that such hierarchies exist.

He believed that all the elements in a social order are distinctions within a totality, but that to the extent that they *are* distinct, the political and cultural elements are causally less dominant that the economic. The character of the society is predominantly—*not exclusively*—determined by its peculiar mode of production, especially by the way in which surplus value is extracted from its workers—for example, by slavery, serfdom, or wage-labor. Similarly in an organism there are key functions, such as the circulation of the blood, that contribute more than other functions to the maintenance of the whole.

Differentiation of structure and integration of function are complementary features. Wholes exercise a configurational control over sub-wholes, and sub-wholes function (a) in sub-ordination to their controlling agency, (b) in supra-ordination to their own parts, and (c) in co-ordination with other parts on the same level as themselves. This kind of hierarchy operates with respect to both biological and social organisms, whether it be the action of a nervous system or a complex socio-economic order.

One important kind of hierarchy in the individual human organism is the pattern of repression. The best known interpretation is that of Freud. According to his theory, dreams and myths are the disguised expression of repressed wishes that are powerfully operative in the "unconscious." When the "libido" or "id," the deep instinctive force of life, is repressed by the critical faculties, it assumes a multitude of disguises to circumvent the repression. I have called attention to the analogy between the theory of Freud and that of Marx in the preceding chapter. The insight shared by both men is that illusory forms of thought can often be explained in terms other than conscious motivations. Marx's *social* unconscious, the (non-exclusive) determination of "ideology" by underlying "materialistic" forces, matches Freud's *psychological* unconscious, the determination of myth and "rationalization" mainly by deep instinctive forces. According to Marx, social repression has unfortunate consequences, such as crippling alienations. Similarly according to Freud, psychological repression has unfortunate effects, such as disabling anxieties. For both men the "cure" involves the exposure of the hidden causes and the substitution of conscious control in place of blind groping.

An organic whole conceived in this way is a better

model for the Marxian theory than the base-superstructure model. It preserves the concept of different degrees of dominance or subordination which is the core of the base-superstructure model, but avoids its mechanical and reductionist connotations. Although Marx made extensive use of the organic model, he had not in his own thinking clearly distinguished it from the base-superstructure model. The two models often appear side by side with apparent inconsistency. They should be distinguished, and the organic model recognized as the more inclusive and accurate, incorporating as it does the principle of dominance and subordination, but avoiding reductionism.

To make clear just what "hierarchy" means, we must distinguish between what is most dominant in terms of *effects* from what is most determinant in terms of *causes*. In Greco-Roman society, for example, the *polis* (city state), and in medieval society the Catholic Church, played the dominant role in terms of effects but not the most determinant role in terms of causes. In answering an objection by a German-American newspaper to his doctrine of base and superstructure, Marx wrote:

> In the estimation of that paper, my view that each special mode of production and the social relations corresponding to it, in short, that the economic structure of society, is the real basis on which the juridical and political superstructure is raised, and to which definite social forms of thought correspond; that the mode of production determines the character of the social, political, and intellectual life generally, all this is very true for our own times, in which material interests preponderate, but not for the middle ages, in which Catholicism, nor for Athens and Rome, where politics, reigned supreme. . . . This much, however, is clear, that the middle ages could not live on Catholicism, nor the ancient world on politics. On the contrary, it is the mode in which they gained a livelihood that explains why here politics, and there Catholicism, played the chief part. For the rest, it requires but a slight acquaintance with the Roman republic, for example, to be aware that its secret history is the history of its landed property. On the other hand, Don Quixote long ago paid the

> penalty for wrongly imagining that knight errantry was compatible with all economical forms of society.[35]

Marx is making a very important observation. The dominant element and even the subordinate elements in the effects (e.g., knight errantry) *must* be compatible with the economy, but the chief *determinant* element among the causes, namely, the mode of production, need not be *dominant* among the effects. As Michael Harrington remarks:

> In capitalism, the society of *homo economicus,* one has the unusual situation in which the economic is both determinant and dominant. . . . Organic wholes, be they human bodies or human societies, can have determinant preconditions and dominant functions. . . . [36]

In the human mind-body, for example, no organ can operate without the heart—it is the most determinant of all the organs, but the mental activity of the brain and the central nervous system is the more dominant psychologically. Similarly in the Middle Ages the feudal system was the more determinant, but religion was the more dominant among the effects in the psychological and cultural life of the people.

We would err, and betray what Marx says elsewhere, if we were to conclude that the economy was *alone* efficacious. As elements within an organic whole, politics in ancient society and religion in medieval society were constantly interacting and interweaving with the economy. All three factors—economy, polity, and religious culture—were dialectically interactive, being cause-and-effect of one another. Within this organic hierarchy, to repeat, the mode of production is predominant in the causes but not necessarily in the effects.

Hierarchy can be inadequately understood as a set of relations of superordination and subordination *among indi-*

[35]Marx, *Capital* (Chicago: Charles H. Kerr & Company, 1906), Vol. I, p. 94, f.n.
[36]Michael Harrington, *The Twilight of Capitalism* (New York: Simon and Schuster, 1976), pp. 68–69.

viduals. Marx maintained, for example, that the rich employer exercises far more power than the poor worker. In this sense he recognized a hierarchy of power among persons, but he explained this disproportionate power more in terms of social structure than vice versa. The "great man" such as Napoleon, may also exercise a predominant control or influence over lesser men. Although Marx discounted "the great man theory of history," he did not altogether dismiss it. In discussing historical accidents he said:

> These accidents . . . fall naturally into the general course of development and are compensated for, again, by other accidents. But acceleration and delay are very dependent upon such "accidents" which include the "accident" of the character of those who at first stand at the head of the movement.[37]

We can agree with Marx that such accidents should not simply be dismissed as unimportant. One might recall the attempted assassination of Franklin D. Roosevelt early in his first term as President, when he narrowly escaped death and Mayor Cermak of Chicago was killed in his stead. Suppose Roosevelt had suffered the same fate as President Kennedy suffered. A mediocre Vice President, John Nance Garner, would have been elevated to the presidency in a time of severe crisis. Such an "accident" would surely have made a considerable difference.

Hierarchy can also be understood as the tyranny of impersonal forces over individual purposes. Engels characteristically employs an inorganic model—the parallelogram of forces described in physics—to indicate the dominance of the impersonal:

> History makes itself in such a way that the final result always arises from conflicts between many individual wills, of which each again has been made what it is by a host of particular conditions of life. Thus there are innumerable intersecting forces, an infinite series of parallelograms of forces

[37]Marx and Engels, *Selected Correspondence 1846–1895*, p. 311. Letter of Marx to Kugelman, April 17, 1871.

which give rise to one resultant—the historical event. This again may itself be viewed as the product of a power which, taken as a whole, works *unconsciously* and without volition. For what each individual wills is obstructed by everyone else, and what emerges is something that no one willed.[38]

This passage bears some resemblance to Marx's theory of the impersonal operation of the market system, but it misses what is most essential in Marx's structuralism. Engels speaks of the clash of *individual wills* in cancelling one another—Marx speaks of the dialectic of *discrepant structures,* such as the forces and relations of production.

Hierarchy, as Marx conceives it, is less like the parallelogram of forces and more like the configuration of an organism. In the organism each organ has a structure that is related to the structure of the other organs and to the structure of the organism as a whole. It is a structure of structures and not simply a structure of individual cells. There is some justification for classifying Marx as a structuralist along with such writers as Jean Piaget and Claude Levi-Strauss. In society viewed as a structured organism, the mode of production is dominant among the causes, but all the elements in the organic hierarchy are interdependent—hence it is false to say that production alone determines historical events, or that all other elements are simply derived from the economy.

We can now distinguish three versions of base-superstructure. The fundamentalist version, because of its reductionist character, is flatly incompatible with the organic model. The dialectical version is more nearly compatible, but, as stated by Engels, it retains too many traces of economic reductionism and external relations. The organic version, as hierarchical structure, is an integral part of the organic model. To say that the base-superstructure has simply been incorporated into the organic model would be a misleading way to characterize the transformation. The base-superstructure (to use Hegel's favorite term) has been

[38]*Ibid.,* p. 476. Letter of Engels to J. Bloch, September 21, 1890.

aufgehoben—suspended, conserved, and lifted up—in being absorbed into the organic whole. All the familiar features of the base-superstructure model—the forces and relations of production, the state and the legal system, the ideological and non-ideological forms of culture—reappear in a more subtle and coherent structure.

5. Lingering Questions and an Attempted Answer

The exact relation between the base-superstructure and the organic model is still not clear. How profound a transformation must the former undergo to be incorporated into the latter? Consider the case of Lenin. He finally adopted at least verbally an organic theory:

> Society is not a simple, mechanical accumulation of these or those institutions, the simple, mechanical accumulation of these or those phenomena. . . . It is rather a social organism, holistic system of social relations, the social formation.[39]

Despite this statement, Lenin continued to speak in the same old way about base and superstructure. He did not realize what a difference it makes to accept the organic model.

To pose the issue more concretely let us recall Marx's distinction between the determinant in the causes and the dominant in the effects. Marx contended that the slave mode of production in Greece largely determined that the politics of the city-state was dominant, and that similarly the feudal mode of production in the Middle Ages largely determined the dominance of Catholicism. How could he prove these claims? For example, just how does the economic realm connect up with the religious realm? If we take seriously the interpenetration implied by the doctrine of internal relations, religion is so much a part of economic

[39]Lenin, *Philosophical Notebooks* (Warsaw, 1956), pp. 191–192. Quoted by Piotr Sztompka, *System and Function* (New York: Academic Press, Inc., 1974), p. 172.

life that it is hard to understand how economic activities comprising one realm can cause or explain religious phenomena in another realm.

What is meant by "explains" in this context? If Marx clings to his theory of internal relations, he cannot employ a Humean type of causal explanation. Hume's sharp analytical distinction between cause and effect fits a doctrine of external rather than internal relations. But if a Marxist does not accept the Humean type of explanation, what kind of explanation is acceptable?

We are confronted by a whole nest of questions. Can we explain religious beliefs and practices by simply paying attention to the way in which people make their living? Do economic and religious life coexist and mutually condition one another, or does the first precede and the second follow in temporal sequence? If we were given enough information about feudal economy would we see that a certain form of religion (Catholicism) must ensue? If so, is the "must" a logical as well as a causal entailment? Are the religion and the economy united in a larger organic configuration? Is the economy the more basic causally in all times and places? If not, what accounts for the difference? Until a Marxist can answer these questions he or she has not resolved the puzzles of historical explanation, but perhaps neither has any one else.

One major difficulty is to explain how a single kind of "determinant"—the mode of production—can determine such variant effects as Catholicism in the Middle Ages and politics in Greece. A Freudian who contends that the Oedipus Complex explains why one person becomes an artist and another person becomes a scientist faces the same kind of difficulty. There must be something besides the common factor to explain the difference. A Marxist might reply that there was a different mode of production in Greece (slavery) than in medieval Europe (feudalism), and that this difference accounts for the different effects. But slavery has existed elsewhere without the politics of the city-state and feudalism has existed without Catholicism. The factors are sometimes tied and sometimes not. What seems to be required to resolve these questions is a more subtle and complex theory of causality.

Louis Althusser, in response to the need, distinguishes between three conceptions of causality: linear, teleological, and structural. He rejects linear causality, the temporal sequence of single cause and single effect, as too simple; he rejects teleological causality, the "expression" of mind or spirit, as too idealistic; and he accepts structural causality alone as representative of Marx's maturity. Structuralism maintains that the cause of the effects is the complex structure of the whole "social formation," including the economy, the polity, and the ideology and science at a certain stage and place of social development. The causality is nothing external—it is the interrelations among all these elements:

> This implies . . . that the effects are not outside the structure, are not a pre-existing object, element or space in which the structure arrives to *imprint its mark*: on the contrary, it implies that the structure is immanent in its effects, a cause immanent in its effects in the Spinozist sense of the term, that *the whole existence of the structure consists of its effects,* in short that the structure, which is merely a specific combination of its peculiar elements, is nothing outside its effects.[40]

It might be objected that this structuralist theory of causality goes beyond anything conceived by Marx. Althusser admits that Marx did not succeed in explicitly formulating this theory of causality, but he contends that it is implicit in a number of passages. The following quotation from the *Grundrisse* is an example in which the skeleton of the base-superstructure model is discernible in the context of the structural whole:

> In all forms of society there is one specific kind of production which predominates over the rest, whose relations thus assign rank and influence to the others. It is a general illumina-

---

[40]Louis Althusser/Etienne Balibar, *Reading Capital* (London: NLB, 1970), pp. 188–189.

tion which bathes all the other colours and modifies their particularity. It is a particular ether which determines the specific gravity of every being which has materialized within it.[41]

Althusser interprets this passage as meaning that "the complex whole has the unity of a structure articulated in dominance."[42] The elements in the social formation are organized in a certain hierarchy under the powerful influence of the economy, itself an integral part of the formation. That the organic totality is structured and hierarchical is as essential to its nature as that it is a complex unity.

The totality is a dialectical unity of "contradictions." The principal but far from the sole contradiction is the conflict between the forces and the relations of production.

> The "contradiction" is inseparable from the total structure of the social body in which it is found, inseparable from its formal conditions of existence, and even from the instances it governs; it is radically affected by them, determining, but also determined in one and the same movement, and determined by the various levels and instances of the social formation it animates: it might be called overdetermined in its principle.[43]

The term "overdetermined" is borrowed from Freud, who means by it, among other things, the condensation of a number of unconscious thoughts and impulses in a single, highly charged image. Althusser means by overdetermination "the fusion of an accumulation of contradictions."

> If . . . a vast accumulation of "contradictions" come into play in the same court, some of which are radically heterogeneous—of different origins, different sense, different levels and points of application—but which nevertheless merge into a ruptural unity, we can no longer talk of the sole, unique power of the general "contradiction."[44]

[41]Grundrisse (Nicolaus), pp. 106–107.
[42]Althusser, For Marx (London: Allen Lane, 1969), p. 202. The analogy with "the integrative action of the nervous system" (Sherrington's phrase) may be helpful in understanding "the unity of a structure articulated in dominance."
[43]Ibid., p. 101.
[44]Ibid., p. 100.

Citing Engels' statement that the economy is determinative "in the last instance," Althusser declares that if this is taken to mean that ultimately the economy is *alone* determinative, we have to conclude that the "last instance" never arrives:

> The economic dialectic is never active in the *pure state*; in History, these instances, the superstructures, etc.—are never seen to step respectfully aside when their work is done or, when the Time comes, as his pure phenomena, to scatter before His Majesty the Economy as he strides along the royal road of the Dialectic. From the first moment to the last, the lonely hour of the "last instance" never comes.[45]

Even when the economy exerts its powerful sway there is always a multiplicity and coalescence of causes. Base-superstructure has been absorbed into the many-sided structural totality.

Althusser's interpretation of structural causality is an important contribution to Marxism. My disagreement with him is mainly twofold: first, he exaggerates the discontinuity between the early "humanist" and later "scientific" works of Marx, and, second, he tries to expunge from Marxism its humanist elements. He leaves out the "inner dialectic" of human needs and potentialities driving toward fulfillment. Although his structural causality is a great advance beyond linear causality, he does not really explain why and how the "economic base" largely determined that politics in Greece and Catholic religion in medieval Europe were dominant. If he had not omitted the inner dialectic his attempted explanation would have been more adequate. In the chapters that follow I shall combine the inner and the outer dialectic in a more comprehensive statement of Marx's "organic" causality.

[45]*Ibid.*, p. 113.

3

Organic Development

1. Historicism

The base-superstructure model, if conceived as a metaphor drawn from architecture, connotes stability and not change. Marx strains or even contradicts the model by interpreting it dynamically, but there is no such contradiction or strain when he turns to the organic model. In his Preface to the first and Afterword to the second edition of *Capital* he reverts to this model because an organism, as he says, is "constantly changing." Homeostasis—dynamic inner equilibrium—is its principle of stability, but this is a *moving* equilibrium and the equilibrium is never perfect. An organism is "well balanced" or in "dynamic equilibrium" if it has not only achieved homeostasis but has established a *modus vivendi* between its inner play of forces and its external environment. In this inward adjustment and outward adaptation it is continually in process of development. This is true of organisms at every level, whether plants, animals, or human mind-bodies; and if "organism" is extended to include societies, the organic life-process applies to "social organisms" too.

Because of Marx's strong emphasis on historical processes he has been called an "historicist." The terms "historicist" and "historicism" were given intellectual currency by Ernst Troeltsch in *Der Historismus und Seine Probleme* (Tübingen, 1922).[1] He meant by historicism (in German

[1]See the article by Maurice Mandelbaum, "Historicism," in *The Encyclopedia of Philosophy*, ed. by Paul Edwards (New York: The Macmillan Company and the Free Press, 1967), Vol. 4, pp. 22–25.

Historismus) a tendency to interpret all knowledge and all human experience in a context of historical change. But the word has been used in a variety of ways. Maurice Mandelbaum has defined it as follows:

> Historicism consists in the attempt to take seriously (in a philosophic sense) the fact of change. It sees behind every particular fact the one ultimate fact of change: every particular is treated with relation to the process of change out of which it arises, and this process is seen as immanent in it.[2]

That Marx was a historicist in this sense is indisputable. History was for him the main social science. Even economics, upon which he expended infinite pains, seemed to him less important for its own sake than for the light it shed upon historical development. He sought to disclose the economic forces that were propelling capitalist industrial society toward communism.

A more elaborate and idiosyncratic meaning of historicism is stated by Karl R. Popper in *The Poverty of Historicism* and *The Open Society and Its Enemies*.[3] He defines historicism as the doctrine that there are laws of historical development and that, on the basis of knowledge of these laws, it is possible to make large-scale historical prophecies. His conception of historicism entails two further doctrines. First, a society is an "organic unity," and as such it is more than the additive sum of its parts. This contention strongly suggests "that there is a close connection between historicism and the so-called *biological or organic theory* of social structures—the theory which interprets social groups by analogy with living organisms."[4] Second, like any organic being, the society is much more profoundly conditioned by its past than is a physical aggre-

---

[2]Maurice Mandelbaum, *The Problem of Historical Knowledge* (New York: Harper & Row, 1967), pp. 88–89.
[3]See Karl R. Popper, *The Poverty of Historicism* (Boston: Beacon Press, 1957—first published in *Economica*, Vol. 11. 1944 and Vol. 12, 1945); and *The Open Society and Its Enemies*, 5th edition revised and enlarged (London: Routledge & Kegan Paul, 1966).
[4]*The Poverty of Historicism*, p. 19.

gate. Hence to understand it and its future we must know its history. In combination these two doctrines imply that a holistic methodology is applicable to historical explanation. The social scientist must survey broad sweeps of time as well as broad sweeps of coexistent data in space. Despite great erudition and critical acumen, Popper is not reliable as an historian of ideas, and his characterization of "historicism" is not what is generally meant by the term. I mention it because he identifies it with Marxism.

Popper names Plato, Hegel, and Marx among the philosophers who are historicists. Comparison of Marx with Plato and Hegel will help to clarify what is distinctive about Marx's "historicism."

2. Plato and Marx

Because of his classical education and enduring interest in Greek culture, Marx was conversant with Plato's philosophy. In his preliminary notebooks to his doctoral dissertation, in the dissertation itself, and in his later works, there are scattered references to Plato. Despite these references, I see no reason to suppose that Plato greatly influenced Marx, but a comparison of their ideas will be illuminating.

In characterizing justice in the Republic, Plato depicted the soul as the state writ small and the state as the soul writ large. In the soul, reason is the faculty of judgment, spirit (will and the martial emotions) enforces the decisions of reason, and appetite consists of impulses and passions that need to be governed. Within an integrated personality, reason controls spirit, and reason and spirit together control appetite. The structure of the state matches, not by accident, the tripartite structure of the soul. There are three classes—the wise rulers ("guardians"), the police-soldiers ("auxiliaries"), and the laborers—corresponding respectively to reason, spirit, and appetite. The two well-integrated systems—the soul and the state—mesh in a mutual integration. Each mental faculty and each social class is coordinated organically with every other.

According to Popper's interpretation of Plato, history is governed by a law of historical decay. The ideal state, as sketched in the Republic, is designed to escape this historical movement of degeneration. There are various devices to keep the system static: separation and hierarchy of classes, intensive regulation and censorship, and communism of property and family life among the guardians and auxiliaries. Nevertheless, the ideal state will not last forever—once it is disrupted by a relaxation of controls, the state and its citizens will pass through successive stages of decay: timocracy, oligarchy, democracy, and tyranny.

In comparing Plato and Marx writers have frequently pointed to communism as a common doctrine, but the similarity is superficial. For Plato communism, as primarily a device to instill group solidarity in the ruling classes, is restricted to the guardians and auxiliaries. For Marx communism, as the means to freedom and equality in a classless society, will envelop the whole social order.

A more fundamental likeness is the acceptance by both Plato and Marx of a largely economic interpretation of history. In tracing the rise and fall of states Plato emphasizes such economic factors as the division of labor, the development of imperialism, and the conflict of economic classes. According to his theory of historical decay, internal economic strife and class war fomented by economic self-interest are the main forces of revolutionary transformation. Plato combines this historical materialism with a non-materialist metaphysics.

These doctrines, the historical and the metaphysical, are logically independent. To suppose that "the materialistic interpretation of history" implies a certain type of metaphysics, such as cosmic materialism, is a mistake. The fact that Marx was a historical materialist, in the sense of stressing the mode of production, does not commit him to a metaphysical position, such as a "dialectical materialism" extended to embrace the whole universe. Unlike Engels he says almost nothing in his mature works about the metaphysical nature of the universe, and it is problematical to what extent he agreed with Engels. Even if he did agree, he never bothered to sketch a cosmic metaphysics, or make his agreement indubitable.

The main similarity between Plato and Marx is that they adopt an organic theory of society. In Plato this theory takes the form of an analogy between the individual psyche and the city-state. He conceives of both the well-integrated soul and the aristocratic state as an organic whole in which every function is so dependent on every other function that any substantial alteration in one affects the others. In Marx the organic theory is not couched in terms of such a literal analogy between the soul and the state. It is best interpreted as a heuristic model.

Plato is less of an "historicist" in Mandelbaum's definition of the term than Marx. Far from seeing "behind every particular fact the one ultimate fact of change," Plato contrasts the Heraclitean flux of sensory phenomena with an alleged eternal order beyond the reach of sense perception. Transcending the world of "appearances" are the static archetypes for justice, wisdom, courage, temperance, and other social values. The problem is to return as nearly as possible to conformity with the archetypes and thus to arrest history. There is the recurrent suggestion that archetypal models were approximated in the remote past, and that history has been a decline from this golden age. In contrast, Marx accepts the historical world as ultimate and, despite crises and setbacks, progressive.

Plato is not only less of a historicist, but much less of an empiricist than Marx. As the character Socrates says in the *Philebus*:

> I am sure that all men who have a grain of intelligence will admit that the knowledge which has to do with being and reality, and sameness and unchangeableness, is by far the truest of all.[5]

Plato's distinction between rational "knowledge" of the unchanging Forms and empirical "opinion" concerning the

[5]Plato, *Philebus*, #58. (Jowett's translation.)

changing particulars implies that historical cognition is inferior in kind. The hierarchy of reason, spirit, and appetite in the individual and of guardians, auxiliaries, and craftsmen in the state commits him to a static ethics and politics. Plato would like so far as possible to preserve this hierarchy. Marx's opposing view is epitomized in the words of Engels:

> Everything that is real within the realm of the history of mankind is bound to become unreasonable after a while; hence it is already by definition unreasonable, is afflicted with unreasonableness from the very beginning. . . . Everything that exists deserves to perish.[6]

According to the Marxian theory of dialectical development "the principle of negativity" is constantly at work in history. Every historical stage, however much it may claim reasonableness, suffers from a warped perspective, and is consequently condemned by its one-sidedness to be superseded. Even communism, Marx tells us in the *Economic and Philosophical Manuscripts* is not a final stage of historical development.[7]

3. Dialectic in Hegel and Marx

Whereas Plato probably exercised no great influence on Marx, the immense influence of Hegel is incontestable. Even when Marx adopted alternative positions, he may have been reacting to that "mighty thinker." In the *Economic and Philosophical Manuscripts*, he declares that "the outstanding achievement of Hegel's *Phenomenology*" is "the dialectic of negativity as the moving and creating principle."[8] This "dialectic" is the principle of contradiction in all moving

---

[6]Friedrich Engels, *Ludwig Feuerbach and the Outcome of Classical German Philosophy* (New York: International Publishers, 1941). p. 11.
[7]Marx, *Economic and Philosophical Manuscripts, in* Marx, *Early Writings*, trans. and ed. by T.B. Bottomore (London: C. A. Watts & Company, 1963), p. 167. Perhaps Marx is referring to "crude" or immature communism rather than the highest form of communism.
[8]*Economic and Philosophical Manuscripts*, p. 202.

things. "Contradiction is the root of all movement and life," declares Hegel. "Only insofar as it has a contradiction in itself does anything move, or have impulse and activity."[9] Similarly he declares that "life, as life, involves the germ of death, and . . . the finite, being radically self-contradictory, involves its own self-suppression."[10]

A logician might object that contradiction applies to propositions but not to living beings. To this objection Hegel replies:

> Instead of speaking by the maxim of Excluded Middle (which is the maxim of abstract understanding) we should rather say: Everything is opposite. Neither in heaven nor in earth, neither in the world of mind nor of nature, is there anywhere such an abstract "Either-or" as the understanding maintains. Whatever exists is concrete, with difference and opposition in itself. . . . Contradiction is the very moving principle of the world: and it is ridiculous to say that contradiction is unthinkable. The only thing correct in that statement is that contradiction is not the end of the matter, but cancels itself. (Negation of the negation.)[11]

Hegel furnishes numerous examples of "contradiction" in real life, including the following from the human sphere:

> To illustrate the presence of Dialectic in the spiritual world, especially in the provinces of law and morality, we have only to recollect how general experience shows us the extreme of one state or action suddenly shifting into its opposite: a Dialectic which is recognized in many ways in common proverbs. Thus summum jus summa injuria: which means, that to drive an abstract right to its extremity is to do a wrong. In political life, as everyone knows, extreme anarchy and extreme despotism naturally lead to one another. The perception of Dialectic in the province of individual Ethics is seen in the well-known adages, Pride comes before a fall: Too much wit outwits itself. Even feeling, bodily as well as men-

[9]Hegel, *Wissenschaft der Logik* (Hamburg: G. Lasson, 1963), Vol. II, p. 58.
[10]*The Logic of Hegel*, trans. by William Wallace (Oxford at the Clarendon Press, 1892), p. 148.
[11]*Ibid.*, p. 223.

tal, has its Dialectic. Every one knows how the extremes of pain and pleasure pass into each other: the heart overflowing with joy seeks relief in tears, and the deepest melancholy will at times betray its presence by a smile.[12]

By such real-life contradictions Hegel means opposed, antithetical tendencies that work in contrary directions, each ailing from too-limited scope or perspective and bent on dominating the whole field.

The finitude and perishability of things, he tells us, lies "in the want of correspondence between their immediate being and what they essentially are."[13] This "contradiction between essence and existence" is a very fundamental idea in both Hegel and the early Marx. No living being that exists, they declare, is adequate to express its "essence"— the latent depths and potentialities of its nature. Potentiality striving to realize itself breaks through the fetters of existence. Every living thing and every social formation must evolve new conditions and forms of life if it is to fulfill itself. Marx in his later writings ceases to use the term "human essence," but he retains the concept of a "contradiction" between human potentialities and the fetters of actual human existence.

An example supplied by Hegel that strongly impressed Marx is the relation between "lordship and bondage." Many books have pointed out the relevance to Marxism of this section of the *Phenomenology of Mind*. I shall summarize it briefly. Human beings need to respect and aid each other in order to fulfill themselves, and they also need recognition and self-respect. The contradiction between master and bondsman arises when some people try to wrest recognition and benefit from others without reciprocating. This may lead to armed struggle and the subjugation of the vanquished. By such unjust means class relations are established—the victor becoming master, or lord, and the vanquished becoming bondsman, or slave. The relation is then

[12]*Ibid.*, pp. 150–151.
[13]*Ibid.*, p. 223.

mediated by material objects—the products of the hard labor of the subjugated class provide surplus for the lord. At
first he has much the superior position, but in the long run
of history this superiority is undermined. He cannot enjoy
the fullest self-respect when the workers upon whom he
depends fear and hate him, nor can he experience in his
relation with the bondsmen the free mutuality and affec-
tionate ties that are the mark of satisfactory human relations. Paradoxically he has lost his independence by becoming a master: he must depend upon the toilers not only
for physical sustenance but also for recognition of himself
as master. In compensation he falls back upon an idle
round of enjoyments: he is simply a consumer. The
workers, in contrast, are the real producers, and through
their mastery of things in the work process, they achieve
understanding of their historical role and knowledge of material reality. Eventually the tables will be turned and the
worker will achieve independence. Only when the master-
bondsman distinction is annulled will essence and existence cease to be antagonistic.

Marx may have had this argument in mind when he
said "that Hegel grasps the self-creation of man as a process, . . . and . . . he, therefore, grasps the nature of labour,
and conceives objective man (true, because real man) as the
result of his own labour."[14] Hegel's conceptions of the self-
creation of mankind through labor and the dialectical development of man and society, with all the revolutionary
social and political implications of these conceptions, are a
major source of Marxian theory. Marx, of course, pushed
these revolutionary implications much farther than Hegel.

I have emphasized change, but organic change goes
hand in hand with continuity. The distinguishing characteristic of all living organisms, as Bergson so strongly emphasized, is *duration* conceived as continuous and irreversible progression. *Lived* time is not just a perishing but a
conservation in which the stage that is "negated" is pre-

[14]*Economic and Philosopohical Manuscripts*, trans. by Bottomore, p. 202.

served in altered form. For example, the innocence of childhood is "contradicted" by the fever of adolescence, but the transformed qualities of both the child and the adolescent are preserved in the mature adult. *Aufheben* is the term used by Hegel and Marx to designate this process of maturation, but the German word has no exact English equivalent. It is usually translated by some uncommon English locution, such as "sublation" or "supersession," but this sophisticated terminology loses much of its flavor. *Aufheben* (the present process) or *aufgehoben* (the past or completed process) is, so to speak, a synthesis of three English terms, *cancel, preserve,* and *lift up.* It thus combines the negative (annul, abolish), the positive (save, conserve), and the transformative (transcend, sublimate). Hegel and Marx used the word to designate action whereby a higher quality or characteristic supersedes a lower by transforming its nature. They thought that action of this sort is the essence of organic development, applying to both individuals and societies. To this extent they agree.

Nevertheless the differences between them are sharp. Hegel interprets both man and the cosmos in idealistic terms, conceiving the world of objects as the embodiment of spirit, and man's relation to this world as primarily cognitive. Marx believes in a naturalistic interpretation of life and its underlying conditions, and thinks that man's relation to the world is or ought to be mainly one of activity ("practice"). He charges that Hegel's understanding of reality is abstract rather than concrete and realistic: "For its real mode of existence is abstraction."[15] His emphasis on economic forces and material needs differs radically from Hegel's emphasis on culture and spirituality. The Marxian vision of the abolition of economic classes and the state has no counterpart in Hegel.[16]

[15]*Ibid.,* p. 200.

[16]For an illuminating comparison see Jean-Yves Calvez, "Hegel and Marx," with a comment by David McLellan in *The Legacy of Hegel: Proceedings of the Marquette Hegel Symposium 1970,* ed. by J.J. O'Malley, K.W. Algozin, H.P. Kainz and L.C. Rice (The Hague: Martinus Nijhoff, 1973).

While recognizing these profound differences, we should not exaggerate them. Duncan Forbes remarks that "Hegel's philosophy of history, in principle at any rate, incapsulates and postulates a materialist or economic interpretation of history."[17] "Civil society"—the arena of material needs and economic conflicts—is described by Hegel in language similar to Marx's account of "bourgeois society." Both recognize (Marx to a greater extent than Hegel) the importance of human labor in shaping the course of history. Marx thinks that Hegel's great accomplishment is to have worked out a comprehensive account of man as a historical being who creates through his own labor the socioeconomic world.

> The outstanding achievement of Hegel's *Phenomenology*— the dialectic of negativity as the moving and creating principle—is, first, that Hegel grasps the self-creation of man as a process, objectification as loss of the object, as alienation and transcendence of this alienation, and that he, therefore, grasps the nature of *labour,* and conceives objective man (true, because real man) as the result of his *own labour.*[18]

Nevertheless there is more than a touch of exaggeration in Duncan Forbes' contention that Hegel "postulates a materialist or economic interpretation of history." If these words refer to a theory that regards the economic basis as largely determining the intellectual superstructure, there is no evidence for such a view in the writings of Hegel. Far more representative of Hegel's convictions is his remark:

> Every day I am more and more convinced that theoretical work has more effect in the world than practical work; once the realm of our ideas is revolutionized, actuality must follow along.[19]

[17]Hegel, *Lectures on the Philosophy of World History* (Cambridge University Press, 1975), p. xxii.
[18]*Economic and Philosophical Manuscripts,* p. 202.
[19]Letter of Hegel to Friedrich Immanuel Niethammer, October 28, 1808. Quoted by Auguste Cornu, *The Origins of Marxian Thought* (Springfield, Ill.: Charles C Thomas Publisher, 1957), p. 120.

Hegel's so-called "materialist" emphasis is "incapsulated" within an idealistic metaphysics, an authoritarian politics, and a cultural interpretation of history, all of which Marx repudiates.

As I maintain throughout this book, Marx does not swing to the opposite extreme of a reductionist "historical materialism," unless it be temporarily and in isolated passages. Base and superstructure are reductionist in implication if considered in abstraction, but they are not reductionist if regarded as reciprocal moments within an organic whole. Rather they signify the principle of hierarchy that characterizes any complex organism. When the base-superstructure model is "incapsulated" (to use Forbes' term) within the more inclusive organic model, neither model is flatly rejected. The organic model is commodious enough to include the residue of truth in the base-superstructure model, and at the same time to include alienation and other non-materialist factors in the shaping of history.

No longer need we consider Marx's theory of history as exclusionary. Max Weber and R. H. Tawney contend that religion has exercised a more originative role than reductive "Marxism" admits. Rudolf Stammler maintains that legal systems condition the economic order. Georges Sorel and Hendrik de Man have insisted that myths and ideals often play an important role. Others have said that Marx was not sufficiently aware of the irrational elements in human motivation: folk traditions, nationalistic sentiments, racial prejudices, group neuroses, unconscious or semi-conscious impulses. If Marxists accept the organic model, they can admit all of these factors to the extent that they are verified by historical research. This admission need not exclude the strongest emphasis on the mode of production.

4. The Historical Dialectic of Essence and Existence

Among the Hegelian concepts influencing Marx were "existence" and "essence." The distinction between these concepts is among the oldest in philosophy, but in its use by existentialist philosophers it is also quite modern. Aristotle distinguished between the two but so do Sartre and Heidegger.

To say of anything that it exists is simply to indicate *that* it is; to speak of its essence is to refer to *what* it is. The existence is the *actuality* of the thing, the essence is its *qualitative nature*. Aristotle used the word "essence" to denote the basic properties that make the thing what it is, in contrast with those properties that the thing may happen to possess but that it need not have to be itself. A human being may be sunburned, for example, but would still be a human being and even the same person if he or she were not. We should distinguish between those properties that are "accidental" and so non-essential (e.g., sunburned) and those properties that are essential (e.g., being an animal who can reason). Also we should distinguish the essence of an individual (what makes a particular person the man he is) and the essence of the species (what makes human beings human).

Essence is distinguished from existence in either of two ways. First, we may indicate *what* a thing is without indicating *that* it is. After an essence is characterized more or less exhaustively, the question may remain whether any such being exists. Readers of Shakespeare know a good deal about Hamlet whether or not there was ever a Prince of Denmark with these characteristics. The question of a thing's existence is therefore *additional* to the question of its characteristics. Second, we can distinguish between what a thing is *potentially* from what it is *actually*. A male baby, for example, is potentially a man, but not a giraffe, an earthquake, or even a woman. Potentiality, as the latent underlying nature that tends toward realization, is part of the essence but not part of the existence. The baby grows up and becomes a man, but not until this point of maturity does his full-fledged manhood exist.

With these distinctions in mind, we can understand the historical dialectic of essence and existence as conceived by Hegel and Marx. All organic beings are replete with potentialities. Human beings, as part of their species-nature, strive to fulfill them. Because they are internally related to their environment, they cannot realize them in isolation but only in fellowship with others and in "metabolic" interaction with nature. This directional and dialectical character of human life is the natural basis of history. So far as the *existent* nature of things—for example, the class structure of society—limits and frustrates the human *potential*, there is a contradiction between essence and existence. The existence "negates" essence in the sense of blocking or suppressing it. Human beings in this contradictory state must either remove the existential fetters or sink into an inauthentic and dehumanized condition.

Hegel believes that freedom is the essential attribute of spirit and that spirit is the essential attribute of the human species. Life is a massive drive toward coherence and totality; the individual becomes more free in becoming more whole and less isolated. The subjective world of feeling and thought must be harmonized with the objective world of institutions and culture. Thereby the spirit triumphs over its institutional fetters: "the dichotomy between its essence (or what it is in itself) and its real existence is overcome, and it has attained satisfaction: it has created its own world out of its inner essence."[20]

On the one hand, the individual expands his interests and loyalties until he has mentally absorbed—internalized—the social order in which he lives. On the other hand, the nation-state and its culture are differentiated in all their fullness and this differentiation is manifested in the enriched lives of the citizens. The duality between subject and object and between essence and existence is thus overcome. The history of society is spirit making itself actual by breaking through innumerable barriers and moving toward this consummation. As the germ bears in itself the whole nature of the tree, so does the spirit in its germination contain in potentiality the whole history of its development.

[20]Hegel, *Lectures on the Philosophy of World History*, p. 58.

Marx likewise believes that man is potentially a free and universal being and that his existential situation fetters and distorts this potentiality. The movement of history is to strike off these fetters and to make the transition from human bondage to human freedom. As in Hegel's philosophy, freedom is conceived as the unity of the subjective and objective worlds. It means overcoming the object-subject split—becoming at one with oneself and other people and one's environment. Hegel envisages the climax of the historical process as the synthesis of divergent interests in the state and the achievement thereby of a civic humanity. In contrast, Marx envisages the goal as the universality of the classless society. He regards the state as largely an instrument of class domination, and he seeks to resolve the conflict between essence and existence by revolutionary social action. As the culmination of predictable history, communism will remove the fetters of class division, "It is the true solution of the conflict between existence and essence."[21]

Some interpreters maintain that the distinction between essence and existence is characteristic of the thinking of the young but not the mature Marx. R. Pascal in his edition of *The German Ideology*, for example, notes that in this work completed in 1846 Marx "makes his final reckoning with this concept of 'self-estrangement' *(Entfremdung)*," a concept integrally linked with the distinction between essence and existence.[22] Louis Althusser is perhaps the best known advocate of the view that the doctrine of *Entfremdung* and the contrast between existence and essence are confined to Marx's youth, when he was allegedly sowing his philosophical wild oats. On this point, a number of interpreters, such as Daniel Bell, Sidney Hook, and Lewis Feuer, have agreed with Althusser.

[21]*Economic and Philosophical Manuscripts,* p. 155.
[22]Marx and Engels, *The German Ideology: Parts I and III,* ed. by R. Pascal (New York: International Publishers, 1939), p. 202. Pascal fails to note that the concept of estrangement or alienation appears several times in *The German Ideology.* See the quotations corresponding to notes 35 and 36 below.

I have already remarked that this sharp separation between the young and the old Marx is untenable. Although the term "human essence" seemed to the later Marx too abstract and static in connotation, he by no means abandoned the view that there is a *relatively* constant human nature that is fettered by the inhuman condition of existence. He still thought of man as alienated in capitalist society, and he still used the terms "human nature" and "species-being."

In this respect he differs from "existentialism" as characterized by Jean-Paul Sartre. "Existence precedes essence," declares Sartre, man has no "nature"—he is radically incomplete and unfinished.

> What is meant here by saying that existence precedes essence? It means that, first of all, man exists, turns up, appears on the scene, and, only afterwards, defines himself. If man, as the existentialist conceives him, is indefinable, it is because he is nothing. Only afterward will he be something, and he himself will have made what he will be. Thus there is no human nature. . . . [23]

Marx believed that man is in the making and makes himself; but he denied that human nature is a featureless jelly ready to be cast into any mold. Its full realization requires the "all-round" actualization of human potentialities in a long and tortuous historical process. In holding these beliefs Marx is more like Hegel than like Sartre.

5. Alienation

So much has been written about alienation that I hesitate to add to the literature already extant, but I shall relate it to the concept of organic development.

In a state of alienation, declared Hegel, "there is no living union between the individual and his world; the ob-

[23]Jean-Paul Sartre, *Existentialism* (New York: Philosophical Library, 1947), p. 18.

101

ject, severed from the subject, is dead."[24] The essence of alienation is this separation between subject and object; man finds himself cut off from a world that is adverse and alien to his impulses and desires. His ties with organic being have been broken; his growth toward a genuinely human life has been throttled.

That alienation is a kind of separation is recognized by Richard Schacht and Bertell Ollman. Schacht declares that the term "alienation" has for Marx the meaning of "separation through surrender."[25] For example, the product of labor is separated from the worker by being surrendered by him to his capitalist employer. Surrender (Entausserung) is here the means to separation (Entfremdung). I think separation, not surrender, is the fundamental meaning of alienation, although Entausserung is sometimes employed by Marx as almost synonymous with Entfremdung. Some alienation is the result of deprivation rather than surrender. Ollman, without emphasizing the concept of surrender, interprets alienation as separation from an organic whole. Nonalienated life is a comparatively seamless web of internal relations; alienation occurs when one or more of these relations is broken and life thereby is segmented. Man is estranged from his work, his products, his fellow men, his own deeper self, and his natural environment.

> What is left of the individual after all these cleavages have occurred is a mere rump, a lowest common denominator attained by lopping off all those qualities on which is based his claim to recognition as a man. Thus denuded, the alienated person has become an "abstraction."[26]

The interpretation of Ollman (minus the concept of the whole universe as a gigantic web of internal relations)

[24]G.W.F. Hegel, *Early Theological Writings* (Chicago: University of Chicago Press, 1948), p. 303.
[25]Richard Schacht, *Alienation* (Garden City, N.Y.: Doubleday & Company, 1970), p. 111.
[26]Bertell Ollman, *Alienation: Marx's Conception of Man in Capitalist Society* (Cambridge at the University Press, 2nd. ed., 1976), p. 134.

fits Marx's model of organic totality. Alienation is the negative moment, the impairment and disruption of organic development.

It has been regarded by some philosophers as a soul-sickness based on the inevitable nature of human existence. Every man, they say, is entrapped in his skin and hemmed in by his ego. Like a marooned castaway, he is confined to the desolate island of his separate identity. Marx rejects this interpretation. He regards alienation as an historically produced evil—not a malady rooted in nature or human nature. It is not what happens *separately* to each man; it happens to men in groups and masses; and it varies in quality, incidence, and intensity with historical circumstances. Because it has been made by man it can be unmade by man.

I shall confine my discussion to the following: (1) alienation in the work process, (2) alienation of man from his products, (3) alienation of man from nature, (4) alienation of man from his species-being. These four kinds of alienation interpenetrate.

(1) *Alienation in the work process.* Marx emphasizes the interdependence of two sources of alienation, the *process* and the *product* of labor.

> Alienation appears not merely in the result but also in the *process* of *production.* . . . How could the worker stand in an alien relationship to the product of his activity if he did not alienate himself in the act of production itself?. . . . The alienation of the object of labour merely summarizes the alienation in the work activity itself.[27]

That human life is treated as other than it is, as nonhuman, is not alone characteristic of modern capitalist production. The organization of mass-production with standardized boss-driven labor is called by Lewis Mumford a "megamachine." The regimentation of the human components into the "megamachine" was

> first achieved in Mesopotamia and Egypt, and later in India, China, Persia, and in the Andean and Mayan cultures. . . .

[27]*Economic and Philosophical Manuscripts*, p. 124.

> With mordant symbolism, the ultimate products of the mega-machine in Egypt were colossal tombs, inhabited by mummified corpses; while later in Assyria, as repeatedly in every other expanding empire, the chief testimony to its technical efficiency was a waste of destroyed villages and cities, and poisoned soils; the prototype of similar "civilized" atrocities today. . . . Whether the military or the labor machine came first, they had the same organization. . . . In both cases, the fundamental unit was the squad, under the supervision of a gang boss.[28]

Marx's account of the collective work-process under "oriental despotism" parallels Mumford's description of the megamachine.[29] Also the slaves of ancient Greece and Rome and the serfs of medieval Europe were frequently degraded to a subhuman level. As Georg Lukács has said: "Oppression and an exploitation that knows no bounds and scorns every human dignity were known even to pre-capitalist ages."[30]

This was not always the case. In the peasant's interaction with nature and the medieval craftsman's skill, work often attained dignity and intrinsic worth. With the advent of capitalism, these gains were largely cancelled by mechanical drudgery. The worker was estranged—in this sense "separated"—from his work.

> What constitutes the alienation of labour? First, that the work is external to the worker, that it is not part of his nature; and that, consequently, he does not fulfill himself in his work but denies himself, has a feeling of misery rather than well-being, does not develop freely his mental and physical energies but is physically exhausted and mentally debased. The worker, therefore, feels himself at home only during his leisure time, whereas at work he feels homeless. His work is not voluntary

[28]Lewis Mumford, The Myth of the Machine: Technics and Human Development (New York: Harcourt, Brace and World, 1967), pp. 12, 192.
[29]See Karl A. Wittfogel, Oriental Despotism (New Haven: Yale University Press, 1957) and George Lichtheim, "Oriental Despotism" in The Concept of Alienation and Other Essays (New York: Random House, 1967).
[30]Georg Lukács, History and Class Consciousness (Cambridge: Massachusetts Institute of Technology Press, 1968), p. 90.

but imposed, *forced labour*. . . . Finally, the external character of work for the worker is shown by the fact that it is not his own work but work for someone else, that in work he does not belong to himself but to another person.[31]

This characterization of alienated work appears in the Paris *Manuscripts* of 1844, but it is also described unforgettably in Chapter VIII, "The Working Day," of Volume I of *Capital*. Although this chapter is not entitled "Alienation," it depicts alienation in its most brutal form.

(2) *Alienation of man from his products*. As Marx declared, alienation in work and alienation of the worker from his products are two sides of the same coin. Human beings create the products of industry, but these products then have a "life" and "will" of their own.

> The object produced by labour, its product, now stands opposed to it as an *alien being*, as a *power independent* of the producer. . . . The more the worker expends himself in work the more powerful becomes the world of objects which he creates in face of himself. . . . The worker puts his life into the object, and his life then belongs no longer to himself but to the object.[32]

The products function as "independent beings endowed with life," and enter "into relations both with one another and the human race." An "inhuman power"—the set of economic forces controlling the market—governs the products, rather than the worker's own will.

"Objectification"—a key Marxian term derived from Hegel—is the process by which man projects and expresses himself in external objects. Its common mode, the productive activity, is not necessarily an evil—on the contrary, it is an invaluable means of the humanization of nature and the cultivation of humankind. Without the integration of man and nature through the productive process life would not rise above an animal level. Hegel mistakenly equated alienation with objectification, believing that it is an inevi-

[31]*Economic and Philosophical Manuscripts*, pp. 124–125.
[32]*Ibid.*, p. 122.

table (but not necessarily a permanent) result of the "externalization" of oneself in objects. Marx was the first to disentangle the two meanings: he regarded alienation as a perverted form of objectification. It is an aberration caused by historical circumstances, occurring when man's existence is in conflict with his essence. This kind of conflict is said to be endemic to capitalist production. The worker is alienated from the products of his activity, which belong to another (the capitalist) and which are governed by the impersonal mechanism of the market.

Marx's most profound analysis of this form of alienation is his account of "fetishism" in *Capital*, but it is foreshadowed by his discussion of money-economy in his early writings.

> In money the unfettered dominion of the estranged thing *over* man becomes manifest. The rule of the person over the person now becomes the universal rule of the *thing* over the *person*, the product over the producer. [33]

The term "fetishism" is derived from the critique of religion. According to Feuerbach, the creations of religious thought, spirits and gods, seem to have a life of their own. The powers and capacities that men attribute to these supernatural beings are, in fact, their own powers and capacities projected into a fictitious world and magnified by the religious imagination. Statements about the supernatural world are disguised statements about human traits and needs. It is similar with the products of the human hand in the world of commodities. They appear to have an independent life of their own, acting and reacting on one another in accordance with economic laws. Although their economic value is realized only in exchange, that is, by means of a *social* process, this value appears to be an objective property of the commodities.

[33]"Excerpts from James Mill's *Elements of Political Economy*" (1844) in *Marx, Early Writings*, trans. by Rodney Livingstone and Gregor Benton (New York: Random House, 1975), p. 270.

> It is an enchanted, perverted, topsy-turvy world, in which
> Mister Capital and Mistress Land carry on their goblin tricks
> as social characters and at the same time as mere things.[34]

The social relations between men assume in human eyes the fantastic guise of relations between things. Fluctuations of price, inflations, and deflations, employment and unemployment, the crippling effects of the division of labor and the unjust distribution of wealth, are all seemingly independent of the will and desire of the producers. The economic system becomes heartless: people are treated as if they were things, and things are regarded as if they were human. Marx called this capitalist inversion of people and things the fetishism of commodities.

Alienation of the producer from his product is not restricted to capitalist production. The slave is deprived of the use and benefit of his products, and the serf must surrender a substantial proportion of his produce to the feudal lord. The fruits of their labor tyrannize over them and intensify their alienation. Alienation of men from the products of their labor has been a constant feature of history:

> This fixation of social activity, this consolidation of what we
> ourselves produce into a material power above us, growing
> out of our control, thwarting our expectations, bringing to
> naught our calculations, is one of the chief features in histori-
> cal development up till now.[35]

The fetishism of commodities is particularly characteristic of capitalism. In pre-capitalist economies production on the whole aims at the creation of use-values rather than exchange-values. Hence economic relations are usually more direct and personal than in the capitalist economy of commodity-production and market-exchange. Marx does attribute "fetishism" to commodities produced in a "simple exchange" economy. This type of production and exchange is transitional and not distinctly capitalist, but since it is the

[34]*Capital* (Chicago: Charles H. Kerr & Company, 1909), Vol. III, p. 966.
[35]*The German Ideology*, in Marx/Engels, *Collected Works* (New York: International Publishers, 1976), Vol. 5, pp. 47–48.

107

beginning of capitalism it may be proper to include it within the "capitalist epoch."

(3) *Alienation of man from nature.* Marx characterizes primitive man's awareness of nature as a form of alienation:

> Consciousness is ... from the very beginning a social product, and remains so as long as men exist at all. ... At the same time it is consciousness of nature, which first confronts men as a completely alien, all-powerful and unassailable force, with which men's relations are purely animal and by which they are overawed like beasts. ... [36]

Because primitive man is not master of himself and his environment, he feels terrified and powerless ("alienated") in the face of nature.

In reaching this conclusion Marx was influenced by Feuerbach's interpretation of religion. Religion, according to Feuerbach, is the fantasy of alienated man. The fact that it is primordial indicates that alienation characterized human life from the beginning. When human beings do not feel in harmony with nature they compensate by the illusions of supernaturalism. God is an empty figment apart from the ideal qualities that they find in themselves and attribute to Him. He is the reification of idealized human traits—a reification that occurs because men are at odds with their human and natural environment. Hence the overcoming of alienation is inseparable from the reconciliation of individual men with nature.

> Including *external* nature; for as man belongs to the essence of Nature,—in opposition to common materialism; so Nature belongs to the essence of man,—in opposition to subjective idealism. ... Only by uniting man with Nature can we conquer the supernaturalistic egoism of Christianity.[37] (My italics.)

These ideas of Feuerbach were present in Marx's mind when he wrote the *Economic and Philosophical Manuscripts* in 1844.

[36]*Ibid.,* p. 44.
[37]Feuerbach, *The Essence of Christianity* (New York: Harper & Brothers, 1957), p. 270.

Even at this early stage of his career Marx was not wholly in accord with Feuerbach. He *agreed* with Feuerbach's criticism of religion and his linking together of humanism and naturalism. He *disagreed* with Feuerbach's concept of a static human "essence" and his passive stance toward nature. We are confronted at this point by two different theories of cognition—as a reflection of nature ("Feuerbach's theory) and as an organic transformation of nature (Marx's).[38] Feuerbach believed that man's knowledge of nature is a faithful reflection of objective qualities. Marx had an activist and practical orientation toward nature in knowing and transforming it. This is implied by his idea of *humanized* nature, which possesses no forms or qualities inherent in itself and *preceding* human—that is, *social—conciousness.*

> The *human* significance of nature only exists for *social* man, because only in this case is nature a *bond* with other men, the basis of his existence for others and of their existence for him. Only then is nature the *basis* of his own *human* experience and a vital element of human reality. The *natural* existence of man has here become his *human* existence and nature itself has become human for him.[39]

Marx thinks that man's basic nature, including his sensory reaction to the external world, is created by man himself through the historical process. "The cultivation of the five senses is the work of all previous history."[40] Apart from this historical process nature "is nothing to man."

Human beings are alienated from nature when their productive relations are fundamentally awry. The alienation occurs when the worker "is related to the *product of*

---

[38]See the illuminating discussion by Leszek Kolakowski, *Marxism and Beyond* (London: Pall Mall Press, 1968), pp. 62–71. For Feuerbach's statement of his theory see especially *Principles of the Society of the Future*, sections 36, 37, 45, 48. Engels and Lenin, deviating from Marx, also embraced a reflectionist epistemology.

[39]*Economic and Philosophical Manuscripts*, p. 157.

[40]*Ibid.*, p. 161.

labour as an alien object which dominates him. This relationship is at the same time the relationship to the sensuous external world, to natural objects, as an alien and hostile world."[41] When alienation in the productive process wrests from the worker "the object of production . . . , it also takes away his *species-life*, his real objectivity as a species-being, and changes his advantage over animals into a disadvantage in so far as his inorganic body, nature, is taken from him."[42] The symbiotic harmony of man with nature is ruptured: nature-for-man becomes nature-against-man.

(4) *Alienation of man from his species-being.* The alienation of man from his own humanity ("species-being") assumes two intertwined forms. First, there is a disparity between his actual condition and his human nature: existence and essence are in conflict. Second, there is an estrangement of man from other men. Instead of being members of a true community, they confront one another as enemies.

> When man stands over against himself, other men stand over against him also. . . . The estrangement of man from his essential being means that a man is estranged from others, just as each is estranged from his essential humanity.[43]

This dehumanization cannot be understood apart from Marx's concept of man, but an adequate discussion of the concept would require more space than I can spare. Although whole books have been devoted to the subject,[44] I shall mention only a few salient characteristics.

[41]*Ibid.*, pp. 125–126.

[42]*Ibid.*, p. 128.

[43]*Ibid.* in a passage translated by Alasdair MacIntyre, *Marxism* (London: SCM Press, 1953), pp. 50–51. I have preferred MacIntyre's translation to Bottomore's.

[44]Among older books see Vernon Venable, *Human Nature: The Marxian View* (New York: Alfred A. Knopf, 1945). For a recent account see John Plamenatz, *Karl Marx's Philosophy of Man* (Oxford: Clarendon Press, 1975). Also see Bertell Ollman, *Alienation: Marx's Concept of Man in Capitalist Society*; Erich Fromm, *Marx's Concept of Man* (New York: Frederick Ungar Publishing Company, 1969); and Lucien Séve, *Man in Marxist Theory and the Psychology of Personality* (Atlantic Highlands, N.J.: Humanities Press, 1978).

In terms of deep-rooted but largely unrealized potentialities man is (1) social, (2) productive, (3) universal and free, and (4) whole. I shall illustrate Marx's views regarding these characteristics by brief quotations.

(1) Marx thinks of human beings as inherently social:

> Since the essence of man is the true community of man, men, by activating their own essence, produce, create this human community, this social being which is no abstract, universal power standing over against the solitary individual, but is the essence of every individual, his own activity, his own life, his own spirit, his own wealth.[45]

(2) Man is a producer, a maker, in a sense unique to the human species. In a passage quoted at greater length in Chapter I, Marx declares:

> Of course, animals also produce. They construct nests, dwellings, as in the case of bees, beavers, ants, etc. But they only produce what is strictly necessary for themselves and their young. They produce only in a single direction, while man produces universally. They produce only under the compulsion of direct physical needs, while man produces when he is free from physical need and only truly produces in freedom from such need. Animals produce only themselves, while man reproduces the whole of nature. . . . Thus man constructs also in accordance with the laws of beauty.[46]

(3) Marx links together the freedom of the individual person and the universality of the human community. The thrust toward freedom and universality is inherent in man's very constitution.

> Man is a species-being . . . in the sense that he treats himself . . . as a universal and consequently free being.[47]

> Man . . . is free not through the negative power to avoid this or that, but through the positive power to assert his true individuality. . . . If man is social by nature, he will develop his

[45]"Excerpts from James Mill's *Elements of Political Economy*," p. 265.
[46]*Economic and Philosophical Manuscripts*, p. 128.
[47]*Ibid.*, p. 126.

true nature only in society, and the power of his nature must be measured not only by the power of the separate individual but by the power of society.[48]

(4) Human life is a drive toward concreteness and totality. Organic wholeness is characteristic of human nature in its integrity. Man realizes "his manifold being in an all-inclusive way, and thus as a whole man," by "seeing, hearing, smelling, tasting, touching, thinking, observing, feeling, desiring, acting, loving."[49]

These characteristics represent essential human nature in its historical unfolding. Although more potential than actual, they operate as drives toward human fulfillment. Dehumanization is the repression and distortion of these drives. It produces fractured people in a fractured society.

Among the principal causes of alienation are poverty and the division of labor. Nothing is more dehumanizing than extreme poverty.

> Not having . . . is a most dismal reality; . . . the man who has nothing is nothing, for he is cut off from existence in general, and still more from human existence. . . . Not having is . . . a very positive having, a having, of hunger, of cold, of disease, of crime, of debasement, of imbecility, of all inhumanity and abnormality.[50]

Although the division of labor is another major cause of dehumanization, Marx does not condemn it from every point of view. He recognizes that it is a form of social production that has been historically necessary for the increase of wealth. But it intensifies the split between labor and capital, and it has been carried to the point of extreme fragmentation. Poverty and division of labor are not "causes" in the sense of being *external* determinants of

[48]*The Holy Family* in Marx/Engels, *Collected Works* (New York: International Publishers, 1975), Vol. 4, p. 131.
[49]*Economic and Philosophical Manuscripts*, p. 159.
[50]*The Holy Family*, p. 42. That Marx and his family suffered appalling poverty is evident from reading Maximilien Rubel and Margaret Manale, *Marx Without Myth: A Chronological Study of His Life and Work* (Oxford: Basil Blackwell, 1975).

alienation—they are *internally* related to alienation and therefore interpenetrative with it.

6. The Relation of Alienation to the Two Models of Historical Interpretation

Marx's account of alienation is consistent with his historicism. The human nature that suffers dehumanization is itself created in the long course of history. The traits that Marx calls man's "species-being" are "the slumbering powers" of which he speaks in *Capital* (see below, page 214). They are the relatively enduring human potentialities that are shaped and awakened by the historical process. Nothing in Marx's account of alienation is inconsistent with historicism as "the attempt to take seriously the fact of change" (Mandelbaum's wording). Alienation and its overcoming constitute the "inward journey" of mankind's historical odyssey.

Just how much emphasis is placed on alienation depends on the model of historical explanation accepted. If the interpreter of Marx has solely in mind the base and superstructure model, he may regard alienation as little more than a by-product of economic forces, or consider it an aberration of Marx's youth that was corrected in his sober manhood. Shlomo Avineri has remarked:

> Such a view, considering only the objective side of historical development and not its subjective development, . . . sees in man and in human will only an object of external circumstances and, *mutatis mutandis*, of political manipulation. Both the cruelty and harshness of Bolshevism and the intellectual wastelands of Social Democracy grow directly from this mechanistic twist. . . . [51]

The position of Louis Althusser is somewhat harder to classify. He represents a compromise between the older "scientific Marxism" of Communist Party orthodoxy and

[51]Shlomo Avineri, *The Social and Political Thought of Karl Marx* (Cambridge at the University Press, 1969), p. 144.

the newer structuralist orientation of Levi-Strauss and others. Rejecting a simple one-way concept of cause and effect, he recognizes that the elements of the total structure are linked to each other in all sorts of relations of interdependence, and that the total configuration exercises a pervasive influence upon its constituents. But he still clings, at least halfheartedly, to Engels' contention that "the economic necessity . . . in the last analysis always prevails," and he contends that the mature Marx eliminated humanism except as an "ideology."

> In 1845, Marx broke radically with every theory that based history and politics on an essence of man. This unique rupture contained three indissociable elements. (1) The formation of a theory of history and politics based on radically new concepts: the concepts of social formation, productive forces, relations of production, superstructure, ideologies, determination in the last instance by the economy, specific determination of the other levels, etc. (2) A radical critique of the *theoretical* pretensions of every philosophical humanism. (3) The definition of humanism as an *ideology*.[52]

This rejection of humanism as applicable to the mature Marx lends a near-mechanist cast to Althusser's thought. It is best described, in the words of Nicos Poulantzas, as "a gestalist mechanism."[53]

Althusser's interpretation of Marx's intellectual development is not wholly unfounded. Marx appears to have reacted against his humanistic theory of alienation in favor of economic determinism shortly after he wrote the *Economic and Philosophical Manuscripts*. In a letter to Pavel V. Annenkov, a Russian man of letters, on December 28, 1846, he wrote:

[52]Louis Althusser, *For Marx* (New York: Pantheon Books, 1969), p. 227. Lucien Sève, *op. cit.*, agrees with Althusser that there is a profound rupture between the young (pre-1845) and the older Marx, but he finds it in the contrast between a "speculative" and a "scientific" humanism and not between humanism and anti-humanism.

[53]Nicos Poulantzas, "Vers Une Theorie Marxiste," *Les Temps Modernes*, no. 240 (1966), p. 1981.

Are men free to choose this or that form of society for themselves? By no means. Assume a particular state of development in the productive forces of man and you will get a particular form of commerce and consumption. Assume particular stages of development in consumption and you will have a corresponding social order, a corresponding organization of the family and of the ranks and classes. Presuppose a particular civil society and you will get particular political conditions which are only the official expression of civil society.... Men's material relations are the basis of all their relations.[54]

Likewise Marx declared in *The German Ideology* (1846) that "civil society is the true source and theatre of all history."

This conception of history ... relies on expounding the real process of production—starting from the material production of life itself—and comprehending the form of intercourse connected with and created by this mode of production, i.e., civil society in its various stages, as the basis of all history.... [55]

In the *Communist Manifesto* (1848) Marx turned against the conception "of Human Nature, of Man in general, who belongs to no class, who has no reality, who exists only in the misty realm of philosophical fantasy." These statements are a prelude to his summary of the base-superstructure theory in the Preface to *A Contribution to the Critique of Political Economy* (January 1859). The reader who heeds only these passages naturally would conclude with Althusser that Marx abandoned his earlier humanism.

Althusser cites Marx's *Theses on Feuerbach* as marking the decisive break with his early humanism. The sixth the-

---

[54]Marx/Engels, *Selected Correspondence 1843–1895*, ed. by Dona Torr (New York: International Publishers, 1936), pp. 7–8.

[55]*The German Ideology* in *Collected Works*, pp. 53–54. Marx's term "civil society" is borrowed from Hegel, who emphasizes the economic aspects of civil society but regards them as elements within an organic whole. If this Hegelian connotation is borne in mind, the above references to "civil society" are not as reductionist as they might appear.

sis is said to be an attack on Feuerbach's theory of the human essence:

> Feuerbach resolves the essence of religion into the essence of man. But the essence of man is no abstraction inherent in each single individual. In its reality it is the ensemble of the social relations.

Marx charges that Feuerbach is compelled by his nonhistorical approach "to abstract from the historical process . . . and to presuppose an abstract—*isolated*—human individual."[56] If we note what Feuerbach actually says, however, he is *not* postulating "an abstract—*isolated*—human individual."

> The single man *in isolation* possesses in himself the essence of man neither as a *moral* nor as a *thinking* being. The essence of man is contained in the community, in the unity of man with man—a unity, however, that rests on the *reality* of a distinction between "I" and "You."[57]

Marx's ambiguous phrase, "the ensemble of human relations," may not have the same meaning as Feuerbach's term "community." But both Marx and Feuerbach conceive the human being as a focus of human relations; both insist that sociality should *enhance*, not diminish, individuality; and both characterize human beings as impoverished by a life of abstract thought and in need of sensuous and interpersonal experiences. Marx is being accurate when, in the Paris *Manuscripts*, he commends Feuerbach for "making the social relationship of 'man to man' the basic principle of his theory."[58]

Feuerbach himself comes close to asserting that the human reality is "the ensemble of social relations." This seems to be the meaning of his contention that "there is no

---

[56]See *Theses on Feuerbach* in Marx/Engels, *Collected Works*, Vol. 5, pp. 3–5.

[57]*Principles of the Philosophy of the Future* in *The Fiery Brook: Selected Writings of Ludwig Feuerbach*, trans. with an introduction by Zawar Hanfi (Garden City, N.Y.: Doubleday & Company, 1972), p. 110.

[58]*Economic and Philosophical Manuscripts*, p. 110.

me without you. I depend on you: No *Thou*—no *I*."[59] As Marx W. Wartofsky has said in interpreting Feuerbach:

> The *species being* does not exist in itself, but only in the relation, the interaction, of *I* and *Thou*. . . . The community, the commonalty, is *not* an entity, therefore not a hyposta- tized, independent being, but a relation, or as Marx was to say (in the *Theses on Feuerbach*), an *ensemble of relations*.[60]

Both Marx and Feuerbach interpret human nature as *rela- tional*. There is of course a difference. In Feuerbach the relations are more sentimental, personal ("man to man"), and unhistorical; in Marx the relations are spelled out in much greater detail, social, economic, cultural, and above all, historical. But the difference is not between a human- ism and a non-humanism, or between an isolated individu- alism and a "scientific socialism." Indicative of consider- able agreement is the fact that Feuerbach, toward the end of his life, hailed *Capital* as Marx's "great critique of political economy."[61]

In the first thesis Marx repudiates both speculative ide- alism and reductive materialism, and in later theses he in- sists on the efficacy of practical thought:

> Man must prove the truth, i.e., the reality and power, the this-worldliness of his thinking in practice. . . . The philoso- phers have only *interpreted* the world in various ways; the point is to *change* it.

"Materialists," in their notion of one-way causality, forget that there is a dialectical interaction between thought and things, men and situations. People are changed *by* chang- ing circumstances; circumstances are changed *by* changing people.

---

[59]Feuerbach, "On *The Essence of Christianity* in relation to *The Ego and Its Own*" (a reply to Max Stirner), quoted by Marx W. Wartofsky, *Feuer- bach* (Cambridge University Press, 1977). p. 425.
[60]Wartofsky, *ibid.*, p. 426.
[61]Feuerbach, Letter to Friedrich Kapp, April 11, 1868, cited by Wartofsky, pp. 451–452.

> The materialist doctrine concerning the changing of circum-
> stances and upbringing forgets that circumstances are
> changed by men and that the educator must himself be edu-
> cated. This doctrine must, therefore, divide society into two
> parts, one of which is superior to society. The coincidence of
> the changing of circumstances and of human activity or self-
> change can be conceived and rationally understood only as
> *revolutionary practice.*[62]

The meaning of this ellipitical passage seems to be as follows. The proponents of "the materialist doctrine" think of
human beings as passive creatures that are wholly determined by external circumstances. They conceive social
transformation as the manipulation of an inert social mass
by an elite of right thinking leaders who, in turn, have been
determined by circumstances. In seeking to instill revolutionary ideas in the workers by external manipulation, they
forget that as "educators" they must themselves be educated. The process of education can only be rationally understood as a change in consciousness on the part of *both*
the educated and the educators. Whenever the role of con-
sciouness—the function of *self*-changing—is neglected, the
ideological basis is laid for one part of society—the self-de-
clared revolutionary vanguard—to raise itself above the rest
of society and to try to manipulate it. To do so is to forsake
the very meaning of revolutionary practice.

There is no reason to think that Marx abandoned his
humanism or theory of alienation in his mature works. In
Capital the word "alienation" *(Entfremdung)* is rare but the
doctrine is not. The discussion of exploitation, dehumanization, fetishism, and class conflict traverses the same
ground as in the *Paris Manuscripts,* but with a vastly augmented body of evidence and a much firmer grasp of the
economic aspects of alienation. Although Marx no longer
used the term "human essence," he still distinguished be-

[62]In translating this thesis, Engels omitted the term "self-change," thus
partially obscuring the meaning. Unfortunately his translation, published
as an Appendix to his book *Ludwig Feuerbach and the Outcome of Classical German Philosophy,* is frequently quoted.

tween "human nature in general" and "human nature as modified in each historical epoch."[63] In the Grundrisse the word "alienation" as well as the doctrine recurs frequently and the humanism is as insistent as ever.

In the foregoing account of alienation I have quoted mainly from the early writings, but the idea of alienation and its overcoming is a permanent part of Marx's thought. In his Speech on the Anniversary of the People's Paper (1856) he declared: "All our invention and progress seem to result in endowing material forces with intellectual life, and in stultifying human life into a material force."[64] Similarly in the omitted "sixth chapter" of Capital (published for the first time in 1933), Marx speaks of "the personification of objects and the reification of people"—the very essence of alienation.[65] Much of the argument of the Grundrisse and Capital can be interpreted as an elaboration of this theme. The overcoming of alienation is the reversal of this relation: human beings are treated as human beings and things as things. This conception of alienation and its overcoming is the core of Marx's humanism.

Marx reacted against Feuerbach's reflectionist and unhistorical theory of knowledge and his static notion of "the human essence," but not against humanism. During the remainder of his life he tried to make his base-superstructure model more workable by introducing qualifications and exceptions. Gradually the lineaments of his organic model emerged in clearer perspective. He apparently never thought of the base-superstructure and organic models as alternatives. The explanation may be that he regarded the former as the more abstract and the latter as the more concrete. The difference is in the level of abstraction rather than in flat contradiction.

One advantage of the organic model is that it clarifies what Marx means by alienation. The meaning is simply

[63]Capital, I, p. 668.
[64]Speech on the Anniversary of the People's Paper, in Karl Marx, Selected Writings, ed. by David McLellan (Oxford University Press, 1977), p. 338.
[65]Selected Writings (McLellan), p. 515.

that organic unity is impaired. When Marx speaks of the "social organism" he does not mean that it is a seamless unity, "organic" through and through. Especially in the later pathological stages of a social order, there are tragic conflicts and schisms. Marx is like Schiller in contrasting man's *actual* schizoid condition with his *potential* nature as a healthy organism. According to the editors of the *Letters on the Aesthetic Education of Man*, Schiller realized that

> if the analogy of an organism is to be invoked at all, then it can no longer be in terms of the simple antithesis, common enough in his day, between a mechanical "aggregate of elements" and a living "organized whole".... It had to include notions of imbalance, asymmetry, dominant principle, and hierarchical subordination, all of them characteristic of living forms, and becoming increasingly marked with increasing differentiation.[66]

The doctrine of alienation is thus an integral part of Marx's mature theory of dialectrical development. Both the self and society become more rich and complex by a process of splitting and differentiation. The division-fraught realities of the actual world are the internal motor of revolutionary transformation. Both the schisms of alienation and the socio-economic conflicts are mighty forces of historical change. Although there is a difference of viewpoint in the later writings, it is largely Marx's more acute realization that alienation and economic malaise are two faces of the same coin.

7. The Objective Stages of Historical Development

Alienation and its supersession may be called the subjective aspect of historical development; the transformation of society from one socio-economic formation to another may be called its objective aspect. In the famous Preface to *A*

[66]Elizabeth M. Wilkinson and L.A. Willoughby, Introduction to Friedrich Schiller, *On the Aesthetic Education of Man* (Oxford at the Clarendon Press, 1967), p. lxxxiv.

Contribution to the Critique of Political Economy Marx declared: "In broad outlines we can designate the Asiatic, the ancient, the feudal, and the modern bourgeois modes of production as so many epochs in the progress of the economic formation of society."[67] In addition to these four epochs there is an initial primitive and a future communist stage. In calling these stages "epochs" in economic progress, Marx did not mean that they necessarily follow in historical sequence. He repudiated the view that every geographical area must pass through all six stages one after another. He simply meant that each successive stage is further removed from barbarism and closer to the future stage of advanced communism.

The pre-capitalist economic formations are discussed in *The German Ideology* (1846), the *Grundrisse* (1857–1858), *A Contribution to the Critique of Political Economy* (1859), *Capital* (1867 onwards), articles contributed to the *New York Daily Tribune* (1853 onwards), and letters of various dates. Marx also jotted down a great many pages of excerpts and notes based on his extensive reading of ethnological literature (1879—1882).[68] The stages of socio-economic development may be summarized as follows:

(1) *Primitive Communities*. In the closing years of his life, Marx was influenced in his interpretation of primitive society by the work of Lewis H. Morgan, the American anthropologist. Morgan in *Ancient Society* (1877) maintained that property distinctions played only a minor role in primitive societies; that social cohesion based on kinship groups preceded the rise of the family, economic classes, and the state; and that the society of the future would resemble the communal institutions of primitive men. "It will

[67]Preface to *A Contribution to the Critique of Political Economy* (Chicago: Charles H. Kerr & Company, 1904), p. 13.
[68]Se Eric J. Hobsbawm, Introduction to Marx, *Pre-Capitalist Economic Formations* (New York: International Publishers, 1965); Lawrence Krader, *The Ethnological Notebooks of Karl Marx* (Assen, Netherlands: Van Gorcum and Company, 1972); Krader, *The Asiatic Mode of Production* (Assen: Van Gorcum and Company, 1975); and Karl A. Wittfogel, *Oriental Despotism*, *op. cit.*

be a revival, in a higher form," said Morgan, "of the liberty, equality, and fraternity of the ancient gentes."[69] Making use of Marx's copious notes, Engels wrote *The Origin of the Family, Private Property and the State* (1883) in which he extolled Morgan's work. Marx based his interpretation not only on Morgan but on classic sources, such as Tacitus' *Germania* and Caesar's *Gallic Wars,* and on modern authorities, such as Georg Maurer, Johann Bachofen, and Nikolai Mikhailovsky.

Marx's most concise early statement of the characteristics of primitive society is in *The German Ideology:*

> The first form of property is tribal property. It corresponds to the undeveloped stage of production, at which a people lives by hunting and fishing, by cattle-raising or, at most, by agriculture. In the latter case it presupposes a great mass of uncultivated stretches of land. The division of labour is at this stage still very elementary and is confined to a further extension of the natural division of labour existing in the family. The social structure is, therefore, limited to an extension of the family: patriarchal chieftains, below them the members of the tribe, finally slaves. The slavery latent in the family only develops gradually with the increase of population, the growth of wants, and with the extension of external intercourse, both of war and barter.[70]

Slavery, when fully developed as a mode of production, constitutes a later stage.

In subsequent formulations this sketch was filled out and modified. Marx realized that primitive societies were complex and various, but he was too old and ill to make use of his voluminous notes to write a sophisticated interpretation.

(2) *Asiatic Society.* Marx described the Asiatic mode of production in articles that he contributed to the *New York Daily Tribune* in 1853 and subsequently. Not far removed

[69]Lewis H. Morgan, *Ancient Society,* ed. by Leslie A. White (Cambridge, Mass.: Harvard University Press, 1964), p. 467. Originally published in 1877.
[70]*The German Ideology,* pp. 32–33.

from primitive communism, the Asiatic society was characterized by the absence of private property in land. The inhabitants lived in villages and cultivated the surrounding land in common, as in the ancient Mexican *ejido* system. Hand-weaving and spinning, or other forms of domestic handcraft, were combined with hand-tilling in agriculture. Because of arid climatic conditions, irrigation on a great scale was a necessary function of a centralized government. In addition to the hydraulic works, gigantic constructions such as the Great Wall of China and the Pyramids of Egypt were the products of regimented labor. Colossal statues and temples were erected to glorify the central despotism. With the exception of these constructions and locales of the central government, the occupations and dwelling-places were decentralized. Village isolation, which was heightened by the absence of roads, left the rural communities "almost without intercourse with other villages." This meant "the dissolution of society into pulverized and disconnected atoms" unable to withstand the despotic force of the government.[71] The result was a remarkably static economy.

> The simplicity of the organization for production in these self-sufficient communities . . . supplies the key to the secret of the unchangeableness of Asiatic societies, an unchangeableness in striking contrast with the constant dissolution and refounding of Asiatic States, and the never-ceasing changes of dynasty. The structure of the economic elements of society remains untouched by the storm clouds of the political sky.[72]

Marx regarded this constellation of factors as a distinctive system and contrasted it with both slavery and feudalism.

Although "the Asiatic mode of production" embraced the greater part of Asia, it was, in a sense, a misnomer. It appeared, with variations, in ancient Egypt, Byzantium, and the Aztec, Mayan, and Inca empires. A semi-Asiatic

[71]*New York Daily Tribune*, August 8, 1853, reprinted in Marx and Engels, *On Colonialism* (Moscow: Foreign Languages Publishing House, no date), p. 79.
[72]*Capital*, I, pp. 393–394.

society took root in Russia, where village communities and state despotism developed without hydraulic public works. However, the paradigm examples were in Asia.

(3) *Ancient (or Classical) Society.* In southern Europe primitivism was superseded by the slave-owning and urban-oriented societies of Greece and Rome. Several tribes united to form a city, "a polis," and this process was repeated again and again. Whereas Asian history is a kind of undifferentiated unity of village and country, ancient classical history is the history of cities, such as Athens, Syracuse, Corinth, Rome, and Carthage—cities originally based on land ownership but in course of time evolving commerce and crafts. In its developed form, the ancient mode of production was characterized by the predominance of chattel slavery. The bias of the land-owning aristocracy was directed against the free artisans as well as the slaves. As private property increased, the structure of society based on communal institutions and with it the democratic power of the people decayed. At this stage

> The division of labour is already more developed. We already find the opposition of town and country; later the opposition between those states which represent town interests and those which represent country interests, and inside the towns themselves the opposition between industry and maritime commerce. The class relations between citizens and slaves are now completely developed.[73]

From these antagonisms Greco-Roman civilization never recovered.

> The slaves died out again and again, and had constantly to be replaced by new ones. Slavery remained the basis of the entire production process. The plebeians, midway between freemen and slaves, never succeeded in becoming more than a proletarian rabble.[74]

Economically and technologically the cities became increasingly interdependent, but they remained an anarchic

[73]*The German Ideology*, p. 33.
[74]*Ibid.*, p. 84.

bundle of independent city-states competing in commerce, colonization, and military aggression. When the Macedonian and Roman empires imposed a measure of political unification, the decay of the civilization was already far advanced. "Rome indeed never became more than a city; its connection with the provinces was almost exclusively political and could, therefore, easily be broken again by political events."[75] Weakened by war and rent by class conflicts, the classical civilization finally succumbed to enemies from within and without.

(4) *Feudal Society*. Feudalism was a synthesis of classical and Germanic influences.

> The last centuries of the declining Roman Empire and its conquest by the barbarians destroyed a considerable part of the productive forces; agriculture had declined, industry had decayed for want of a market, trade had died out or been violently interrupted, the rural and urban population had decreased. These conditions and the mode of organization of the conquest determined by them, together with the influence of the Germanic military constitution, led to the development of feudal property.[76]

In his later formulations Marx put greater emphasis on the Germanic tribal influence, with its communal institutions and strong kinship ties.

The economic basis of feudalism was primarily agricultural. In course of time the farmland in western and central Europe was divided into "manors." A manor was a landed estate held by a lord and worked by tenants and serfs. The tenants, resembling modern sharecroppers, were higher in the hierarchy than serfs but definitely subordinate to the lord. The serfs worked not only their own holdings but the lord's demesne as well. Although exploited, they were freer than slaves. Whereas the slaves were property that could be bought and sold, the serfs could not be separated from their plots of land. If the lord transferred the manor to another,

[75]*Ibid.*
[76]*Ibid.*, p. 34.

the serf remained on the land and served his new lord. Although he could not be sold off his land, neither could he leave it. There were various degrees of subordination among the serfs, some with more burdens and fewer rights than others. There was also an order of rank among the lords. The lord of the manor was often a vassal of another lord higher up in the scale.

In the later Middle Ages the towns grew larger and the traders and craftsmen prospered.

> The gradually accumulated small capital of individual crafts-men and their stable numbers, as against the growing popula-tion, evolved the relation of journeyman and apprentice, which brought into being in the towns a hierarchy similar to that in the country. Thus property during the feudal epoch primarily consisted on the one hand of landed property with serf labour chained to it, and on the other of the personal labour of the individual who with his small cpaital com-mands the labour of journeymen. The organization of both was determined by the restricted conditions of production—the scanty and primitive cultivation of the land, and the craft type industry. . . . Apart from the differentiation of princes, nobility, clergy and peasants in the country, and masters, journeymen, apprentices and soon also the rabble of casual laborers in the towns there was no important division.[77]

(5) *Modern Capitalist Society.* Marx's account of pre-capitalist societies rests on far less research than his de-scription and analysis of captialism. He was interested in these earlier societies mainly as they bore on the origins and development of the capitalist system. The distinguish-ing features of capitalism are commodity production, sur-plus-value, and free labor. Commodity production—pro-duction not for immediate use but for profitable exchange on the market—is not unique to capitalism, but it is far more prevalent in capitalist society than in any previous social order. Also the extraction of surplus value from the worker is not unique to capitalism. The form of this extrac-tion, however, distinguishes capitalism from other eco-

[77]*Ibid.,* pp. 34–35.

nomic systems: the worker is paid in wages less than the value of what he or she produces. Free labor, as the predominant form of employment, is a feature unique to capitalism. The worker sells his labor power on the market, and differs in this respect from the serf, the slave, the Asiatic toiler, and the member of a primitive commune. These characteristics of the capitalist system will be examined more fully in Chapter 5.

(6) *Communism.* Marx was convinced that historical forces are moving inexorably toward revolution. The only way in which "contradictions" can be resolved is by a revolutionary transformation of the relations of production. This restructuring will be the most profound revolution that the human race has ever known.

Marx thought that the lineaments of the future communist society are reasonably clear. (i) The fundamental principle of the economic system will be production for use and not production for profit. The institutional basis of the system will be the social ownership of the means of production. In the *Communist Manifesto* Marx spoke of ownership vested in the state, but in his later works he declared that "united co-operative societies are to regulate national production upon a common plan."[78] (ii) Marx defined the state as the coercive instrument of class-domination and predicted that the state in this sense will disappear in a classless society. The change need not terminate all law and administration. Marx seemed to recognize the necessity of some kind of administrative and legal agencies to form and execute the "common plan." In a marginal jotting that Marx made in 1874 while reading Bakunin's *Statism and Anarchy,* he remarked that "when class rule has disappeared, there will no longer be any state in the *present political sense* of the word."[79] (My italics.) Hearkening back to his usual characterization of the *political* state as rooted in class structure, he did not rule out non-coercive

---

[78]Marx, *The Civil War in France* in *Selected Works,* 2 vol. edition (New York: International Publishers, no date), II, p. 504.
[79]*Selected Writings* (McLellan), p. 563.

law and administration when the "present political" character of the state will have ceased to exist. The "associated producers" and not the coercive state will directly control the economy. (iii) Sufficient livelihood and ample leisure and cultural opportunities will be available to all. This transformation will bring an end to the "old division of labor" and "the alien relation between men and what they produce." (iv) Freedom will be the goal and consummation of the communist revolution. By "freedom" Marx means self-realization in and through community.

> Only within the community has each individual the means of cultivating his gifts in all directions. ... In the real community the individuals obtain their freedom in and through their association.[80]

An individual's fulfillment will be measured by the extent and intensity of his relations to other things and particularly to other people.

> The real intellectual wealth of the individual depends entirely on the wealth of his real connections. Only this will liberate the separate individuals from the various national and local barriers, bring them into practical connection with the production (including intellectual production) of the whole world and make it possible for them to acquire the capacity to enjoy this all-sided production of the whole earth (the creations of man).[81]

True to the concept of organic unity, Marx conceives freedom in terms of organic ties.

In *The Critique of the Gotha Program* he distinguishes between two phases of communism. The first, commonly termed "socialism," is a transitional phase in which the new order bears scars from the past. There must be compromises to insure survival of the new society. The state must maintain iron control against counter-revolution and for-

[80]*The German Ideology*, p. 78.
[81]*Ibid.*, p. 51.

eign attack; and to provide incentives, the more efficient and dedicated workers must be compensated with higher rewards. The principle of distribution will be "To each in accordance with his productivity."

Socialism will be transcended in the second phase of communism. The coercive state, in the words of Engels, "will wither away," and a different distributive principle will prevail. Marx declares in a famous passage:

> In a higher phase of communist society, after the enslaving subordination of the individual to the division of labour, and therewith also the antithesis between mental and physical labour, has vanished; after labour has become not only a means of life, but life's prime want; after the productive forces have also increased with the all-round development of the individual, and all the springs of cooperative wealth flow more abundantly—only then can the narrow horizon of bourgeois right be crossed in its entirety and society inscribe on its banner: From each according to his ability, to each according to his needs.[82]

Marx never predicts how long will be the transition from the first to the second phase.

8. A Multilinear and Organic Theory of History

Marx's interpretation of history is frequently misdescribed. A Soviet Russian "manual," for example, has thus characterized his theory:

> All peoples travel what is basically the same path. ... The development of society proceeds through the consecutive replacement, according to definite laws, of one socio-economic formation by another. Moreover, a nation living in the conditions of a more advanced formation shows other nations their future just as the latter show that nation its past.[83]

[82]The Critique of the Gotha Program in Selected Works, II, p. 566.
[83]Otto V. Kuusinen and others, Fundamentals of Marxism-Leninism (Moscow: Foreign Languages Publishing House, 1963), p. 125. This work was compiled by a staff of Russian academicians. As a source of Marx's ideas it is unreliable.

In Marx's lifetime a Russian ethnologist, N. K. Mikhailovsky, asserted that Russia, like every other country, would be forced to pass through a stage of capitalist development. When he attributed this opinion to Marx, the latter replied:

> He has to transform my sketch of the origins of capitalism in Western Europe into a historical-philosophical theory of a universal movement necessarily imposed upon all people, no matter what the historical circumstances in which they are placed. . . . But I must protest.

Marx then pointed out that in the early history of Rome, big estates and large financial capital resulted from the expropriation of land-holding peasants. Centuries later similar developments occurred in the rise of capitalism. But what happened in Rome was not the emergence of capitalism.

> The Roman proletarians did not become wage earners, but an idle mob, more abject even than the erstwhile "poor whites" of the southern States of the USA. Beside them grew up a system of production which was not capitalist, but was based on slavery. Thus we see that events of a striking similarity, but occurring in different historical contexts, produced quite different results. The key to these phenomena can be discovered quite easily by studying each of these developments separately, but we shall never succeed in understanding them if we rely on the *passe partout* of a historical-philosophical theory whose chief quality is that of being supra-historical.[84]

This caution against overgeneralization is reflected in other passages. Of the types of societies which Marx distinguished in *The German Ideology*—the primitive, ancient, feudal, and modern bourgeois—he remarked that "they can only serve to facilitate the arrangement of historical material, . . . but they by no means afford a recipe or schema . . . for neatly trimming the epochs of history."[85] As a typology based on Western evolution, they are not sequential in any

[84]Marx, *Selected Writings in Sociology and Social Philosophy*, ed. by T.B. Bottomore and Maximilien Rubel (London: Watts & Company, 1956), pp. 22–23.
[85]*The German Ideology*, p. 37.

other context. The Asiatic mode falls outside of the sequence, and Marx did not believe capitalism to be a necessary prelude to socialism.

He was aware of many phases and directions of historical development even at the primitive level. In a draft of a letter to Vera Zasulich, a Russian correspondent, he declared:

> Primitive communities are not all cut to a single pattern. On the contrary, taken together they form a series of social groupings, differing both in type and in age, and marking successive phases of development.[86]

His comments in the *Grundrisse* and in his ethnological notebooks indicate a considerable grasp of the diversities and complexities of primitive societies.

He pointed out various ways in which civilization evolved from its primitive origins. In the south of Europe, primitivism was superseded by the slaveholding societies of Greece and Rome, but in the Germanic north, the tribal type of society persisted throughout the Greco-Roman period. The feudal institutions of medieval Europe derived mainly from the kinship societies ("gentes") in the north rather than from the decaying slave system to the south. In Asia primitivism evolved into neither chattel slavery nor feudalism but into a distinctively Asiatic pattern. As contrasted with what happened in Europe, technology and the industrial middle class in Asia played a minor role, and the social order remained comparatively stagnant century after century. The Asiatic societies were not all of a uniform pattern—they might be centralized or decentralized, more or less despotic, and variously organized. Feudalism was largely confined to Western Europe, and capitalism was no more than a late importation in the Orient. The attribution of unilinear determinism to Marx is flatly contradicted by the relevant texts.

Marx clung to a multilinear theory for two reasons.

[86]Letter of Marx to Vera Zasulich, March 8, 1881 (third draft) in *Pre-Capitalist Economic Formations*, p. 144.

First, he was too much the social scientist to impose a *rigid* schematism on the data of history. He conceived the typology of historical development as little more than a heuristic device, not as a Procrustean bed to which history must be fitted by violent foreshortening. Second, he recognized the importance of the organic context in producing a unique configuration of historical events. In his reply to Mikhailovsky, he remarked "that events of a striking similarity, but *occurring in different historical contexts*, produced quite different results." (My italics.) His conception of an organic totality prevented him from abstracting a single line of development, such as the expropriation of the peasantry, and considering it as alone determinative. In *The German Ideology*, he employed the base-superstructure model but not to the exclusion of organic wholeness:

> This conception of history thus relies on expounding the real process of production—starting from the material production of life itself—and comprehending the form of intercourse connected with and created by this mode of production, i.e., civil society in its various stages, as the basis of all history; describing it in its action as the state, and also explaining how all the different theoretical products and forms of consciousness, religion, philosophy, morality, etc., etc., arise from it, and tracing the process of their formation from that basis; thus *the whole thing can, of course, be depicted in its totality (and therefore, too the reciprocal action of these various sides on one another).*[87] (My italics.)

The very concept of a complex organic whole implies a non-repetitive character. Exact repetition, as in the same brand of spark plugs, tends to be a mark of the mechanical. The notion that every society moves forward uniformly and irresistibly like an escalator is more a mechanistic than an organic concept.

Even when Marx refers to the material basis of the society, we can interpret his meaning too narrowly. In the above quotation from *The German Ideology*, he speaks of

[87]*The German Ideology*, p. 53.

"the material production of life itself" as belonging to the base. The biological factors of family and kinship relations are strongly emphasized by Marx in his account of primitive and Asiatic societies and by Engels in *The Origin of the Family, Private Property and the State*. I know of no reason to believe that Marx would disagree with the following statement by Engels of the "two-fold character" of the productive process:

> The social organization under which the people of a particular historical epoch and a particular country live is determined by both kinds of production: by the stage of development of labor on the one hand and of the family on the other. The lower the development of labor and the more limited the amount of its products, and consequently, the more limited also the wealth of the society, the more the social order is found to be dominated by bonds of kinship.[88]

Likewise basic is the natural environment. "In all the forms of society in which land ownership is the prevalent form," declares Marx, "the influence of the natural element is the predominant one."[89] The classical ideal of the free citizen is based on land-ownership.

> The ancients unanimously commended farming as the *activity proper* to free men, the school for soldiers. . . . "No Roman was permitted to lead the life of a petty trader or craftsman."[90]

In a letter to Engels dated August 6, 1866, Marx commended a "very important work" by Pierre Tremaux, *Origine et Transformations de l'Homme et des Autres Betes*, declaring that Tremaux had taken "a very significant step beyond Darwin" in his interpretation of the effects of geological formations on human beings. When Engels, in re-

---

[88]Engels, *The Origin of the Family, Private Property and the State* (New York: International Publishers, 1942), pp. 5–6.

[89]Marx, *The Grundrisse*, ed. David McLellan (New York: Harper & Row, 1972), p. 41.

[90]*Pre-Capitalist Economic Formations*, p. 76. The sentence enclosed in quotation marks is excerpted by Marx from Dionysius of Halicarnassus, *Roman Antiquities*, Bk. IV, Ch. 25.

ply, disparaged the book, Marx continued to praise its basic idea that geological elements, especially the soil, exercise an important influence on human development (letter of October 3, 1866).[91]

The aesthetic element in production is also an important factor. Marx speaks with admiration of the "dignity" of the guild system with its craftsmanship "half the expression of artistic creation, half its own reward."[92] Genuine artistic production is not motivated primarily by economic considerations:

> The same kind of labour may be productive or unproductive of commodities. For example, Milton, who wrote *Paradise Lost*, was an unproductive worker. On the other hand, the writer who turns out factory-made stuff for his publisher is a productive worker. Milton produced *Paradise Lost* for the same reason that a silk worm produces silk. It was an activity of his nature. Later he sold the product for five pounds.[93]

As I pointed out in Chapter I, few interpreters of human nature have gone so far as Marx in recognizing that the aesthetic drive is part of man's "species-being." He lamented the alienation of modern "economic man" in his aesthetic and artistic life, but he realized that artistic development is not entirely dependent on, or proportional to, economic development. There may be retrogression in the arts while there is progress in the economic order, and vice versa.[94]

Scientific and philosophical ideas may likewise be accommodated within an organic concept of historical development. In denying that ideas have an *independent* history, Marx was not belittling the role of consciousness. He was insisting that the agents of history are "real living individuals" and that "consciousness" is "solely . . . their consci-

---

[91]Maximilien Rubel and Margaret Manale, *Marx Without Myth*, p. 218.
[92]*Pre-Capitalist Economic Formations*, pp. 76, 98.
[93]*Theories of Surplus Value*, selections trans. by G.A. Bonner and Emile Burns (London: Lawrence & Wishart, 1951), p. 186.
[94]See *The Grundrisse*, ed. McLellan, pp. 44–46.

ousness."[95] The attempt to separate thought and action is false.

> The production of ideas, of conceptions, of consciousness, is . . . directly interwoven with the material activity and the material intercourse of men—the language of real life. . . . Consciousness can never be anything else than conscious being, and the being of men is their actual life-process.[96]

Marx here insists on life's organic wholeness and integrity. The organic totality model—not a reductionist version of the base-superstructure model—is the best key to Marx's interpretation of history. Although some passages are reductionist, they are exaggerations or exceptions.

To sum up the argument of Chapters 1–3, Marx makes use of two models of historical explanation (omitting the dialectical model which is incorporated in the other models). The first model is base and superstructure. Almost all interpreters have considered this the key to an understanding of Marx. Stated simplistically, it maintains that the "economic base" determines the political and cultural superstructure. So understood it is reductionist and misrepresents the full range and complexity of Marx's thought. Even Engels' amended ("dialectical") version tends toward an externalistic theory of relations and the ultimate reduction to the economic base. The strength of the base-superstructure model is that it embodies an idea central to Marx's theory, namely, that the mode of production plays the dominant causal role in history. This idea, when reinterpreted, can be detached from the first model and as the principle of hierarchy incorporated in the second.

The second model is organic totality, comprising both a synchronic and a diachronic aspect. The synchronic aspect (structure) is the whole looked at in cross-section. The hierarchical order and mutual dependence of its parts are comparable to a living organism. The mode of production is causally dominant, but all the elements in the hierarchy

[95]*The German Ideology*, p. 37.
[96]*Ibid.*, p. 36.

are interactive. Hence it is false to say that production alone is basic and everything else is derivative. The diachronic aspect (process) is the social organism viewed in its historical development. Hegel and Marx agree that the dynamism of history is the conflict of opposites: in Hegel, the battle of ideas or cultural forces; in Marx, the conflict between dynamic technology and static class structure, and between the bourgeoisie and the proletariat, or between other economic classes. Marx and Hegel, each in his own way, recognize an inner dialectic: the conflict between essence and existence, the gap between need and fulfillment, the schisms and fragmentations of alienation. There is progress in human development—a chequered movement through bondage and alienation toward freedom and rationality. The forces of historical change are not solely economic and the course of development is not unilinear. The remaining chapters deal with organic disunity and disfunction. Chapter 4 examines the ways in which the concrete wholeness of the "social organism" is impaired by abstraction, and Chapter 5 considers the approaching crisis and revolutionary transformation of capitalist society.

4

The Abstract and
The Concrete

1. Marx and the Expressivist Movement

The interpretations of Marx antedating the publication of the *Economic and Philosophical Manuscripts* generally depicted him as anti-romantic. He clung, it was said, to the belief in reason, science, and progress, the attainment of a universalist society, the full rational development of human potentialities—the basic faith of the Enlightenment. This faith was enriched with ideas from four sources: German idealist philosophy, especially the system of Hegel; the materialist reaction to Hegelian idealism, notably Ludwig Feuerbach's naturalistic humanism; British classic economic theory exemplified in Adam Smith and David Ricardo; and French theories of socialism and communism. From these diverse sources, it was said, Marx evolved the complex synthesis known as "scientific Marxism." The older interpreters of Marx, such as Kautsky, Plekhanov, and Lenin, in elaborating this "scientific" version, were not aware of the voluminous unpublished writings of Marx in which his more philosophical ideas were expounded. They drew heavily on the later works of Engels, leaping to the conclusion that "the two founders of scientific socialism" agreed in all essentials.

The Marxian scientific synthesis, allegedly, contrasts sharply with anti-Enlightenment movements such as existentialism. This is the impression conveyed not only by traditional "Marxists" but by many existentialists and their interpreters. For example, William Barrett in his sympathetic study of existentialism, *Irrational Man*, contends that "existentialism is the counter-Enlightenment come at last to philosophic expression," and that Marx, as a scion of the Enlightenment, is opposed in spirit to existentialism.[1] Among existentialist philosophers, Sartre appears to be a strong sympathizer with Marxism, but even he is ambivalent. More typical of the attitude of the existentialists is the remark of Nicolai Berdyaev: "For Marx class is more real than man."[2] This remark expresses the existentialist charge against Marx, namely, that he submerges the individual in the social mass.

Georg Lukács, almost alone among the older interpreters, discerned in *Capital* and other published works of Marx a theory of "reification" and "alienation" that was later confirmed by disclosure of the unpublished writings. Lukács' *Geschichte and Klassenbewusstsein* (1923) was in this respect an outstanding intellectual feat. Subsequent to the publication of the Paris *Manuscripts* and other early writings, many interpreters have "discovered" a humanist Marx. According to Robert Tucker, for example, the *Economic and Philosophical Manuscripts* disclose a romantic, almost a religious, thinker. Erich Fromm contends that there is a powerful existentialist current in the *Manuscripts*. Adam Schaff, frequently citing the early works, refutes the charge that Marx subordinates the human individual to the collectivity. Lucio Colletti, Istvan Mézáros, and Shlomo Avineri, while agreeing with this interpretation, have found a basic continuity in Marx's humanist thought from early to late. In light of the evidence now available, we can conclude that the older interpretations of Marx are misleading. Despite obvious differences, Marx and the existentialists are alike in two respects—an intense awareness of human alienation and a strong reaction against abstraction.

[1]William Barrett, *Irrational Man* (New York: Doubleday and Company, 1958), p. 244.
[2]Nikolai Berdyaev, *The Meaning of the Creative Act* (New York: Macmillan-Collier, 1955), p. 287.

The revolt against abstraction is perhaps the most pervasive characteristic of the existentialist movement. F. Temple Kingston, in his book on French existentialism, has said:

> All of the existentialists admit that human beings in this century are threatened to an unusual degree in their very existence by abstract philosophies, by all-powerful states, and by the misuse of scientific inventions.[3]

Hostile critics complain that Marx represents the opposite stance: the mass-anonymity of collectivism, the machinations of bureaucracy, the technological standardization of life—all of which contribute to an "abstract" mode of existence. I shall maintain, on the contrary, that Marx's writings from the early *Critique of Hegel's "Philosophy of Right"* (1843) to the late *Notes on Adolph Wagner* (1879–1880), represent a sustained polemic against abstraction.

The attack on abstraction is related to the view that expression is natural to organic life. A dog, for example, naturally growls or wags its tail, and a human being laughs, blushes, scowls, or otherwise expresses his or her feelings. The connection between outward expression and inner states was investigated by Charles Darwin in his *Expression of the Emotions in Man and Animals* (1872). His evolutionary interpretation of emotional patterns of behavior from lowly animals to humankind indicates how organically based are these expressive features. More recently psychologists, such as Rudolf Arnheim and Carroll C. Pratt, have investigated artistic expression.[4] Here, too, they have found a natural correspondence between inner state and outward form. Whether the expression is artless or artistic,

[3]F. Temple Kingston, *French Existentialism: A Christian Critique* (Toronto: University of Toronto Press, 1961), p. 26.

[4]See Rudolf Arnheim, *Art and Visual Perception* (Berkeley and Los Angeles: University of California Press, 1969) and Carroll C. Pratt, *The Meaning of Music* (New York: McGraw-Hill Company, 1931).

the world of organisms—even as lowly as insects[5]—is as teeming with expression as it is teeming with life.

The concept of "expression" is pivotal in the stream of thought that Charles Taylor has called "the expressivist tradition." In his masterly book on Hegel, he uses the terms "expressivist" and 'expressivism" to denote a way of thinking and feeling that stresses "unity" and its expressive manifestations. "Expressivism" regards freedom, in the sense of authentic self-expression, as a basic value, and defines "expressive unity" as the unity of the individual person with himself, nature and his fellow men. Human purposes and fulfillments are the unfoldment of the potentialities of the unique individual in his organic wholeness.

> The central notion is that human activity and human life are seen as expression. . . . Each individual . . . has his own way of being human, which it cannot exchange with that of any other except at the cost of distortion and self-mutilation. . . . Since we are expressive beings, our life is a unity, it cannot be artificially divided into distinct levels: life as against thought, sentience as against rationality, knowledge as against will. Man is not an animal with reason added, but a totally new indivisible form.[6]

The concept of the unique individual's organic development and expressive realization, Taylor asserts, is one of the key ideas of the modern age. Representing a post-Enlightenment "climate of opinion," it contributed greatly not only to the rise of romanticism and revolution in the late eighteenth century but to the civilization that has developed subsequently. "In different forms, it is one of the major *idees-forces* which has shaped the contemporary world."[7]

In maintaining that there is a strong expressivist current in both Hegel and Marx, Taylor is not denying that

[5]See Charles Darwin, *The Expression of the Emotions in Man and Animals* (Chicago: University of Chicago Press, 1965), p. 349: "Even insects express anger, terror, jealousy, and love by their stridulation."
[6]Charles Taylor, *Hegel* (Cambridge University Press, 1975), pp. 14, 15, 21.
[7]*Ibid.*, p. 18.

there is also a potent influence from the Enlightenment. He regards Marx's theory as a confluence of the two streams.

> The fact is that from the beginning, his position was a synthesis between the radical Enlightenment, which sees man as capable of objectifying nature and society in science in order to master it, and the expressivist aspiration to wholeness. This is what he meant in speaking of communism as the union of humanism and naturalism.[8] Expressive fulfillment comes when man (generic man) dominates nature and can impress his free design on it. But at the same time he dominates nature by objectifying it in scientific practice. . . . In this vision, objectification of nature and expression through it are not incompatible, any more than they are for a sculptor who may make use of engineering technology in constructing his work.[9]

Taylor interprets the transition from Marx's early philosophical works to his later economic treatises as a shift of emphasis rather than a change of view. To those who disagree Taylor replies:

> Many Marxists, and others, would object to this interpretation of Marxism, which places it in what I have called the expressivist tradition. Of course, Marxism is more than this. But I do not think we can understand it and its impact if we try to abstract from this dimension.[10]

At the same time Taylor warns that Marxism includes more than expressivism. The expressivist thinkers in general eschewed functional or causal explanation in order to concentrate on meaning, and their interpretation of meaning tended to be subjective. Marx, on the other hand, maintained that our expressions, such as action that produces value, can be analyzed causally and objectively. This balanced approach, both expressivist and scientific, lifts his

[8]In the *Economic and Philosophical Manuscripts*, trans. and ed. by T.B. Bottomore (London: C.A. Watts & Co., 1963), p. 155, Marx declares: "Communism as a fully developed naturalism is humanism, and as a fully developed humanism is naturalism."
[9]Charles Taylor, *Hegel*, pp. 551–552.
[10]*Ibid.*, p. 547.

synthesis above the battle between the romantics and the anti-romantics.

2. The Expressivist Influence of Schiller

Taylor traces the expressivist tradition to such figures as Leibniz, Rousseau, and Herder, and finds it exemplified in the great romantics Goethe, Schelling, and Fichte. He maintains that both Hegel and Marx were profoundly influenced by it. In its impact on Marx, the expressivist ideas of Schiller and Feuerbach are especially relevant.

Friedrich Schiller was a major contributor to the literary and aesthetic tradition in which Marx was immersed as a young man. Marx spent much of his time during his student years writing verse, and his reading of poetry was a lifelong passion. To help him in his poetic labors he copied lengthy passages from Lessing's *Laokoön* and Winckelmann's *History of Ancient Art.* Later he studied the aesthetic treatises of Solger and Hegel, K. A. Böttiger's *Mythological Art* and Johann Grund's *Greek Painting,* and copied long extracts from Vischer's *Aesthetik.* He even planned to write an article on aesthetics for the *New American Cyclopedia* (1857–1858) at the request of its editor, Charles Dana, but the project had to be abandoned. We know that he was well acquainted with the works of Schiller, not only the poetry but the aesthetic treatises. In a newspaper article (1842) he said that Schiller is "the prophet of the new movement of minds,"[11] and he mentioned Schiller frequently in his later years. As S.S. Prawer has said, "Marx left his readers in little doubt that he respected Schiller as a great writer," even though his tastes in poetry ran more to Goethe and Shakespeare.[12] He was already familiar with Schiller's ideas when he wrote the *Economic and Philo-*

---

[11]See Karl Marx/Frederick Engels, *Collected Works* (New York: International Publishers, 1975), 1, p. 291.

[12]S.S. Prawer, *Karl Marx and World Literature* (Oxford at the Clarendon Press, 1976), p. 361. For numerous references by Marx to Schiller consult Prawer's index under "Schiller," p. 444.

sophical Manuscripts in 1844, but the similarity between the *Manuscripts* and the *Letters on the Aesthetic Education of Man* may have been less the result of any direct influence of Schiller on Marx than the immersion of both in a common expressivist tradition. For example, Schiller's idealization of the natural humanity of the Greeks in contrast to the artificiality and dehumanization of modern life was based in large part on Winckelmann's *History of Ancient Art*—the book that had inspired Marx in his student days. Among the ideas of Schiller that reappear in Marx are the alienating effects of the division of labor, the need to restore unity and concreteness to life, and the historical development of human capacities.

The development sketched by Schiller consists of three stages: first, the relatively undifferentiated unity of early society; second, the splitting of the social order into specialized functions and hostile classes; and third, the reintegration of mankind at the advanced level made possible by the keying up of aptitudes in the second stage. This is a spiral progression, in which the second stage is the antithesis of the unitary first stage, and the third stage is a return to unity at a higher, more differentiated level.

The initial, undifferentiated stage applies especially to the ancient Greeks:

> At that first fair awakening of the powers of the mind, sense and sensibility did not as yet rule over strictly separate domains; for no dissension had as yet provoked them into hostile partition.[13]

This idyllic unity came naturally to the Greeks, like the original Paradise to Adam and Eve, but if the manifold human potentialities were ever to be developed it was necessary to taste the fruits of evil. Humanity had to advance

---

[13]Friedrich Schiller, *On the Aesthetic Education of Man in a Series of Letters*, edited and translated by Elizabeth M. Wilkinson and L.A. Willoughby (Oxford: Clarendon Press, 1967), p. 31. See also Schiller's famous essay "On Naive and Sentimental Poetry." For Marx's similar view of Greek life and culture see his *Grundrisse*, translated by Martin Nicolaus (Harmondsworth: Pelican Books, 1973), pp. 111, 488.

through an intermediate stage of fragmentation to a new kind of wholeness and integrity.

The second stage—the development embodied in the division of labor—has been achieved at a frightful cost. "Instead of rising to a higher form of organic existence," society has "degenerated into a crude and clumsy mechanism."

> State and Church, laws and custom, were now torn asunder; enjoyment was divorced from labour, the means from the end, the effort from the reward. Everlastingly chained to a single fragment of the Whole, man himself develops into nothing but a fragment; everlastingly in his ear the monotonous sound of the wheel that he turns, he never develops the harmony of his being, and instead of putting the stamp of humanity upon his own nature, he becomes nothing more than the imprint of his occupation or of his specialized knowledge. . . . Thus little by little the concrete life of the Individual is destroyed in order that the abstract idea of the Whole may drag out its sorry existence, and the State remains for ever a stranger to its citizens since at no point does it ever make contact with their feeling.[14]

This "abstract" stage of conflict and alienation is necessary for human progress, but it cannot satisfy our human demands for happiness and fulfillment.

> If the manifold potentialities in man were ever to be developed, there was no other way but to pit them one against the other. This antagonism of faculties and functions is the great instrument of civilization—but it is only the instrument; for as long as it persists, we are only on our way to becoming civilized.[15]

The third stage, which lies in the future, is the reunification and filfillment made possible by the second stage. Schiller's ideal is to restore "the concrete life of the individual" by the free play and reconciliation of the diverse sides of human nature. The psychological basis of this restoration is the interrelation between the three fundamental human drives—

[14]*Ibid.*, pp. 35, 37.
[15]*Ibid.*, p. 41.

the sensuous-drive of bodily needs, the form-giving drive of reason, and the play-drive of the imagination. The first two drives tend to conflict and the third mediates and harmonizes them. The object of the sense-drive is Life, which denotes all material existence presented to our senses. The object of the form-drive is structure or Form in its widest acceptation. The object of the play-drive, Beauty, is the synthesis of Life and Form, and may be characterized as "Living Form." The word "play" is used not in the limited meaning of a game or pastime but as the freedom of imagination in the vivacious exercise of its powers. Only when man's rational and sensuous needs are reconciled in play is human nature restored to its wholeness and integrity.

> Though it may be his needs that drive man into society, and reason which implants within him the principles of social behavior, beauty alone implants within him a social character. Taste alone brings harmony into society, because it fosters harmony in the individual. All other forms of perception divide man, because they are founded exclusively either upon the sensuous or upon the spiritual[16] part of his being; only the aesthetic mode of perception makes of him a whole, because both his natures must be in harmony if he is to achieve it.[17]

The free, formative activity of the aesthetic imagination is characteristic of the artist, but by no means limited to him. By means of aesthetic education, it can become the common possession of all. Schiller's theory is remarkable not only for deploring the one-sided development and alienation of the individual in an age of specialization but in advocating a profound cultural revolution that would transform both the individual and the social order.

No one who has read carefully the *Letters on the Aesthetic Education of Man* and the *Economic and Philosophi-*

[16]The German adjective *"geistegen"* is here translated "spiritual." Reginald Snell (in Schiller, *On the Aesthetic Education of Man*, New Haven: Yale University Press, 1954) translates *"geistegen"* as "intellectual," which seems to me to fit the context better.
[17]Schiller, *On the Aesthetic Education of Man in a Series of Letters*, p. 215.

cal Manuscripts can fail to see that Schiller and Marx are in considerable agreement. In their attack upon abstractions and plea for a more concrete existence, in their depiction of the dehumanizing effects of the division of labor, in their delineation of alienation and its overcoming, in their concept of the wholeness and integrity of the aesthetic mode of experience, in their belief that mankind must pass through a stage of fragmentation before achieving a high level of civilization, they are in basic accord. They differ, however, in their means and priorities. As Stefan Morawski has written, Schiller "had dreamt that the world would be rescued from need and suffering by aesthetic man." Marx, in contrast, "was to turn Schiller's conception inside out; it was *political* man who was required for the rescue and realization of aesthetic humankind.".[18]

3. Feuerbach on Abstraction and Concreteness

The influence of Feuerbach was decisive in the most formative period of Marx's young manhood (1841–1844). In January 1842 Marx tendered this advice to theologians and philosophers:

> Free yourselves from the concepts and prepossessions of existing speculative philosophy if you want to get at things differently, as they are, that is to say, if you want to arrive at the *truth*. And there is no other road for you to *truth* and *freedom* except that leading *through* the stream of fire [the *Feuer-bach*]. Feuerbach is the *purgatory* of the present times.[19]

In 1844 Marx sent to Feuerbach a copy of the Introduction to his *Critique of Hegel's 'Philosophy of Right."* In the letter of transmission he said:

[18]Stefan Morawski, *Inquiries into the Fundamentals of Aesthetics* (Cambridge, Mass.: Massachusetts Institute of Technology Press, 1974), p. 328.
[19]*Writings of the Young Marx on Philosophy and Society*, trans. and ed. by Lloyd D. Easton and Kurt D. Guddat (Garden City, N.Y.: Doubleday and Company, 1967), p. 95.

I don't attribute any exceptional value to this essay but I am glad to have an opportunity of assuring you of the great respect and—if I may use the word—love, which I feel for you. Your *Philosophie der Zukunft*, and your *Wesen des Glaubens*, in spite of their small size, are certainly of greater weight than the whole of contemporary German literature put together. In these writings you have provided—I don't know whether intentionally—a philosophical basis for socialism and the Communists have immediately understood them in this way. The unity of man with man, which is based on the real differences between men, the concept of the human species brought down from the heaven of abstraction to the real earth, what is this but the concept of *society!*[20]

By the time that Marx wrote the *Theses on Feuerbach* in the spring of 1845, the influence of Feuerbach had waned, but the effects remained to some extent throughout Marx's lifetime. So much has been written about this influence that I need say little. The final sentence that I have quoted from the letter to Feuerbach indicates the basic ideas I wish to stress.

The first idea is "the unity of man with man . . . based on the real differences between men." The profound interaction between human beings comes about only when there is a person-to-person relation of genuine mutuality. To repeat a key passage:

The single man *in isolation* possesses in himself the *essence* of man neither as a *moral* nor as a *thinking* being. The *essence* of man is contained only in the community, in the *unity* of man with man—a unity, however, that rests on the *reality* of the distinction between "I" and "You."[21]

This interpersonal relation stands in sharp contrast to the depersonalization of massive, bureaucratic organizations. It combines a strong affirmation of individuality with an equally strong assertion of fellowship.

[20] Letter to Ludwig Feuerbach, August 11, 1844, in Marx/Engels, *Collected Works*, Vol. 3, p. 354.
[21] Ludwig Feuerbach, *Principles of the Philosophy of the Future* in *The Fiery Brook: Selected Writings of Ludwig Feuerbach*, trans. with introduction by Zawar Hanfi (New York: Doubleday and Company, 1972), p. 244.

The second idea is that "the concept of the human species" is "brought down from the heaven of abstraction to the real earth." Rejecting both religious supernaturalism and philosophical idealism, Feuerbach insists that the starting point of philosophy must not be God or the Hegelian 'Idea" but man in his concrete actuality. The flesh-and-blood human being—sensing, feeling, desiring, thinking, imagining—the living person in all the plenitude of his powers—is the real subject of Feuerbach's philosophy. There is an unmistakable existential ring to his exhortation:

> Think not as a thinker, that is, not as one that is confined to a faculty that is *isolated* in so far as it is *torn away* from the totality of the real being of man; think as a *living, real* being ... ; think as one who exists, as one who is *in the world* and is part of the world, not as one in a vacuum of abstraction.[22]

Feuerbach's humanist attack on abstraction is reflected in many passages of the *Economic and Philosophical Manuscripts.*

Among Feuerbach's great achievements, according to Marx, is "to have founded *genuine materialism* and *positive science* by making the social relationship of 'man to man' the basic principle of his theory."[23] In doing so Feuerbach clearly went beyond Hegel, who negated conventional theology, but then "negated this negation" by restoring theological abstractions in the form of Absolute Idealism. Both Feuerbach and Marx rejected Hegelian idealism, but Marx, in turn, went beyond Feuerbach. He was too much the activist and social revolutionary to be permanently satisfied with Feuerbach's philosophy, demanding far greater emphasis on historical development, economic causes, class structure, and revolutionary social practice. He charged that Feuerbach had an inadequate sense of the complexity of human relations; that he clung to a naive theory of the human mind as a passive mirror of

[22]*Ibid.*, p. 240.
[23]*Economic and Philosophical Manuscripts*, p. 197.

sensation; that he was entrapped by an abstract and unhistorical conception of the "human essence."

Although Marx was chary of the term "human essence," (*menschliches Wesen*), he used another favorite term of Feuerbach, "species-being" (*Gattungswesen*), in a revealing passage of the *Grundrisse*. According to Feuerbach's use of this term, the ability of humankind to recognize its own species-being distinguishes it from all other animals: man is conscious not only of himself as an individual but also as a member of the human species, and this grasp of a common nature is the fundamental element in human consciousness. In discussing the social interdependence of human beings in the productive process, Marx repeats the essentials of Feuerbach's characterization, but in the context of his own economic analysis.

> Regarded from the standpoint of the natural difference between them, individual A exists as the owner of a use value for B, and B as an owner of a use value for A. In this respect, their natural difference again puts them reciprocally into the relation of equality. In this respect, however, they are not indifferent to one another, but integrate with one another, have need of one another; so that individual B, as objectified in the commodity, is a need of individual A, and vice versa; so that they stand not only in an equal but also in a social, relation to one another. This is not all. The fact that this need on the part of one can be satisfied by the product of the other, and vice versa, and that the one is capable of producing the object of the need of the other, and that each confronts the other as owner of the object of the other's need, this proves that each of them reaches beyond his own particular need etc., as a *human being* and that they relate to one another as human beings; that their common species-being (*Gattungswesen*) is acknowledged by all.[24]

Marx goes on to say that this species-consciousness "does not happen elsewhere"—that it is a *human* and not a general animal characteristic.

[24]*Grundrisse: Foundations of the Critique of Political Economy (Rough Draft)*, trans. by Martin Nicolaus (Harmondsworth: Penguin Books, 1973), pp. 242–243.

149

The passage is one of many that disprove Althusser's contention that the *Theses on Feuerbach* (1845) and *The German Ideology* (1846) mark a radical break with Marx's early humanism. The distinctive characteristic of this humanism is that it is construed in economic terms. A person is alienated, Marx contends, when he is forced by the economic system to violate his species-being. He is then an "abstract individual," detached from the human community. The economic emphasis should not obscure the fact that Feuerbach had a powerful and lasting albeit diminishing impact on Marx.

4. Hegel and Marx on Abstraction and Concreteness

The influence of Feuerbach was far outweighed by the influence of Hegel. Marx distinguished between the "rational kernel" of Hegel's dialectic that must be preserved and the "mystical shell" that must be discarded.[25] "Abstract" and "concrete" are perhaps the commonest of all terms in the Hegelian philosophical vocabulary. We need to understand what Hegel meant by these terms, how they are related to organic totality, and to what extent Marx agreed.

The word "abstract" is derived from the Latin verb *abstrahere*, "to draw away," meaning to withdraw or separate in thought or in objective matter of fact. In thought, abstracting is the focusing of attention on some part or aspect of an object, usually for the purpose of contemplation or understanding. In every act of mental abstraction there is the residue of those features of the object that are nonfocused. If I abstract the color of an apple, for example, the taste, shape, texture, and weight are not in the focus of my consciousness. Sometimes the verb "to abstract" means not simply to focus but objectively to separate. Hegel, for example, says that to amputate an arm is to abstract it from the human body. Marx likewise uses "abstract" to desig-

[25]*Capital*, Vol. I, trans. by Samuel Moore and Edward Aveling (Chicago: Charles H. Kerr and Company, 1906), p. 25.

nate severance from a larger whole. A human being who lacks social roots—who is detached and alienated—is called by Marx an "abstract person."

The term "concrete" is derived from the past participle of the Latin verb *concrescere*, meaning to grow together. As used by Hegel and Marx, the concrete is that which has organically grown together and remains unfragmented. It is the whole in its integrity. If we think of an object *as a whole*, we are thinking of it concretely. "Concrete" means taken all together—"abstract" means taken piecemeal.

The common tendency is to regard ideas as abstract and objects as concrete. From the standpoint of Hegel and Marx this is a mistake. "Abstract" applies equally to ideas and objects. When I mentally abstract, the abstracted referent (the object that I am isolating in attention) is called an "abstraction." For example, the shape of a table top when focussed in attention is an abstraction, but the *idea* of that shape is an abstraction too. Detached idea and detached object are correlative and share the same degree of abstraction.

The referents to which ideas refer may be either *parts* or *aspects*. A part can be withdrawn, an aspect cannot. The distinction is clear if we think of a machine. If someone asks for the spark plug of an automobile, I can remove it and give it to him; but if he asks for the shape of the automobile, I cannot detach and hand it over. An aspect cannot be unscrewed or pried loose or cut away with an axe, saw, or blow torch. Parts in a machine are such things as plugs, bolts, pistons, gears; aspects are such qualities as shapes, colors, textures, weights.

This distinction between a part which is detachable and an aspect which is not is less applicable to an organism. In an organic unity a "part" resembles an aspect in being nondetachable. (For this reason Hegel thinks it is misleading to speak of the "part" of an organism—it is better to call it an "organ" or a "member.") A foot, for example, cannot be and remain amputated without ceasing to be a foot. It is only in horror stories that one shakes hands long severed from bodies. Admittedly an organ can sometimes be transplanted from one organism to another— even the human heart has been transplanted. But the transplantation must be rapid if the heart is to function. In general, the parts of an organism depend upon one another not only for their functions but for their very existence.[26]

Hegel was profoundly moved by the expressivist current with its emphasis on organic unity. The image that dominated his thought was that of "a whole, integrated life in which man was at one with himself, and men were at one with each other in society" and in symbiotic harmony with nature.[27] Impelled by this expressivist image, Hegel developed a comprehensive philosophy of organicism. According to this philosophy, many things are detached and fragmentary, but the fragments gradually coalesce and take the forms implicit in them. This movement toward organic wholeness can be traced mentally in dialectical logic or historically in the march of events. Each fragment, being one-sided, grapples with its opposite and contradictory fragment. The conflict is eventually resolved in a wider integration, which reconciles the conflicting fragments in a richer, more concrete whole. This new synthesis, in turn, finds *its* contradictory, and the dialectical movement into opposition and transcendence continues. At each new level the opposites are richer and more inclusive, but there is a residual abstractness that leads into new contradictions and syntheses. The progress thus continues from level to level until it culminates in the *"Absolute"*—the point of complete integration. At this level there is no more abstractness, and all the elements are integrated in the one absolutely coherent organic whole. The Absolute is approached in the late stages of history, and it subsists eternally in the totality of the logical categories.

---

[26]For a comprehensive modern discussion of organic *versus* mechanistic explanation in biology see Ernest Nagel, *The Structure of Science* (New York: Harcourt, Brace and World, 1961), Ch. 12.
[27]Charles Taylor, *Hegel,* p. 51. See also pp. 23–25, 39.

The crucial question is whether Hegel can harmonize the ideal perfection of the Absolute with the manifest imperfections of ordinary experience. His phrase, often quoted, that "truth is the whole" implies that the Absolute as "the whole" is concrete and real and the fragment is abstract and comparatively unreal. Hegel's universe has, so to speak, fallen into two halves, appearance and reality. We are left with an ultimate dualism, which contradicts the claim of organic unity. The difficulty is stated pithily by Stephen Pepper:

> All may be organic in the ideal fact of the Absolute, but ignorance and frustration and unsolved problems and the narrow horizons of space and time and the limited span of life are strikingly upon us. These are in flat contradiction to the optimistic serenity of the Absolute. The organicist himself admits them in his progressive categories. He admits that as finite living individuals we cannot attain the Absolute. Then how can he say that in fact there are no fragments? . . . Contradiction thus breaks out even in the Absolute, since the Absolute includes all facts. Organicism thus convicts itself of inadequacy.[28]

Hegel's problem is akin to that of Plato in seeking to reconcile Being, the realm of eternal essences, and Becoming, the realm of changing particulars. In Plato's *Sophist*, the question is asked:

> Oh heavens, can we ever be made to believe that motion and life and soul and mind are not present with perfect being? Can we imagine that being is devoid of life and mind, and exists in awful unmeaningness an everlasting fixture?[29]

Plato tries to bridge the gap between the static forms and the fluctuant particulars by the mediation of soul. In the *Timaeus*, God as the supreme soul is said to be inspired by the forms to mould unstable and disordered matter into "the moving image of eternity." In Hegel's system, *Geist* (Spirit) performs a similar function. The progressive move-

[28]Stephen C. Pepper, *World Hypotheses* (Berkeley: University of California Press, 1942), pp. 308, 314.
[29]Plato, *Sophist* #249. (Jowett's translation.)

ment of history from the abstract to the concrete is the embodiment and expression of *Geist*. Whether and to what extent Hegel thought of *Geist* as self-conscious apart from humankind is a disputed point.[30] But he employs "God" as a synonym of "Spirit," and depicts God as a force or spirit immanent in the world, achieving self-consciousness in the minds of men. For both Feuerbach and Marx this Spirit or God is a superstitious relic of Christian theology.

Marx does not wholly disagree with Hegel. The universe, Hegel believes, is an organic unity made up of component organic unities. Marx recognizes many of these component unities but apparently not a *cosmic* organic unity. Because the philosophical context differs for the two men, the words "abstract" and "concrete" take on a somewhat different meaning for Marx than for Hegel. But they agree in interpreting abstraction as detachment from an organic complex and in noting that organic integration may be more or less intense and comprehensive.

Hegel interprets the cosmic organic unity in accordance with his idealistic principle of the identity of thought and being. The word "thought" is in ordinary language applied both to thinking and to the content thought. When used by an idealist in the former sense we have a more subjective form of idealism; when used in the latter sense we may have a kind of "objective idealism," namely, the doctrine that objective reality is intelligible as a system of logical and internally related categories. That Hegel used "thought" in this sense seems to be universally conceded by his interpreters, but that he also used "thought" in the former "subjective" sense is less clear. In a good many passages he seems to be referring to a cosmic spirit. This Spirit

[30]Compare Charles Taylor, *Hegel*, and J.N. Findlay, *Hegel: A Re-Examination* (New York: Macmillan, 1958) for contrasting interpretations of *Geist*. Likewise disputed is the question whether Marx interpreted Hegel correctly. See, for example, the Introduction by Duncan Forbes to Hegel, *Lectures on the Philosophy of World History* (Cambridge University Press, 1975) and John Maguire, *Marx's Paris Writings* (Dublin: Gill and Macmillan, 1972), Ch. 5.

can be conceived of in either of two ways: as a single cognitive consciousness thinking all things as thought content; or as the totality of rationally connected experiences combined in a logical unity as close as, but not identical with, the unity of a single mind. Whatever be the nature of this cosmic organic unity, detachment from it makes anything to that degree abstract. Only the cosmic unity itself is completely concrete.

Marx rejects both subjective and objective idealism in *toto*. When he speaks of "organic unity" he does not mean the unity of a cosmic Spirit in either of the meanings I have distinguished, and he does not mean the unity of an all-embracing system of logical categories. He means the unity of a human mind-body or the unity of a social order. In his concept of mind-body unity he is much closer to Schiller and Feuerbach than he is to Hegel. In consequence his understanding of concreteness is more aesthetic in Schiller's sense and more naturalistic in Feuerbach's sense than rational in Hegel's sense. The elaborate scaffolding of "absolute idealism" is dismissed as an abstraction from the concrete realities of life and nature. Hegel has taken a high level abstraction, "spirit," severed it from its natural basis in human life and treated it as an independent substance. Spirituality is an aspect of the human mind-body and it cannot exist when severed. As separate "Ideas" that mould history or exist as components of the Absolute, the logical categories are as fictitious as abstract Spirit. All such abstractions presuppose the objects or events from which they are abstracted. Hegel has fallen into the muddle that Whitehead has called "the fallacy of misplaced concreteness"—the "error of mistaking the abstract for the concrete." He has isolated certain aspects of human existence and has "reified" these aspects. In theory he has moved from the abstract to the concrete, but in plain fact he has moved in exactly the opposite direction. This, I believe, is the tenor of Marx's critique of Hegel.

Hegel distinguishes between analytical understanding (*Verstand*) and synthetic reason (*Vernunft*). Understanding

155

mentally abstracts the part or aspect to achieve conceptual clarity, but it thereby violates the integrity of the organic complex. Reason, in contrast, is receptive to the internal drive of fragments toward the integrations which complete them. Marx does not entirely agree with Hegel in these judgments. With his more scientific bent, he is much less averse than Hegel to understanding (*Verstand*). Although he is strongly opposed to an abstract, fragmentary human life, he is not opposed to abstraction as a device of scientific analysis. In his Preface to the first edition of *Capital* he explains that without the method of abstraction the meaning of economic value, as an element in a larger organic whole, cannot be delineated.

> The value-form, whose fully developed shape is the money-form, is very elementary and simple. Nevertheless, the human mind has for more than 2000 years sought in vain to get to the bottom of it, whilst on the other hand, to the successful analysis of much more composite and complex forms, there has been at least an approximation. Why? Because the body as an organic whole, is more easy of study than the cells of that body. In the analysis of economic forms, moreover, neither microscopes nor chemical reagents are of use. The force of abstraction must replace both. But in bourgeois society the commodity-form of the product of labor—or the value-form of the commodity—is the economic cell-form. To the superficial observer, the analysis of these forms seems to turn upon minutiae. It does in fact deal with minutiae, but they are of the same order as those dealt with in microscopic anatomy.[31]

Just as the biologist makes use of the microscope, Marx makes use of abstractions. It is necessary to isolate the part (the economic cell-form) in order to examine it more exhaustively. For the sake of pursuing a scientific purpose, the analyst omits certain parts or aspects that are irrelevant to his immediate purpose. But he should retain a precise and distinct awareness of the methodological omissions, and he should not mistake the abstracted part or element

[31]*Capital*, I, p. 12. Marx's use of the biological term "cell form" indicates that he is still clinging to the organic model.

for the whole. As soon as he accords to it an *exclusive* importance and a *reified* status, he has fallen victim to his method. He has taken what is only a method (namely, abstraction) for the truth itself.

Influenced by his concept of organic totality, Marx employs the method of abstraction in order to return to the organic whole with sharpened insight. He denies that abstractions suffice, either in scientific thought or in real life. The human being in his many-sidedness, not a dehumanized figment of political or economic analysis (such as the "economic man" of the classical economists), is man as he really is. In his economics, Marx adopts both an analytic and synthetic approach. The economist should analytically dissect the superficial unity that appears at first glance and then rebind the parts into a more authentic and richly articulated whole *after* analysis. Although Marx is aware of "the force of abstraction," he never loses sight of his main objective, to comprehend the character and development of capitalist society as a "social organism."

The kind of methodological abstraction to which Marx objects is illustrated in a passage in *The Holy Family*. This method consists in abstracting a universal predicate and treating it as a concrete "substance"—that is as a real, existent thing. Just as Aristotle accused Plato of reifying universals, so Marx accuses Hegel of reifying abstract essences. In explaining the nature of "Hegelian construction," he uses the example of the essence of fruit.

> If from real apples, pears, strawberries and almonds I form the general idea *"Fruit,"* if I go further and *imagine* that my abstract idea *"Fruit,"* derived from real fruit, is an entity existing outside me, is indeed the *true* essence of the pear, the apple, etc., then . . . I am declaring that *"Fruit"* is the "Substance" of the pear, the apple, the almond, etc. . . . . Particular real fruits are no more than semblances whose true essence is *"the* substance"—*"Fruit."*

The abstraction "Fruit" is treated as a self-subsistent substance—the concrete subject of change and development. "The different ordinary fruits," according to this fallacious way of reasoning, "are different manifestations of the life of the 'one Fruit': they are crystallizations of 'the Fruit' itself."[32]

In the *Critique of Hegel's "Philosophy of Right"* Marx again describes this fallacy of abstraction.

> Hegel makes the predicates . . . independent, but independent as separated from their real independence, their subject. Subsequently, and because of this, the real subject appears to be the result; whereas one has to start from the real subject and examine its objectification. The mystical substance becomes the real subject and the real subject appears to be something else, namely, a moment of the mystical subject.[33]

Hegel, for example, interprets political sovereignty in this "mystical" way. Sovereignty, the abstract essence of the state, is treated as if it were reified and to be interpreted as the subject of political activity.[34]

Similarly the Left Hegelians abstract from particular historical persons and events a reified essence which they call "History." "History . . . becomes a person apart, a metaphysical subject of which the real human individuals are merely the bearers."[35] The Hegelians, in this respect, are akin to their master, Hegel, who makes the "Absolute Spirit" the "mystical" subject of historical change and development. Although Feuerbach rejects these idealistic abstractions, he does not entirely escape the abstract mode of reasoning. He still interprets human nature in an unhistorical way, regarding "the human essence" as an "abstraction inherent in each single individual." This criticism of Feuerbach, epitomized in the Sixth of the Theses is not an "epistemological break" from Marx's earlier writings (as Althusser contends), but a continuation of the polemic against abstraction that runs from the beginning to the end of Marx's works.

[32]*The Holy Family* in Marx/Engels, *Collected Works*, 4, pp. 57–58.
[33]Marx, *Critique of Hegel's "Philosophy of Right"* (Cambridge at the University Press, 1970), p. 24.
[34]See *ibid.*, pp. 22–26.
[35]*The Holy Family*, p. 79.

Contrary to all these examples of fallacious abstraction, Marx asserts that the real agents of history are concrete human beings in their social relations.

> History does nothing, it "possesses no immense wealth," it "wages no battles." It is man, real, living man who does all that, who possesses and fights: "history" is not, as it were, a person apart, using man as means to achieve its own aims; history is nothing but the activity of man pursuing his aims.[36]

History is the multiform activities of individuals in "the ensemble of their social relations."

To sum up, Marx himself employs the method of abstraction as a means of understanding the "social organism," but he rebinds the parts thus dissected, and he objects to substitution of an abstraction in place of the concrete totality.

5. Concreteness and Abstraction in Human Life

In his early writings Marx strongly insisted on the concrete and sensuous character of human life. "Man is not an abstract being, squatting outside the world," he declared. 'Man is the human world, the state, society."[37] As an objective being, the human person can fulfill his or her needs and drives only in a sensuously rich milieu.

> The objects of his drives exist outside himself as objects independent of him, yet they are objects of his needs, essential objects which are indispensable to the exercise and confirmation of his faculties. The fact that man is an embodied, living, real, sentient, objective being with natural powers, means that he has real, sensuous objects as the objects of his being, or that he can only express his being in real, sensuous objects.[38]

---

[36]Ibid., p. 93.
[37]Contribution to the Critique of Hegel's Philosophy of Right: Introduction in Early Writings, trans. by Bottomore, p. 43.
[38]Economic and Philosophical Manuscripts, p. 207.

If we employ the word "aesthetic" in its original etymological meaning, namely, "pertaining to the senses," we must conclude that Marx's ideal of human life is strongly aesthetic in tinge. By the term "senses," Marx means "not only the five senses, but also the so-called spiritual senses, the practical senses (desiring, loving, etc.)."[39] The realization of the human potential brings into play the whole concrete person, including his individuality, his emotional and sensory versatility, and his capacity for love and fellowship.

> Man appropriates his manifold being in an all-inclusive way, and thus as a whole man. All his *human* relations to the world—seeing, hearing, smelling, tasting, touching, thinking, observing, feeling, desiring, acting, loving—in short, all the organs of his individuality, like the organs that are directly communal in form, are in their objective action (*their action in relation to the object*) the appropriation of this object, the appropriation of human reality. The way in which they react to the object is the confirmation of *human reality*. It is, therefore, just as varied as the determinations of human nature and activities are diverse.[40]

Although this human fulfillment is "aesthetic" in the widest meaning of the term, it includes "aesthetic" fulfillment in its more limited artistic meaning. In a passage that I have quoted at greater length in Chapter 1, Marx distinguishes between men and animals on an aesthetic basis:

> The products of animal production belong directly to their physical bodies, while man is free in face of his product. . . . Thus man constructs also in accordance with the laws of beauty.[41]

---

[39] *Ibid.*, p. 161.

[40] *Ibid.*, p. 159. The words "appropriation" and "objective action" in this quotation need clarification. By objective action (or "objectification") human beings create or transform objects, thus projecting their own qualities into nature. Appropriation occurs when they relate themselves in a human way to these objects. Objectification and appropriation combined make possible the contemplation and enjoyment of a humanized world.

[41] *Ibid.*, p. 128.

Like Schiller in his *Letters on the Aesthetic Education of Man,* Marx links together art and freedom and contrasts the freedom of art with abstract, dehumanized life.

Aesthetic value, he contends, is neither in the object alone nor in the subject (beholder) alone but in the accord between the two. The manner in which an object is realized "depends upon the *nature of the object* and the nature of the corresponding faculty." To realize aesthetic value, therefore, there must be an appropriate object, for example, a musical composition. "Man's musical sense is only awakened by music." But there must also be the subjective capacity:

> The most beautiful music has no meaning for the non-musical ear, is not an object for it, because my object can only be the confirmation of one of my own faculties. It can only be so for me in so far as my faculty exists for itself as a subjective capacity, because the meaning of an object for me extends only as far as the sense extends (only makes sense for an appropriate sense).[42]

Both the aesthetic object sundered from the subject (beholder), and the aesthetic subject sundered from the object, are unreal abstractions.

For Marx this internal relatedness of subject and object applies, *mutatis mutandis,* to all experience in the natural world. Man-in-himself and external-nature-in-itself are abstract and fragmentary moments in concrete, phenomenal nature.

> To say that man *lives* from nature means that nature is his *body* with which he must remain in a continuous interchange in order not to die. The statement that the physical and mental life of man, and nature, are interdependent means simply that nature is interdependent with itself, for man is a part of nature.[43]

As man's being is creatively enriched, nature is humanized and man is naturalized. The humanization of nature and the naturalization of man are two sides of a single process.

[42]*Ibid.,* p. 161.
[43]*Ibid.,* p. 127.

This expressivist ideal of man's harmony with nature is definitely aesthetic in tone.

The contrast between a concrete life of sense-fulfillment and an abstract life of thought is explicit in the Marxian critique of Hegel. Marx complains that in Hegelian philosophy "mind alone is the *true* essence of man, and the true form of mind is thinking mind. . . . Human nature itself is treated as merely *abstract, thinking nature.*"[44] In this criticism Marx evidently had in mind such Hegelian passages as the following:

> The merely felt and sensible . . . is not the spiritual; its heart of hearts is in thought; and only spirit can know spirit. . . . The form of feeling is the lowest in which spiritual truth can be expressed. The world of spiritual existences, God himself, exists in proper truth, only in thought and as thought. If this be so, therefore, thought . . . is the highest and . . . the sole mode of apprehending the eternal and absolute.[45]

This elevation of "thought" above "feeling," the "spiritual" above the "material," and the "eternal" above the "temporal," is contrary to Marx's fundamental convictions. It is an abstraction from the concrete realities of human life and nature.

In language reminiscent of Feuerbach, Marx pits against all such abstractions the figure of "real, corporeal *man,* with his feet planted on the solid ground, inhaling and exhaling all the powers of nature."[46] He attacks Hegel's concept of alienation as abstract and purely intellectual. "For Hegel," he says, "*human life, man,* is equivalent to *self-consciousness.* All alienation of human life is, therefore, nothing but alienation of self-consciousness."[47] Instead of recognizing "the alienated real being of man" Hegel grasps "merely the thought of alienation."

[44]*Ibid.,* pp 201, 214.
[45]*The Logic of Hegel,* trans. by William Wallace (Oxford: Clarendon Press, 1892), pp. 33–34.
[46]*Economic and Philosophic Manuscripts,* p. 206.
[47]*Ibid.,* p. 204.

> The annulment of alienation is also, therefore, merely abstract and vacuous annulment of this empty abstraction. . . . The replete, living, sensuous, concrete activity of self-objectification is, therefore, reduced to a mere abstraction. . . . [48]

Similarly Marx charges that Hegel "stands the world on *its head* and can therefore in his head also dissolve all limitations, which nevertheless remain in existence for bad sensuousness, for real man."[49]

"Bad sensuousness" is the degradation of sensory life. It culminates historically in the slum dwelling and other aesthetic evils of the Industrial Revolution.

> Light, air, and the simplest animal cleanliness cease to be human needs. *Filth,* this corruption and putrefaction which runs in the *sewers* of civilization (this is to be taken literally) becomes the element in which man lives. . . . It is not enough that man should lose his human needs; even animal needs disappear.[50]

This indictment is spelled out in horrifying detail in *Capital.* The facts of human degradation during the heyday of industrial capitalism are very terrible facts, and the economic system that generated them was a very terrible system. The world has changed greatly since Marx wrote, but "bad sensuousness" is still a very present fact.

Marx is even more severe in his attacks on his former associates, the Left Hegelians, than on Hegel himself. Whereas "Hegel's *Phänomenologie,* in spite of its speculative original sin, gives in many instances the elements of a true description of human relations, Herr Bruno [Bauer] and Co. . . . provide only an empty caricature" turning "*real human beings* into *abstract standpoints.*"[51] Throughout his maturity Marx continues to accept the "true" in-

---

[48]*Ibid.,* p. 215.
[49]*The Holy Family,* p. 192.
[50]*Economic and Philosophical Manuscripts,* p. 170.
[51]*The Holy Family,* p. 193. Marx's references to the Left Hegelians ("Bruno and Co.") may convey the misleading impression that they were an organized and cohesive group.

sight of Hegel and to reject the "superficialities" of the Left Hegelians.

Marx points out in *The Holy Family* how undeceived by idealistic abstractions are the industrial workers, for example, in the mills and workshops of Manchester or Lyons.

> They are most painfully aware of the difference between *being* and *thinking*, between *consciousness* and *life*. They know that property, capital, money, wage-labour and the like are no ideal figments of the brain but very practical, very objective products of their self-estrangement and that therefore they must be abolished in a practical, objective way for man to become man not only in *thinking*, in *consciousness*, but in mass *being*, in *life*.[52]

The attack on the intellectual abstractions of Hegel and his leftwing followers is thus directly linked to revolutionary *praxis*.[53]

The word "abstraction" for Marx means more than simply *intellectual* abstraction. It means the detachment of any element from the organic unity of the whole mind-body and its milieu. Isolated passion is as much an abstraction as isolated reason. It is nonsense to believe

> that one could satisfy one passion, separate it from all the others, without satisfying oneself, the whole living individual. If this passion assumes an abstract, separate character, hence if the satisfaction of the individual occurs as the satisfaction of a single passion . . . the reason is not to be found in *consciousness*, but in *being*; not in thinking, but in living; it is found in the empirical development and self-expression of

---

[52]*Ibid.*, p. 53.

[53]The word "praxis" was introduced into social theory by August von Cieszowski, a Pole who associated with the Left Hegelians in Berlin and Paris. Marx used the term to denote both "the unity of theory and practice" and the transformation of the environment by human productive activity.

the individual, which, in turn, depends on the conditions of the world in which he lives.[54]

To isolate a fragment of oneself, whether this fragment be intellectual, passional, or volitional, and to act as if the fragment were the whole, is to lose the aliveness and integrity of the total organic person in the ensemble of his social relations. This is precisely what Marx means by abstraction in ordinary life.

6. The Polemic Against Political Abstraction

Political abstraction occurs when the state is detached from the "civil society" (Hegel's term for the socio-economic order). There is a bifurcation of life into two spheres—the "political" and the "civil," the "public" and the "private." In the political sphere the slogans of "liberty, equality, fraternity" are loudly proclaimed—in the economic sphere acquisitive and exploitative goals are aggressively pursued. In *theory* man is a member of a political community—in *fact* he is "an individual separated from the community, withdrawn into himself, wholly preoccupied with his private interest and acting in accordance with his private caprice."[55] Because the political sphere is detached from civil society, it is "unreal," abstract.

Marx distinguishes between two kinds of rights: the rights of the citizen and the rights of the private individual.

> Political rights . . . can only be exercised if one is a member of a community. Their content is *participation* in the *community* life, in the *political* life of the community, the life of the state. They fall in the category of *political* liberty. . . . [56]

---

[54]Marx/Engels, *Gesamtausgabe* (Frankfurt-Berlin-Moscow: Marx-Engels-Lenin Institute, 1927–   ), I, 5, p. 242, as translated by Erich Fromm, *Beyond the Chains of Illusion* (New York: Simon and Schuster, 1962), pp. 105–106. I am indebted to Fromm for calling my attention to this passage.
[55]"On the Jewish Question" in *Early Writings*, trans. by Bottomore, p. 26.
[56]*Ibid.*, pp. 22–23.

These "rights of the citizen," such as the right to vote and form political associations, are distinguished from the rights of the private individual. The right to "liberty" in the latter sphere is the freedom of private individualism.

> Liberty as a right of man is not founded upon the relations between man and man, but rather upon the separation of man from man. It is the right of such separation. The right of the *circumscribed* individual, withdrawn into himself.... It is the right of self-interest. This individual liberty, and its application, form the basis of civil society. It leads every man to see in other men, not the *realization*, but rather the *limitation* of his own liberty. It declares above all the right "to enjoy and to dispose of *as one will*, one's goods and revenues, the fruits of one's work and industry."[57]

The distinction between these two kinds of rights is indicative of a schism in society. The main basis of the state is the underlying economic system with its divisions and antagonisms. The political community, in contrast, is abstract and specious rather than concrete and substantial. Consequently the rights of the citizen are largely nominal.

The bifurcation of life into the two spheres is reflected in Hegel's political philosophy. He distinguishes "civil society" as consisting mainly of economic activity, from political community in which human beings allegedly overcome their economic egoism and strive for the common good. Marx cannot acccept this dichotomy of state and civil society. As long as it exists "the modern state.... leaves the *real man* out of account or only satisfies the *whole* man in an illusory way."[58] The facts are just the reverse of what Hegel alleges. He thinks that the state reconciles and synthesizes the competing interests of civil society, but in reality it is the bulwark of private interests. A true community will be possible only when the bifurcation ends.

Marx's argument against Hegel's political philosophy

[57]*Ibid.*, pp. 24–25.
[58]*Contribution to the Critique of Hegel's Philosophy of Right: Introduction*, p. 51.

is based on a fundamental premise, namely, that "the individual *is* the *social* being."

> Though man is a unique individual—and it is just his particularity which makes him an individual, a really *individual* communal being—he is equally the *whole*, the ideal whole, the subjective existence of society as thought and experienced. He exists in reality as the representation and real mind of social existence, and as the sum of human manifestations of life.[59]

This creed is the guiding light of Marx's political and economic thought. It is affirmed in his mature works, for example, the *Grundrisse*, as well as in his early writings. The bifurcation of the state and civil society is rejected because it contradicts this creed.

The bifurcation characterizes "bourgeois society" but not ancient Greece or medieval Europe. Marx agreed with Schiller that in the Greek *polis* there was no fundamental cleavage between private and public interest. So long as a person was a free man and not a slave, he was an integral member of the *polis*. The slave, of course, was a private man and not a citizen, but the free man was a member of a real concrete community."The *res publica* was the real private concern, the real content of the citizen, and . . . the political state as political was the true and sole content of the citizen's life and will."[60] Similarly in the Middle Ages the political and economic structures coincided. The socioeconomic distinctions of serf and lord were also the political distinctions of subject and sovereign.

> The spirit of the Middle Ages can be expressed thus: the classes of civil society and the political classes were identical because civil society was political society, because the organic principle of civil society was the principle of the state.[61]

[59]*Economic and Philosophical Manuscripts*, p. 158.
[60] *Critique of Hegel's "Philosophy of Right,"* edited with introduction and notes by Joseph O'Malley (Cambridge at the University Press, 1970), p. 32.
[61]*Ibid.*, p. 72.

According to Marx "this identity has disappeared." The radical split between the public and the private spheres is a phenomenon of capitalist society.

Marx asks the question, what is the relation between political and human emancipation? The two are by no means identical. "A state may be a *free state*, without man himself being a *free man*."[62] Political emancipation in bourgeois society is too abstract and limited in scope to be the sphere of *human* emancipation. Instead there must be a revolution of the whole economic and social structure.

> We have seen: a social revolution possesses a *total* point of view because ... the *community* against whose separation from himself the individual is reacting, is the *true* community of man, *human* nature. In contrast, the *political soul* of revolution consists in the tendency of the classes with no political power to put an end to their *isolation from the state* and from *power*. Its point of view is that of the state, of an abstract *totality* which exists *only* through its separation from real life and which is *unthinkable* in the absence of an organized antithesis between the universal idea and the individual existence of man.[63]

The inadequacy of mere political emancipation is inherent in the abstract nature of the political sphere. Emancipation of political man cannot suffice because man is greater than the citizen and human life is greater than political life.

Marx does not deny that this emancipation is a forward step. "*Political* emancipation certainly represents a great progress," he declares. "It is not, indeed, the final form of human emancipation, but it is the final form of human emancipation *within* the framework of the prevailing social order."[64] In the *Communist Manifesto*, Marx reiterates that "the first step in the revolution of the working class is to raise the proletariat to the position of ruling class, to win

[62]"On the Jewish Question" in *Early Writings*, p. 11.
[63]"Critical Notes on 'The King of Prussia and Social Reform'," in Marx, *Early Writings*, trans. by Rodney Livingstone and Gregor Benton (New York: Random House, 1975), p. 419.
[64]"On the Jewish Question," p. 15.

the battle of democracy." Fragmentary though this victory be, it is a necessary step toward the emancipation of human nature.

In this section I have been quoting mainly from the early writings because they most clearly reveal the philosophical basis of Marx's polemic against political abstractions, but it would be a mistake to suppose that Marx abandoned this polemic in his later works. It underlies his attack on political ideology in *The Eighteenth Brumaire of Louis Bonaparte* (1852); it is presupposed by the denunciation of abstract slogans in *The Civil War in France* (1871) and *Critique of the Gotha Program* (1875), and it is recalled and confirmed in the Afterword to the second edition of *Capital* (1873). In the Afterword Marx recapitulates the main point of his critique of Hegel in 1843 and 1844: whereas Hegel had turned reality upside down by making predicates into subjects and real subjects into predicates, Marx undertakes to turn reality right side up again.

7. The Polemic Against Economic Abstraction

The title of one of Marx's books is *A Contribution to the Critique of Political Economy* and the subtitle of his most famous book, *Capital*, is *A Critique of Political Economy*. These titles suggest that the author was less intent on writing a treatise than a *critique* of economics. "Though *Capital* contains an economic theory," remarks Henri Lefebvre, "it is not a treatise on political economy. It contains something else and more important: a way of superseding political economy, through radical criticism of it."[65]When Marx's writings on economics are regarded as a humanist critique, we begin to discern a critical theme—the attack upon abstraction—running throughout the innumerable pages. The criticism is directed against both the economists and the economy.

[65] Henri Lefebvre, *The Sociology of Marx* (New York: Random House, 1969), p. 16.

The charge against the bourgeois economists is that their "science" is too abstract. John Stuart Mill, for example, is charged with isolating "production as distinct from distribution etc.," and with regarding economic phenomena "as encased in eternal general laws independent of history."[66] Mill is here charged with a double abstraction—first, detachment of production from the other elements in the economy, and second, detachment of economic phenomena from the concrete facts of history.

In accordance with Marx's contention that the economy is an organic totality, the separation of any element except for purposes of analysis is considered a mistake. It might be thought, for example, that "population" is sufficiently concrete to serve as "the foundation and the subject of the entire social act of production."

> However, on closer examination this proves false. The population is an abstraction if I leave out, for example, the classes of which it is composed. These classes in turn are an empty phrase if I am not familiar with the elements on which they rest. E.g. wage labour, capital, etc. These latter in turn presuppose exchange, division of labour, prices, etc. For example, capital is nothing without wage labour, without value, money, price, etc. Thus, if I were to begin with population, this would be a chaotic conception [Vorstellung] of the whole, and I would then, by means of further determination, move analytically towards ever more simple concepts [Begriff] from the imagined concrete towards ever thinner abstractions until I had arrived at the simplest determinations. From there the journey would have to be retraced until I had finally arrived at the population again, but this time not as the chaotic conception of the whole, but as a rich totality of many determinations and relations.[67]

This passage is a clear statement of Marx's contention that analysis should precede but not supersede synthesis, the analytic and the synthetic being reciprocal and interdependent. It is necessary to employ the "force of abstraction" in

[66]Marx, Grundrisse: Foundations of the Critique of Political Economy, p. 87.
[67]Ibid., p. 100.

order to move beyond a "chaotic conception" of the whole economy. But after analysis has arrived at "ever thinner abstractions," it is imperative to retrace the journey by a process of synthesis. The economist who uses this method successfully will recover a sense of the whole, no longer as a chaotic impression, but "as a rich totality of many determinations and relations." Marx's accusation against the economists is that they remain stuck at some abstract point that represents only a facet of reality.

Another kind of abstraction is indicated in Marx's charge that Mill encased economic processes "in eternal general laws independent of history." Marx contends that economic facts must always be understood in the context of a specific organic whole—the social order in its totality—which has an historical beginning, development, and end. There is no economic factor independent of this structure (the synchronic dimension) and process (the diachronic dimension).

In his attack on the economists Marx emphasizes that their "economic laws" are abstractions from the historical process. He distinguishes, for example, between capitalist society, where commodity-production is general and dominating, and feudal society, where commodity-production also takes place but production for immediate use is far more common. Smith, Ricardo, and Mill, he charges, are neglectful of such historical facts, writing as if "the laws of economics" are eternal. This characteristic error—the eternalization of the transitory—is not confined to the defenders of capitalism. In his *Notes on Adolf Wagner* (1879–1880), Marx pillories the half-socialist Wagner for substituting an abstract economic man, whose character and situation are curiously stationary, in place of concrete human beings in a changing historical world.[68] Similarly in *The Poverty of Philosophy* (1847) he condemns the anarchist Proudhon for depicting economic concepts as eternal logi-

[68]See Marx, *Texts on Method*, trans. and ed. by Terrell Carver (Oxford: Basil Blackwell, 1975), pp. 161–219.

cal truths. "Thus these ideas, these categories," he remarks, "are as little eternal as the relations they express."[69] The reference here is to social relations that change more rapidly than psychological relations. But even human nature, with its psychological relations, changes in the long course of history. Marx directs against the economists the type of criticism that he had advanced in his *Theses* of 1845 against Feuerbch, whose mistake was to abstract "the human essence" from the historical process.

When Marx turns from the economists to the economy, he is concerned not with abstraction in theory but with abstraction in everyday life. By abstraction in the work process he means in part the fragmenting effect of the extreme division of labor. "This makes man, as far as is possible, an abstract being, a lathe, etc., and transforms him into a spiritual and physical abortion."[70] In the older handicraft industries, a watch or a table was the individual product of a skilled craftsman. Very different is the work of a modern factory hand, devoting himself hour after hour, day after day, year after year to "the perpetual operation of one and the same limited operation." These endless routines "mutilate the labourer into a fragment of a man, degrade him to the level of an appendage of a machine, destroy every remnant of charm in his work and turn it into a hated toil."[71] The contrast between the independent craftsman and the factory worker is a recurrent theme:

> In handicrafts ... the workman makes use of a tool, in the factory, the machine makes use of him. There the movements of the instruments of labour proceed from him, here it is the movements of the machine that he must follow. In [hand] manufacture the workmen are parts of a living mechanism. In the factory we have a lifeless mechanism independent of the workman, who becomes its mere living appendage. ... At the

[69]Marx, *The Poverty of Philosophy* (New York: International Publishers, no date), p. 93.
[70]Marx on James Mill's *Elements of Political Economy* in *Early Writings*, trans. by Rodney Livingstone and Gregor Benton, p. 269.
[71]*Capital*, I, p. 708.

same time that factory work exhausts the nervous system to the uttermost, it does away with the many-sided play of the muscles, and confiscates every atom of freedom, both in bodily and intellectual activity. The lightening of the labour, even, becomes a sort of torture, since the machine does not free the labourer from work, but deprives the work of all interest.[72]

When we read such passages we recall Schiller's indictment of the division of labor, which destroys "the concrete life of the Individual" and turns him "into nothing but a fragment."

Another cause of abstraction is the concentration of private property in the means of production. Under the pressure of capitalist competition, large companies destroy or absorb small companies. Great corporations, trusts, associations, cartels develop, and life becomes more and more dominated by massive impersonal organizations. For the workers, who are no longer owners of the means of production, the control of their lives passes into the hands of capitalists and managers with whom they have no personal acquaintance.

Thus, on the one hand, we have a totality of productive forces, which have, as it were, taken on a material form and are for the individuals no longer the forces of the individuals but of private property, and hence of the individuals only in so far as they are owners of private property themselves. . . . On the other hand, standing over against these productive forces, we have the majority of the individuals from whom these forces have been wrested away, and who, robbed thus of all real-life content, have become abstract individuals. . . . [73]

The inherent tendency of capitalism, Marx contends, is to concentrate economic power in the hands of the few. Thereby the multitude of workers are largely deprived of self-direction and become cogs in the economic machine.

The worker sells his labor-power in order to make a living. Because his labor-power is inseparable from his per-

[72]*Ibid.*, pp. 461–462.
[73]*The German Ideology*, ed. by R. Pascal (New York: International Publishers, 1939), pp. 65–66.

173

son, he is forced to trim his personality to the level of a commodity.

> Labour does not only create goods: it also produces itself and the worker as a *commodity*, and indeed in the same proportion as it produces goods. . . . Production does not only produce man as a *commodity*, the *human commodity*; in conformity with this situation it produces him as a *mentally* and *physically* dehumanized being.[74]

In later formulations Marx distinguished between labor and labor-power and between the worker and his capacity to work; but he still charged that the effect of the factory-and-market system was to fragment and dehumanize. The worker under capitalism, of course, is not a slave—he has a modicum of freedom—but his freedom is severely circumscribed by the necessity to sell his labor-power.

Every useful thing that is produced by labor-power may be looked at from two points of view, either as use-value or as exchange-value. On the one hand, it is an assemblage of qualities that make it useful in satisfying a human want. Each commodity, or class of commodities, is qualitatively distinct, whether it be bread or heroin, houses or weapons, iron ore or a circus performance. But on the other hand a commodity may be exchanged on a quantitative basis for a wide variety of other commodities. The effect of this reduction of use-value to exchange-value, of quality to quantity, is to transform concrete commodities into economic abstractions.

> If then we leave out of consideration the use-value of commodities, they have only one common property left, that of being products of labour. But even the product of labour itself has undergone a change in our hands. If we make abstraction from its use-value, we make abstraction at the same time from the material elements and shapes that make a product a use-value; we see in it no longer a table, a house, yarn, or any other useful thing. Its existence as a material thing is put out of sight. Neither can it any longer be regarded as the product of

[74]*Economic and Philosophical Manuscripts*, pp. 121, 138.

> the labour of the joiner, the mason, the spinner, or of any other definite kind of productive labour. . . . There is nothing left but what is common to them all; all are reduced to one and the same sort of labour, human labour in the abstract. . . . A use-value, or useful article, therefore, has [exchange]-value only because human labour in the abstract has been embodied or materialized in it. How, then, is the magnitude of this value to be measured? Plainly, by the quantity of the value-creating substance, the labour, contained in the article.[75]

According to Marx, the exchange-value of a commodity is determined by the "socially necessary labor time" embodied in it. Socially necessary labor time is the time required for production under normal conditions, with average degree of skill and intensity, using machinery that is standard in the given industry. The determination of exchange-value is thus a process of averaging and abstracting. Except under conditions of barter the medium of exchange-value is the abstraction of money or credit.

Capitalism is based on value in exchange. Its foundation is quantitative ("money-making") rather than qualitative. Behind the monetary abstractions lurk the concrete realities of economic life—the qualitative diferences in use-values and in kinds and conditions of labor. Professional economists and even non-professionals are prone to focus on the exchange relations among commodities, unaware or forgetful that the quantitative relations between material things conceal the qualitative differences among commodities and the concrete relations among people. When they speak of values, rents, wages, credits, profits, and so forth, as though they were the eternal categories of economics, they obscure the fact that they are simply the manifestations of a special form of social organization ("capitalism") in a particular historical period. Under capitalism both the worker and the employer are enmeshed in abstractions. They deal with their fellow men through the impersonal mechanism of the market, where prices appear to be the substantial realities and human beings merely their instruments.

[75]*Capital*, I, pp. 44–45.

> There is a definite social relation between men, that assumes, in their eyes, the fantastic form of a relation between things. In order, therefore, to find an analogy, we must have recourse to the mist-enveloped regions of the religious world. In that world the productions of the human brain appear as independent beings endowed with life, and entering into relations both with one another and the human race. So it is in the world of commodities with the products of men's hands. This I call the Fetishism which attaches itself to the products of labour, so soon as they are produced as commodities.[76]

Because of the fetishistic attitude that people assume toward commodities, the value of these commodities, which they possess only through their relations with persons, seem to be intrinsic properties exchanging on the market in terms of their fixed objective worth. A diamond, for example, seems *intrinsically* very valuable, whereas, according to Marx's labor theory of value, it would be as cheap as coal if it should require as little labor to obtain it. Hence the human content of exchange values becomes abstract, depersonalized, and, in consequence, heartless.

The abstractness of commodity production is embodied in money as the medium of exchange. Apart from money, exchange is in terms of human qualities.

> Let us assume *man* to be *man*, and his relation to the world to be a human one. Then love can only be exchanged for love, trust for trust, etc. If you wish to enjoy art you must be an artistically cultivated person; if you wish to influence other people you must be a person who really has a stimulating and encouraging effect upon others.[77]

In monetary exchanges, on the other hand, qualities count much less than quantities.

> What I *am* and *can do* is, therefore, not at all determined by my individuality. I *am* ugly, but I can buy the most beautiful woman for myself. Consequently, I am not *ugly*, for the effect

[76]*Ibid.*, p. 83.
[77]*Economic and Philosophical Manuscripts*, pp. 193–194.

of ugliness, its power to repel, is annulled by money. As an individual, I am *lame*, but money provides me with twenty-four legs. Therefore, I am not lame. I am a detestable, dishonourable, unscrupulous and stupid man, but money is honored and so also is its possessor. Money is the highest good, and so its possessor is good.[78]

Again and again—in the *Notes on James Mill*, the *Economic and Philosophical Manuscripts*, the *Grundrisse*, *Capital*, etc.—Marx returns to this theme. In a money-ridden society, the individuality of persons and the qualities of things are alike negated. By reducing all things to a common measure, money produces a "universal confusion and inversion of things." Acquisitiveness takes precedence over all other human traits. To quote Wordsworth:

> The world is too much with us: late and soon,
> Getting and spending, we lay waste our powers.

Human beings are obsessed with the sense of having, and things are valued not for their intrinsic properties but as things to be possessed.

> Private property has made us so stupid and one-sided that an object is only *ours* when we have it, when it exists for us as capital or when it is directly eaten, drunk, worn, inhabited, etc., in short, *utilized* in some way.[79]

"Utilized" not as matchless quality to be appreciated and enjoyed but as object to be acquired and consumed. To "make money" advertisers and salesagents will stimulate any sort of appetite, however unnatural or imaginary it may be. Marx is telling us that our way of valuing objects is undifferentiated and abstract. It suppresses the qualitative nature of each object in a welter of acquisitiveness. The priceless things—such as beauty, love, and honesty—are devalued.

Marx's polemic against abstraction ranges him on the

---

[78]*Ibid.*, p. 191.
[79]*Ibid.*, p. 159.

side of the romantics and the existentialists against the "vulgar materialists." It also touches upon an important modern theme—the crisis in interpersonal relations—a crisis that can be defined as the tyranny of abstractions. Karl Popper has remarked in a striking passage:

> As a consequence of its loss of organic character, an open society may become, by degrees, . . . an "abstract society." It may, to a considerable extent, lose the character of a concrete group of men, or a system of such concrete groups. This point which has been rarely understood may be explained by way of an exaggeration. We could conceive of a society in which men practically never meet face to face—in which all business is conducted by individuals in isolation who communicate by typed letters or by telegrams, and who go about in closed motor cars. (Artificial insemination would allow even propagation without a personal element.) Such a fictitious society might be called a "completely abstract or depersonalized society." Now the interesting point is that our modern society resembles in many of its aspects such a completely abstract society. Although we do not always drive alone in closed motor cars (but meet face to face thousands of men walking past us in the street) the upshot is very nearly the same as if we did—we do not establish as a rule any personal relation with our fellow pedestrians. Similarly, membership in a trade union may not mean more than the possession of a membership card and the payment of a contribution to an unknown secretary. There are many people living in a modern society who have no, or extremely few, intimate personal contacts, who live in anonymity and isolation, and consequently in unhappiness.[80]

The massive forces of change seem to be moving toward an organizational gigantism and standardization that undermine the values of individuality. The depersonalization of existence is not only a threat but a constant reality. Hence springs the crisis of the human person. In his acute perception of this fact Marx belongs to the ethos of the late twentieth century.

[80]Karl Popper, *The Open Society and Its Enemies* (London: Routledge & Kegan Paul, 1966), Vol. I, pp. 174–175.

Crisis and Revolution

1. The Relation of Revolutionary Crisis to Models of Historical Explanation

Marx is the personification of revolution. After his early conversion to communism, he never swerved from his devotion to the revolutionary cause. At times he edged toward the idea of peaceful revolution, but he was committed to violence if peaceful means failed. Because of his intransigent attitude and unrivaled influence, he is the pre-eminent symbol of the revolutionist. Only Lenin rivals him in this respect.

His revolutionary stance sets him apart from others in the use of heuristic models. Although he resembles the "structuralists," the differences are as profound as the resemblances. Richard and Fernande De George have nevertheless included selections from Marx in a structuralist anthology. They have said that Marx, Freud, and Ferdinand de Saussure ("the Father of Modern Linguistics") are the great forerunners of structuralism:

> What Marx, Freud, and Saussure have in common, and what they share with present-day structuralists, is a conviction that surface events and phenomena are to be explained by structure, data, and phenomena below the surface. . . . The attempt to uncover deep structure, unconscious motivations, and underlying causes which account for human actions at a more basic and profound level than do individual conscious decisions, and which shape, influence, and structure these deci-

sions, is an enterprise which unites Marx, Freud, Saussure, and modern structuralists.[1]

Claude Lévi-Strauss, whom many would regard as the greatest of the structuralists, has referred to Marx as one of his "three mistresses" (together with Freud and geology).[2] But in Lévi-Strauss's structuralism there is relatively scant emphasis upon organic sickness and revolutionary transformation. There is little or no account of the contradictions between discrepant structures (e.g., the forces and relations of production), and no emphasis upon dialectical development. Lévi-Strauss conceives human nature as an abstraction (one universal human mind) governed by innate and essential categories of thought. He speaks as if there is always an unconscious infrastructure behind the conscious superstructure. As Miriam Glucksmann writes:

> While this may be the case in Bororo society, it cannot be concluded that in all societies everywhere and at all times there exists a mystified conception of society, and that there is always a real unconscious structure behind the apparent one. In this view, society cannot therefore be acted upon purposefully since the social actors can never have a correct account of its workings. This is a regrettable position: . . . it highlights only the obstacles to social change and so contradicts Lévi-Strauss's professed Marxism. For any Marxist, philosophy must be based on the premise that man makes history and is able to discover the laws of history and society, which may then be acted upon by conscious political action.[3]

In contrast to Marx's principles of "practice" in the Theses on Feuerbach, structuralism asserts no esential link between theory and practice.

[1]Richard T. De George and Fernande M. De George, eds., The Structuralists: From Marx to Levi-Strauss (New York: Doubleday & Company, 1972), p. xii.
[2]Lévi-Strauss, Tristes Tropiques, quoted by Miriam Glucksmann, Structuralist Analysis in Contemporary Social Thought: A Comparison of the Theories of Claude Levi-Strauss and Louis Althusser (London: Routledge & Kegan Paul, 1974), p. 52.
[3]Glucksmann, ibid., p. 90.

Neil J. Smelser has called attention to the similarity between "functional sociology" and Marxism. Functional sociologists, such as Talcott Parsons and Marion J. Levy, have depicted society as an equilibrium system tending toward stability.

> The starting theoretical point of functional theorists' analyses is that societies are faced with a number of functional requisites or exigencies, such as recruitment and socialization of new members in society, the production and allocation of means of subsistence, the regulation of conflict, the maintenance of cultural patterns, and so on.[4]

The function of social regulations and institutions is largely to avoid or ameliorate conflict situations.

That there is some resemblance between these ideas and Marxism is indubitable, but there are outstanding differences. Whereas Marx gives primacy to the mode of production, the functionalists regard the various social levels as more nearly equal. Also they put greater emphasis upon the stabilizing than upon the unstabilizing forces. Even when they discuss "disfunctions"—a concept similar to Marx's "contradictions"—they do not interpret the whole society as tending toward breakdown. Whereas Marx conceives of the inevitable breakdown of capitalist society and its replacement by communism, they are less prone to describe social process in such directional terms. In contrast to both functional society and structuralism, Marx's diagnosis is mainly concerned with grave contradictions in the social structure. Far from advocating value neutrality, he is determined to contribute to revolutionary practice.

The classical economists were likewise more intent on economic equilibrium than disequilibrium. Conservative philosophers, such as Herbert Spencer, used the organic theory of society to defend established privileges against the attacks of the dispossessed. Marx differed from all such theorists, both classical and modern, in being primarily

[4]Karl Marx, *On Society and Social Change*, ed. by Neil J. Smelser (University of Chicago Press, 1973), p. xviii.

concerned with the mortal illness of "bourgeois civilization." He emphasized disequilibrium rather than equilibrium, specific historical processes rather than universal
structural properties, the unity of theory and practice rather
than pure theory. His explanatory models are related to this
revolutionary orientation.

The extent of Marx's agreement and disagreement with
other holistic thinkers should be made clear. Piotr
Sztompka has said that an explanatory theory of society
should answer two questions: "Why do societies hold together and persist?" and "Why do societies fall apart and
change?"[5] Structuralists, functional sociologists, and systems analysts—as well as conservative theorists of social
organicism—answer the first question by developing a holistic theory of society. Marx similarly answers the first
question with his theory of dynamic equilibrium. He
answers the second question with a dialectical theory of
disequilibrium. In this respect he differs from the other ho-
lists, who answer the first question but tend to neglect the
second. For Parsons and Levi-Strauss, not to mention their
many followers, the question of order and persistence takes
precedence over the question of conflict and change. Their
theories are comparatively unhistorical and static; Marx's
theory is historical and dynamic.[6]

Marx also differs from holistic thinkers who try to
answer the second question with a reductionist or mechanistic theory. A kind of equilibrium can be maintained by
mechanical devices, such as a thermostat or the more complex mechanism of a computer. Setting up a model of

[5]Piotr Sztompka, *System and Function* (New York: Academic Press, 1974),
p. 180.
[6]This contrast can easily be overstated. For a persuasive argument that
there is much in common between Levi-Strauss and Marx, see Maurice
Godelier, "System, Structure and Contradiction in *Das Kapital*," in Michael Lane, ed., *Introduction to Structuralism* (New York: Basic Books,
1970). On the relation between Marx's theory and sociological functionalism (including Parsons), see Alan Swingewood, *Marx and Modern Social
Theory* (New York: John Wiley & Sons, 1975), Chapter 8. In Parson's late
publication the conservatism is less pronounced.

"negative feed-back," some "system theorists" have developed mechanistic theories of social control.[7] According to the classical economists and their modern imitators, "the mechanism of supply and demand" maintains economic equilibrium in a similar way. That Marx is unwilling to explain social processes on the basis of a mechanistic model is evident from his emphasis on need-dispositional factors (see section 6 below).

2. Differing Interpretations of Marx

According to the reductive interpretation of the base-superstructure model, the base causes the transformations in the superstructure in a linear time-sequence. Although there may be interaction between superstructure and base, the latter is ultimately determinative. Interpreting Marx in this way, August Thalheimer declared that

> the manner and mode in which men earn their living determines all other aspects of social life. This manner and mode determines, above all, social viewpoints, thoughts, or ideas, i.e., "social consciousness."[8]

Thalheimer, as a leading Communist theoretician, lectured before Marx's manuscripts were drawn from the archives and published, but he could have discovered the error of his interpretation from books published during Marx's lifetime. In *The Poverty of Philosophy,* for example, Marx criticized Proudhon's conception of linear causation:

> M. Proudhon considers economic relations as so many social phases, engendering one another, resulting one from another like the antithesis from the thesis, and realizing in their logical sequence the impersonal reason of humanity. The only drawback to this method is that when he comes to examine a single one of these phases, M. Proudhon *cannot explain it*

---

[7]See, for example, Norbert Wiener, *Cybernetics,* 2nd ed. (Cambridge, Mass.: Massachusetts Institute of Technology Press, 1961).

[8]August Thalheimer, *Introduction to Dialectical Materialism: The Marxist World-View* (New York: Covici, Friede, 1936), p. 185. Lectures delivered at Sun Yat-Sen University, Moscow, to Chinese students.

without having recourse to all the other relations of society; which relations, however, he has not yet contrived to engender by means of his dialectic movement. When, after that, M. Proudhon, by means of pure reason, proceeds to give birth to these other phases, he treats them as if they were new-born babes. He forgets that they are of the same age as the first. . . . The different limbs of society are converted into so many separate societies, following one upon the other. How, indeed, could the single logical formula of movement, of sequence, of time, explain the structure of society, *in which all relations co-exist simultaneously and support one another?*[9]

In this passage Marx accuses Proudhon of transforming Hegel's organic theory of dialectical development into a formula of linear causality. In any concrete social formation, Marx contends, the structural elements originate and develop *interdependently.*

This passage is by no means the only example of Marx's insistence on interdependence. I have quoted examples from such varied sources as the Paris manuscripts, the *Grundrisse, Capital,* and *Theories of Surplus Value.* There are other passages, however, in which the model of base and superstructure seems to be formulated unequivocally and reductively. How should we regard these apparent contradictions?

First, we may conclude that the base-superstructure and organic models are flatly contradictory. Agnes Heller, without referring to these models, finds no great fault in Marx's alleged incoherence:

Like every other thinker of importance, he too refused to sacrifice the *search* for truth in various directions and along various paths on the altar of coherence. . . . The immortality, the living content of Marx's thought . . . , is based precisely on this brilliant lack of coherence.[10]

[9]*The Poverty of Philosophy,* in Marx/Engels, *Collected Works* (New York: International Publishers, 1976), Vol. 6, pp. 166–167. (My italics.)
[10]Agnes Heller, *The Theory of Need in Marx* (New York: St. Martin's Press, 1976), pp. 87–88.

We may accept Marx's incoherence as a gift of genius. Everyone changes his mind to some extent in a life span—especially is this true of a fecund and imaginative thinker. But Heller would surely agree with us that to attribute more inconsistency to Marx than the evidence warrants is unscholarly.

Second, we may cling to the base-superstructure model and regard the organic totality model as an aberration or, at best, a slight amendment. The explanation of historical crisis and revolution will then be linear. The conflicts and disequilibria in the economic base, it will be said, precede and cause the political and cultural revolution. In view of evidence to the contrary, I cannot accept this interpretation.

Third, we may decide that the base-superstructure model misrepresents Marx's fundamental convictions. This is the position of Michael Harrington, who concludes "that Marx and the Marxists made a major contribution to the misunderstanding of Marxism."[11] I find no difficulty in agreeing with Harrington that "the Marxists" misunderstood Marx. You may recall Marx's famous quip: "All I know is that I am not a Marxist." But it is harder to believe he grossly misrepresented himself. Although he was sometimes careless or one-sided in the statement of his ideas, he was not thoroughly mistaken in understanding his own doctrines.

Fourth, we may decide that the two models are not contradictory. The hierarchy of base and superstructure may simply be a constituent within an organic whole. The determining character of the productive system within the society would be no more inconsistent with its organic character than the dominance of the heart and the circulation of the blood is inconsistent with the organic unity of the human body. This synthesis must have occurred to Marx, because he recognizes the validity of both models and never suggests that they are contradictory. The models cease to appear contradictory if we regard them as repre-

[11]Michael Harrington, *The Twilight of Capitalism* (New York: Simon and Schuster, 1976), p. 59. See also Harrington, "Marx versus Marx," *New Politics,* Vol. 1 (Fall 1961), pp. 112–123.

senting different levels in the scale of abstraction—base-superstructure becomes the abstracted hierarchy within the concrete totality. Although there are some apparent and some real contradictions in the details of Marx's exposition,[12] I believe that this fourth interpretation is on the whole correct. More I would not claim.

3. The Organismic Way of Thinking About Crisis

Although the resemblance between a social order and a biological organism should not be exaggerated, organic processes at the biological level are analogous to corresponding processes at the social level. For example, the homeostatic movements in the human body are suggestive of similar movements in society. Homeostasis is defined in the *Larousse International Dictionary* as "a movement within a system, person or group toward equilibrium." This definition implies that the restorations of equilibrium in such diverse structures as a mechanical system, a human organism, and a social group have something in common.

The premise that underlies the concept of homeostasis—namely, that function and malfunction belong to the structure as a whole rather than to any specific member—is as ancient as the science of medicine. According to Pythagoras (circa 580–500 B.C.) the human body is pervaded by certain "opposites," hot and cold, wet and dry; and good health is the result of their due blend and right proportion. The body, like a well-played musical instrument, must be properly attuned, each part in harmony with every other. (Our language, incidentally, still preserves traces of this musical analogy since we speak of "tonic" and "temperament" in medicine as well as in music.) The business of the physician, when harmony is disturbed, is to restore the balance.

[12]On real and apparent contradictions see Raymond Williams' penetrating analysis of such basic Marxian concepts as ideology, causal determination, productive forces, and base and superstructure in *Marxism and Literature* (Oxford University Press, 1977).

Similarly the celebrated Greek physician Hippocrates (circa 460–377 B.C.) contended that the health of the body depends upon the right proportion of warmth, cold, dryness, and moisture corresponding to fire, air, earth, and water. To these, in turn, correspond the bodily fluids, or as they were later called, "humors": blood, phlegm, black bile, and yellow bile (choler). Disease results from the excess or deficiency of any of these properties, and it is to be cured by restoring the natural equilibrium of the body. Hippocrates introduced the term "crisis" to characterize the turning point in a disease when death or recovery hangs in the balance. The physician, he said, should then bring to bear all his remedies to restore the equilibrium.

Basing his ideas on Greek medicine, Plato extended the concept of healthful equilibrium to the soul of man and the entire state. The good life, he maintained, is to be found in the harmonious development and functional cooperation of all the faculties of the soul and all the divisions of the state. In the eighth and ninth books of The Republic, he described the various forms of social pathology that result from the exaggeration and dominance of some one part of human nature. Crisis, he believes, inevitably follows the hypertrophy of a human faculty, such as will, feeling or appetite, and the attendant atrophy of other faculties. But his analysis is distorted by aristocratic bias, so that actually he favors the dominance of a rationalistic elite. Censorship and repression, rather than spontaneous harmony, characterize even his ideal "aristocratic" state.

The notion of humors is elaborated in many medieval treatises and in such Renaissance works as Burton's Anatomy of Melancholy. It becomes a commonplace of popular thought, as we may see from the many references to humors in Shakespeare's plays. Ben Jonson employed it as the basis of his theory of comedy: a comic character, he maintained, is ridiculously unbalanced because he has too much or too little of some humor: blood, phlegm, bile, or choler. The term "humor" still bears this comic connotation.

The humoral theory of disease became obsolete after

dominating medicine for 2000 years; but in principle it is not very different from the modern theory that bodily fluids, such as blood sugar or endocrine secretion, must be kept at the right levels to preserve a healthful balance. Homeostasis—the self-regulatory functioning of the organism in the maintenance of equilibrium—has never ceased to be a basic principle in medicine.

Its importance, for example, was recognized by one of the greatest of Marx's contemporaries, the physiologist Claude Bernard. In his studies of the functions of the liver and the pancreas, of the action of such poisons as carbon monoxide, and of the physiology of the nervous system, he was acutely aware of the working harmony of the organism and the need to restore the harmony when it is impaired. "The word in which Claude Bernard's notions are crystallized," remarks Norbert Wiener, "is homeostasis."[13] Another of Marx's medical contemporaries, Rudolf Virchow, expressed his concept of health and disease in similar terms. His great achievement, as expounded in his Cellular Pathology (1858), was to analyze diseased tissues from the standpoint of cell formation and structure. He maintained that the physical organism functions like a political "state in which every cell is a citizen." Health is like the peaceful cooperation of the citizens and disease is like a civil war.[14]

Similar remarks are made by the great twentieth century physiologist, Walter B. Cannon, whose book The Wisdom of the Body, is a classic exposition of homeostasis. He points out that the physical organism, although very unstable in its constituents, is governed by stabilizing factors that adjust the changes to one another and thereby maintain a state of equilibrium; for example:

> If the hydrogen-ion concentration in the blood is altered ever so slightly toward the acid direction, the especially sen-

[13]Norbert Wiener, "The Concept of Homeostasis in Medicine," in Brandon Lush, ed., Concepts of Medicine (New York: Pergamon Press, 1961), p. 153.
[14]Encyclopedia Britannica (1955 edition), Vol. 23, pp. 178–179.

sitized part of the nervous system which controls breathing is at once made active and by increased ventilation of the lungs carbonic acid is pumped out until the normal state is restored.[15]

If the organism is prevented from regaining equilibrium in the normal way, it seeks balance by a different method. When meningitis destroys synapses in the brain, for example, the recovery consists in new circuits being established. Death results when such equilibrating functions break down completely. In a final chapter Cannon considers the possibility of maintaining social homeostasis by analogous equilibrating factors in society.

The concept of homeostasis is useful in emphasizing the self-regulatory functions of the organism, but it is too static to serve as Marx's model of historical development. As René Dubos has said:

> The word "homeostasis" seems indeed to imply that nature in its wisdom elicits responses that always bring back the organism to the same ideal condition. . . . This is, of course, far from the truth. . . . What characterizes living processes is *homeokinesis* and not homeostasis.[16]

As the words imply, homeostasis is relatively static, homeokinesis is kinetic.

If we are to extend such concepts to society, we must distinguish between static and dynamic equilibrium. A

[15]Walter B. Cannon, *The Wisdom of the Body* (New York: W. W. Norton & Company, 1932), p. 270.

[16]René Dubos, "Environment," in *Dictionary of the History of Ideas* (New York: Charles Scribner's Sons, 1973), Vol. II, p. 126. For argument that we must go beyond the concept of homeostasis to a more kinetic concept, see C.A. Mace, "Homeostasis, Needs and Values," *British Journal of Psychology*, Vol. 43 (1953); Gordon W. Allport, *Pattern and Growth in Personality* (New York: Holt, Rinehart and Winston, 1961); and Walter Buckley, *Sociology and Modern Systems Theory* (Englewood Cliffs, N.J.: Prentice-Hall, 1967). For readings from Buckley and Allport and much other relevant material see Walter Buckley, editor, *Modern Systems Research for the Behavioral Scientist: A Sourcebook* (Chicago: Aldine Publishing Company, 1968).

static equilibrium does not eliminate all change because every society is in constant flux, but the changes consist of slight, or limited and temporary, deviations from the normal pattern of life. There is no cumulative development bringing about fundamental change. Marx's account of the "Asiatic" type of social formation illustrates a relatively static equilibrium. A *dynamic* social equilibrium is one in which cumulative changes, either progressive or retrogressive, are taking place in important parts of the society or in the society as a whole. There is no stable, persisting, "normal" equilibrium, and if we can speak of equilibrium, it must be dynamic. Such an equilibrium occurs when irreversible and fundamental changes take place, yet in balance and harmony with one another so that, at any point of time, the various phases of development are fairly well coordinated with one another. Marx's description of bourgeois society in its heyday of prosperity and expansion approaches this norm of dynamic equilibrium, although even in this stage there were grave conflicts. A dynamic social equilibrium unaccompanied by such conflicts is rare.

As in the rapid onset of a disease, the pace of change accelerates alarmingly during crisis. An historical crisis is a dynamic state, but it differs from a dynamic equilibrium in exhibiting uncoordinated rather than coordinated development. When there is a grievous disturbance of equilibrium, producing a terrifying acceleration of the historical process and little coordination among the societal elements, there is a genuine crisis.

> Only a precipitous change over a short span of time affecting the very vitals of institutions, mores, modes of thought and feeling, power structures, and economic organizations, may rightly be termed a "crisis."[17]

This characterization is akin to Hippocrates' use of "crisis" as a term in medicine. Because of the difference in scale between the individual human organism and the whole so-

[17]Gerhard Masur, "Crisis in History," in *Dictionary of the History of Ideas*, Vol. I, p. 593.

ciety, "a short span of time" has a different meaning in the one case as contrasted with the other. When Thomas Paine wrote The American Crisis in 1776 he said: "These are the times that try men's souls." The period of tensions that he called a "crisis" was considerably longer than the span of time that Hippocrates had in mind. If historians refer to a very protracted period they are likely to speak of an "age of crisis."

In suggesting that there is an analogy between crisis in medicine and crisis in history, I may seem to be introducing a notion that has little relevance to Marx; but we must not forget that he was an exceptionally erudite man. As an inveterate admirer of Greek culture, he must have known about the theories of such Platonic dialogues as the Republic, Statesman, and Timaeus, in which the analogy is employed. His detailed knowledge of Shakespeare's plays made him realize that the theory of humors survived until at least the Elizabethan period. He may have been aware of similar theories among his contemporaries. I cannot judge the probability that Marx would have known the pertinent literature, and I can say only that he was interested in physiology, anatomy, and medicine as in many other subjects. In mid-June of 1864, for instance, he temporarily suspended his writing on economics and studied anatomy and physiology (Carpenter, Lord, Kölliker, Spurzheim, Schwann, Schleiden). On July 4 he wrote to Engels:

> I always follow in your tracks. Thus it is probable that I shall study a lot of anatomy and physiology in my spare time and also attend lectures (where the stuff is demonstrated and dissected ad oculus.)[18]

His reference in the Preface to Capital to "the body as an organic whole," with its cell-structure studied with micro-

[18]Maximilien Rubel and Margaret Manale, Marx Without Myth (New York: Harper & Row, 1975), p. 197. On the state of physiology during Marx's lifetime see John Theodore Merz, A History of European Thought in the Nineteenth Century. (Edinburgh and London: William Blackwood and Sons, 1912), Vol. II, Chs. 8–10.

scopes and chemical reagents, is evidently based on knowledge.

Even if Marx had lacked this knowledge, a similar approach to pathological disturbances was integral to Hegelian philosophy, which he studied assiduously. No one was more devoted to the concept of organic unity than Hegel:

> The limbs and organs . . . of an organic body are not merely parts of it: it is only in their unity that they are what they are, and they are unquestionably affected by that unity, as they also in turn affect it. These limbs and organs become mere parts, only when they pass under the hands of the anatomist, whose occupation, be it remembered, is not with the living body but with the corpse. Not that such analysis is illegitimate: we only mean that the external and mechanical relation of whole and parts is not sufficient for us, if we want to study organic life in its truth. And if this be so in organic life, it is the case to a much greater extent when we apply this relation to the mind and the formations of the spiritual world.[19]

Considered in isolation this passage states the philosophical underpinning for the doctrine of homeostasis. But Hegel combined it with the idea of dialectical development:

> Wherever there is movement, wherever there is life, wherever anything is carried into effect in the actual world, there Dialectic is at work. . . . Neither in heaven nor in earth, neither in the world of mind or nature, is there anything such as an abstract "Either-Or" as the understanding maintains. Whatever exists is concrete, with difference and opposition in itself.[20]

Organic coherence is thus combined in Hegel's philosophy with contradiction.

In the above quotation Hegel seems to be denying the common sense principle that nothing contradictory can exist. The denial can be avoided if we distinguish contradic-

[19]Hegel, *The Encyclopedia of the Philosophical Sciences*, trans. by William Wallace, in Hegel, *Selections*, ed. by J. Loewenberg p. 172.
[20]*The Logic of Hegel*, trans. by William Wallace (Oxford at the Clarendon Press, 1892), pp. 148, 223.

tion in formal logic (the contradictory relation of an affirmative to a negative judgment) from the polarities and contrarieties of real life. Neither Hegel nor Engels always made this distinction. They were misled, for example, by Zeno's paradoxes into supposing that there is an objective logical contradiction in the fact of motion. Such mistakes were later perpetuated in the theory of dialectical materialism.[21] Although contrariety and logical inconsistency are given the same label of "contradiction," they should be distinguished.

Quite apart from questionable details of the *Logic*, Hegel possessed a keen sense of dialectical crisis. This sense is nowhere more evident than in his discussion of drama. The foundation of his theory of comedy and tragedy is summed up by Jacob Loewenberg:

> Life, as Hegel conceives it, is an incessant strife of partisan views. They are partisan because they are particular. . . . Whatever is particular—a particular art, a particular religion, a particular philosophy—is self-absorbed and self-centered and hence never free from bias. The truth is that every particular point of view ineluctably suffers from a warped perspective. The unavoidable tendency of everything particular to emphasize its own particularity Hegel discerns to be the source of all the fatal collisions that render human life so everlastingly unstable.[22]

When we laugh at the eccentricities we have comedy; when we pity the victims of warped perspectives we have tragedy. In comedy the one-sidedness is ridiculous; in tragedy it is catastrophic. In the *Antigone* of Sophocles, for example, Creon's loyalty to the state is inordinate and Antigone's loyalty to the family is just as inordinate; the two characters collide and both go down to destruction. The fate of the protagonists points to the need for a balanced synthesis.

---

[21]See Adam Schaff, 'Marxist Dialectics and the Principle of Contradiction," *Journal of Philosophy*, Vol. 57 (1960), pp. 241–250.
[22]Hegel, *Selections*, ed. by J. Lowenberg (New York: Charles Scribner's Sons, 1929), p. xix.

Marx was an inveterate reader of plays. He knew Greek drama with a thoroughness that only classical scholars can equal, and he could recite scene after scene of Shakespeare by heart. As Lee Baxandal has remarked, "theatrical exuberance was the watchword of the Marx household, with Marx writing drama criticism for German papers, daughter Eleanor becoming a foremost Ibsenite in England, Marx himself frequently reciting, and the whole family constituting a Shakespearean household-performance unit."[23] Marx's knowledge of Greek and Elizabethan plays, when combined with Hegel's dialectical interpretation of comedy and tragedy, must have influenced his interpretation of historical crisis.

The theory of drama carries over into the sphere of human social relations the doctrine of imbalance in the humoral theory of crisis. Marx was quick to see its relation to history:

> Hegel remarks somewhere that all great, world-historical facts and personages occur, as it were, twice. He has forgotten to add: the first time as tragedy, the second as farce. Caussidière for Danton, Louis Blanc for Robespierre, the Mountain of 1848 to 1851 for the Mountain of 1793 to 1795, the Nephew for the Uncle. And the same caricature occurs in the circumstances in which the second edition of the Eighteenth Brumaire is taking place.[24]

The analogy between dramatic conflicts and historical

[23]Lee Baxandall, Review of S. S. Prawer, Karl Marx and World Literature, in The Journal of Aesthetics and Art Criticism (Winter 1977), p. 229

[24]The Eighteenth Brumaire of Louis Bonaparte, in Marx, Selected Works, two volume edition (New York: International Publishers, no date) Vol. II, p. 315. The following editor's footnote is added: "On the Eighteenth Brumaire (according to the calendar introduced in the period of the first French bourgeois revolution), on November 9, 1799, Napoleon I carried out the coup d'etat whereby as First Consul he concentrated supreme power in his hands; in 1804 he declared himself emperor. By the second edition of the Eighteenth Brumaire, Marx means the coup d'etat accomplished by Louis Bonaparte, the nephew of Napoleon I, on December 2, 1851."

events is one of the sources of Marx's dialectical interpretation of crisis.

His familiarity with drama must have reinforced his sense that there is an inward or subjective side to crisis. The difference between tragedy and melodrama and between comedy and farce is largely the presence of the inner drama. As Habermas has written:

> In classical aesthetics, from Aristotle to Hegel, crisis signifies the turning point in a fateful process that, despite all objectivity, does not simply impose itself from outside and does not remain external to the identity of the persons caught up in it. The contradiction, expressed in the catastrophic culmination of conflict, is inherent in the structure of the action system and in the personality systems of the principal characters. Fate is fulfilled in the revelation of conflicting norms against which the identities of the participants shatter.. . . . [25]

Whoever emphasizes only the objective side of crisis misses half of its meaning. Marx had no one-sided interpretation.

The combination of "organic structure" and "dialectical development," the two components of his organic model, is the conceptual foundation of his theory of crisis. By taking account of the rifts and fissures that are present to some degree in any society, Marx develops a model in which the causes of revolution are built in from the outset. When the contradictions in the social organism become very intense and the tempo of change becomes very rapid, the society is in crisis.

4. The Concept of Historical Crisis

The speech of Marx at the anniversary celebration of the *People's Paper*, a Chartist publication, in April 1856, is an eloquent summary of his theory of historical crisis. He be-

---

[25]Jürgen Habermas, *Legitimation Crisis* (Boston: Beacon Press, 1975), p. 2. See also Adolfo Sánchez Vásquez, *Art and Society* (New York and London: Monthly Review Press, 1973), Ch. 6: "The Concept of Tragedy in Marx and Engels."

gins by contrasting the abortive "revolutions" of 1848 with the great revolution that they foreshadowed:

> The so-called revolutions of 1848 were but poor incidents— small fractures and fissures in the dry crust of European society. However, they revealed the abyss. Beneath the apparently solid surface they betrayed oceans of living matter, only needing expansion to rend into fragments continents of hard rock.[26]

Although Marx had extravagant hopes for European revolution in 1848, he was a soberer man when he spoke to his working class audience in 1856. His retrospective judgment was identical with that expressed later by the historian George Macaulay Trevelyan:

> The year 1848 was the turning-point at which modern history failed to turn. . . . Nearly all the despotic Governments of the Continent were overthrown, but nearly all recovered in the course of a year.[27]

Marx distinguished between the crisis of 1848 which "revealed the abyss" and the super-crisis which would rend European society like a colossal earthquake.

The coming revolution, he believed, would be the culmination of profound contradictions:

> There is one great fact, characteristic of this our nineteenth century, a fact which no party dares deny. On the one hand, there have started into life industrial and scientific forces which no epoch of former human history had ever suspected. On the other hand, there exist symptoms of decay far surpassing the horrors recorded of the later times of the Roman Empire. In our days everything seems pregnant with its contrary. Machinery, gifted with the wonderful power of shortening and fructifying human labor, we behold starving and over-

[26]"Speech at the Anniversary of the *People's Paper,*" in Marx, *On Revolution,* ed. by Saul K. Padover (New York: McGraw-Hill Book Company, 1971), p. 59. The following quotations from this speech are from the same source.

[27]George Macauley Trevelyan, *British History in the Nineteenth Century,* 2nd ed. (London: Longmans, Green and Co., 1937), p. 292.

working it. The newfangled sources of wealth, by some strange weird spell, are turned into sources of want. The victories of art seem bought by the loss of character. At the same pace that mankind masters nature, man seems to become enslaved to other men or to his own infamy. Even the pure light of science seems unable to shine but on the dark background of ignorance. All our invention and progress seem to result in endowing material forces with intellectual life, and in stultifying human life into a material force.

Long before the unspeakable blood purges and colossal wars of the twentieth century, Marx describes the startling contradictions of modern civilization.

Hippocrates characterized crisis as the stage when danger and opportunity are at their maximum—*danger* because of the mortal threat of disease, *opportunity* because life still hangs in the balance and remedies may be at hand. A crisis is not only a present evil but a challenge to action in the light of an uncertain future. Marx characterized the double-aspect of the approaching crisis in similar terms. The forces of production are of unparalleled magnitude—industry and science have reached a level of capacity far beyond anything known in the past—but science shines only on the dark background of ignorance, and the newfangled sources of wealth are turned into sources of want. Potentialities are incongruous with achievements: the institutional fetters are holding the potentialities in check. There is a dreadful waste and misuse of resources. Marx turns from these contradictions to his explanation:

> This antagonism between modern industry and science on the one hand, modern misery and dissolution on the other hand, this antagonism between the productive powers and the social relations of our epoch, is a fact, palpable, overwhelming, and not to be controverted.

The antagonism between the productive powers and the social relations, with its "inner dialectic" of needs and potentialities, is the main driving force of history. The most dynamic of the productive powers is the rapid technological development of the instruments of production and the skill and inventiveness of human beings in creating and using these instruments.

This interpretation of history is not simply technological. In speaking of primitive epochs Marx does not use such technological labels as the stone age, the iron age, and the bronze age; likewise in characterizing modern epochs he does not employ technological terms such as eotechnic, paleotechnic, and neotechnic.[28] Instead he distinguishes historical periods by their socio-economic structures: the classless tribalism of the primitive gens; the class relations between slaves and owners, plebians and patricians in Greco-Roman civilization; between lords and serfs, or masters, journeymen, and apprentices in medieval society; between landed aristocrats and farmhands or peasants and between capitalists and industrial workers in bourgeois society. He never forgets that technology functions in a *social* context and that the ultimate source of technology is human labor of hand and brain. "Of all the instruments of production," he declares, "the greatest productive power is the revolutionary class itself."[29]

Doomed by its own inherent laws, capitalism will eventually stumble and fall and break its neck. The movement toward "the abyss" is already evident:

> Some parties may wail over it; others may wish to get rid of modern arts, in order to get rid of modern conflicts. Or they may imagine that so signal a progress in industry wants to be completed by as signal a regress in politics. On our part, we do not mistake the shrewd spirit that continues to mark all these contradictions. We know that to work well the newfangled forces of society, they only want to be mastered by newfangled men—and such are the workingmen. They are as much the invention of modern times as machinery itself. In

[28]Labels of this technological type are employed by Patrick Geddes in several books and by Lewis Mumford in *Technics and Civilization* (New York: Harcourt, Brace and Company, 1934).

[29]Marx, *The Poverty of Philosophy*, in Saul K. Padover, *On Revolution*, p. 24.

the signs that bewilder the middle class, the aristocracy, and the poor prophets of regression, we do recognize our brave friend Robin Goodfellow,[30] the old mole that can work the earth so fast, that worthy pioneer—the Revolution.

In words of fiery prophecy Marx envisages the inexorable outcome:

> To revenge the misdeeds of the ruling class, there existed in the Middle Ages, in Germany, a secret tribunal called the "Vehmgericht." If a red cross was seen marked on a house, people knew that its owner was doomed by the "Vehm." All the houses of Europe are now marked with the mysterious red cross. History is the judge—its executioner, the proletarian.

Marx thus concluded his "little speech in English"—as he termed his address to the assembled workingmen—with the prophecy of proletarian revolution.

5. The Outer Dialectic: Conflict Between Productive Forces and Productive Relations

In his speech Marx points to the conflict between "the productive powers and the social relations" as the acme of dialectical contradictions. His terminology in referring to this conflict varies. He speaks of "forces of production" and "forms of intercourse" in The German Ideology; "productive forces" and "social relations" in The Poverty of Philosophy; "means of production" and "relations of property" in the Communist Manifesto; "the forces of production" and "the relations of production" in the Preface to A Contribution to the Critique of Political Economy. These differences in terminology may indicate subtle shadings in meaning, but the idea that there is a structural conflict within the "base" is common to all the phrasings.

One way of interpreting this conflict is in terms of the

---

[30]A mischievous character known as Puck in Shakespeare's A Midsummer Night's Dream.

theory of "lag" of the American sociologist William F. Ogburn.[31] This theory focuses on different tempos of change: technological innovation develops at a more rapid pace than institutional and cultural transformation; maladjustment results from the incongruity between these fast and slow changes. In Marx's terminology, the forces of production develop more rapidly than the relations of production, and consequently there is a fundamental disequilibrium in the productive system. Revolution consists in the restoration of equilibrium by the transformation of the lagging social relations so as to harmonize with the productive forces.

Despite the contention of Göran Therborn that Marx's theory of crisis is completely different from Ogburn's, [32] the social lag interpretation is incomplete rather than mistaken. According to Marx, the members of the dominant class are resistant to change that would deprive them of their privileges. They use the repressive force of the state and the persuasive force of ideology to block the profound restructuring of human relations without which poverty cannot be abolished. No one is more insistent than Marx that the class structure is an anachronism. In this sense he *does* recognize a fundamental lag.

This is not the whole story. He maintains that there are incompatible *directions* as well as different *tempos* of change. One direction is the movement toward consolidation of wealth and power, especially the swift growth of big business with its contraction in the number of independent establishments. As economic organizations grow in magnitude and shrink in number the hierarchical structures become more elaborate, communication between the various ranks becomes more difficult, and members of the "power

[31]See William F. Ogburn, *On Culture and Social Change,* ed. by Otis Dudley Duncan (Chicago: University of Chicago Press, 1964). Ogburn says that his theory of social lag was derived in large measure from his reading of Marx.

[32]See Göran Therborn, *Science, Class and Society: On the Formation of Sociology and Historical Materialism* (London: NLB, 1976), pp. 358–361.

elite" increasingly regard the masses as pawns to manipulate. The opposite movement is the rapid expansion of the forces of production with its attendant drive toward equal sharing of power and wealth. Consequently, liberation from bondage to material conditions, from poverty and excessive toil, is a demand that is more and more irresistible. Because the expansion of the productive forces is accompanied by rising expectations, the movement toward equality gathers force and momentum. These two movements—the most powerful in modern life—are diametrically opposed. Both social lag and directional conflict figure in Marx's account of the contradiction between the forces and the relations of production.

Marx was not content with a few generalities. Although his exposition of similar contradictions in past civilizations remained sketchy, his analysis of the contradictions of capitalism in the *Grundrisse, Capital,* and *Theories of Surplus Value* is far from brief. I shall present only the barest summary, omitting criticism pro or con.

He begins with "the labor theory of value." An article, if it is to possess economic value, must be (a) the product of labor-power, (b) exchangeable on the market, and (c) socially useful.

> A thing can be a use-value, without having [economic] value. This is the case whenever its utility to man is not due to labour. Such are air, virgin soil, natural meadows, &c. A thing can be useful, and the product of human labour, without being a commodity. Whoever directly satisfies his wants with the produce of his own labour, creates, indeed, use-values, but not commodities. In order to produce the latter, he must not only produce use-values, but use-values for others, social use-values. Lastly, nothing can have value, without being an object of utility. If the thing is useless, so is the labour contained in it; the labour does not count as labour, and therefore creates no value.[33]

---

[33]*Capital* (Chicago: Charles H. Kerr & Company, 1906), Vol. I, pp. 47–48.

Such is the theory not only of Marx, but of Adam Smith and David Ricardo and almost all the economists who preceded Marx.

He added the proviso that exchange value is based upon "socially necessary labour time." This means that the exchange value of a commodity is determined by "the quantity of labour necessary for its production in a given state of society, under certain social average conditions of production, with a given social average intensity, and average skill of the labour employed."[34] It is a theory of averages at the given technological level.

As I have remarked in Chapter I, Marx also added a theory of "surplus value." The worker, lacking capital, is forced to sell his labor-power as a commodity. Its exchange value, like that of any other commodity, is determined by the amount of socially necessary labor time required to produce it. This quantity is the amount of labor needed to maintain the worker, to train him with the requisite skill, and to bring up a certain quota of children who are to replace him on the labor market when he wears out. Ordinarily the wage that the capitalist pays is a rough measure of this exchange value. The laborer, however, normally produces more value than is represented by his wages.

> The labour-process may continue beyond the time necessary to reproduce and incorporate in the product a mere equivalent for the value of the labour-power. Instead of the six hours that are sufficient for the latter purpose, the process may continue for twelve hours. The action of labour-power, therefore, not only reproduces its own value, but produces value over and above it. This surplus-value is the difference between the value of the product and the value of the elements consumed in the formation of that product, in other words, of the means of production and the labour-power.[35]

[34]*Value, Price and Profit* (New York: International Publishers, 1935), p. 33.
[35]*Capital*, Vol. I, p. 232. The twelve hour work-day was common when this passage was written.

Labor-power produces more value than it costs. This unpaid labor-power is the source of profits. Without it capitalism—the private profit-system—cannot exist.

Technology is the most powerful means of business enterprise for increasing the productivity of labor and gaining a competitive advantage over other companies. Large scale production, at a higher technological level, is generally cheaper per unit of output. The smaller companies cannot afford mass production and expensive new machinery; hence they are eliminated in the fierce competition for profits. This explains a fundamental feature of the Marxist model: the unceasing drive for new techniques. Each individual business must improve its technology if it is to survive. Hence technological acceleration is a necessary ingredient of business enterprises.

Because "constant capital" (the cost of plant and machinery) has the function of increasing the productivity of "variable capital" (the cost of labor-power), the proportion of constant to variable capital increases. "If it was originally say 1:1, it now becomes successively 2:1, 3:1, 4:1, 5:1, 7:1, &c"[36] When less and less labor-power is spent on each commodity, the creation of surplus value is decreased and the basis of profit shrinks. This means that the *rate* of profit must decline, although the *mass* of profit, under large-scale production, may rise. The falling rate of profit, in the long run, is a mortal threat to the profit-system.

The machines utilized in large-scale production represent an enormously augmented productive capacity, but under capitalism they compete against workers and displace many of them. Receiving in wages a diminishing proportion of the value they produce, the workers (who are also the bulk of consumers) do not have the buying power to purchase the products that highly mechanized industry can pour forth so prolifically. The result is a constant tendency toward overproduction in relation to effective demand and underproduction in relation to human needs and the capacity to produce. As Engels explained:

[36]*Ibid.*, p. 690.

> Too little is produced. . . . But *why* is too little produced? Not because the [technical] limits of production . . . are exhausted. No, but because the limits of production are determined not by the number of hungry bellies, but by the number of *purses* able to buy and to pay. The moneyless bellies, the labour which cannot be utilized *for profit* and therefore cannot buy, is left to the death-rate.[37]

The increasing disparity between the capacity of society to produce and its capacity to consume makes the profit-system more and more erratic and leads to a crazy succession of inflations and depressions. Employers attempt to safeguard profits by capturing foreign markets and finding cheaper labor power and raw materials in the "underdeveloped" countries. The nations, goaded on by business interests, are driven into imperialistic rivalry and conflict. War may temporarily revive employment and profits, but at the cost of a deeper crisis in the postwar period.

While wealth and power are being concentrated in the hands of the few, the workers become ever more regimented and class conscious. The incongruity between the *social* organization of production in the factory and the *individual* ownership and control of the means of production becomes more flagrant. The government, as an instrument of the ruling class, seeks to preserve class privileges, and the economic elite refuse to surrender their power. The expansion of the technological forces of production is combined with the contraction of the capitalist class. These "contradictions" become more and more intolerable.

> The monopoly of capital becomes a fetter upon the mode of production, which has sprung up and flourished along with, and under it. Centralization of the means of production and socialization of labour at last reach a point where they become incompatible with their capitalist integument. This integument is burst asunder. The knell of capitalist private property sounds. The expropriators are expropriated.[38]

[37]Marx and Engels, *Selected Correspondence 1846–1895*, p. 199.
[38]*Capital*, I, p. 836.

6. The Inner Dialectic of Powers and Needs

The dialectical conflict between the forces and relations of production is matched by an inner dialectic—the disparity between thought and being, ideal and fact, hope and accomplishment, "ought" and "is." The objective social conditions, falling glaringly short of the potential, cannot satisfy human aspirations. Consequently human beings fear and detest the existing order, and in thought soar beyond it. They may leap ahead in fantasy to an idealized future (Utopianism), or return in nostalgic reverie to an idealized past (archaism), or seek escape in religious supernaturalism, or demand revolution and gird for action. Traditional "Marxism" has largely ignored the inward dialectic and has emphasized only the outer. Consequently it has been quick to recognize the crisis of institutions and slow to recognize the crisis of the human person. It has presented a one-sided interpretation of Marx. The existentialists have countered with an equally one-sided emphasis on personal crisis and inner life. Both the "Marxists" and the existentialists fail to realize that Marx himself had supplied the corrective.

If change is only outward, there will be no revolutionary consequences. Inflations and depressions will simply adjust supply to demand and thus restore the economic equilibrium. "The crises are always but momentary and forcible solutions of the existing contradictions, violent eruptions, which restore the disturbed equilibrium for a while."[39] The process of restoring the equilibrium "already implies as a pre-condition the opposite of equilibration and may therefore comprise crisis; the crisis itself may be a form of equilibration."[40] Considered in isolation Marx's economic theory does not entail breakdown and revolution. It entails no more than economic crises that function as necessary restorative forces through which the whole eco-

[39] *Capital*, III, p. 292.
[40] Marx, *Theories of Social Value* (Moscow: Progress Publishers, 1968), II, p. 521. Translation modified.

nomic system is recharged. Even though Marx argues that capitalist crises "will become more and more catastrophic," he maintains that capitalism will not "collapse spontaneously and inevitably through the workings of its internal contradictions."[41] Without the active intervention of human beings *conscious* of their suffering and *determined* to end it, the crises will recur without foreseeable limit. Revolutionary transformation will ensue when and *only when* the inner dialectic of radical needs matches the outward dialectic of socio-economic contradictions.

I have already indicated the nature of the inner dialectic in my discussion of alienation in Chapter 3 and abstraction in Chapter 4. Other factors in this "inner" side of historical development are the unity of theory and practice, the importance of class consciousness, and the elements of mental growth in scientific-technological innovation. The stage of revolutionary transformation requires institutional creativity, which cannot be blind and mindless. I shall now make more explicit the role of needs and powers in revolutionary transformation.

The driving forces of the inner dialectic are "power" and "need." A need arises when there is an impulse that is frustrated, or at least, unconsummated. If it is a choiceworthy need, it is strong and durable enough to be worthy of attention and compatible with a working harmony among genuine needs. Some needs blend well with others and some do not. As Bertrand Russell has remarked, love is better than murder because it suits both parties and murder suits only one. Love is a viable need because it corresponds to powers deep in human nature and blends well with other needs, and murder is not viable because it is incompatible with deep-rooted powers and the needs that spring from them.

Bertell Ollman points out that "power" (Kraft) and "need" (Bedurfnis) are terms frequently used by Marx to denote the basis of human drives. The powers are the dy-

---

[41]Alan Swingewood, *Marx and Modern Social Theory*, pp. 193–194.

namic core of man's natural being pressing toward fulfillment. Synonyms for "power" include "faculty," "ability,"
"function," "capacity," and "potentiality." The needs are
the felt wants that spring from this natural basis. The combination of need and the neglected power to satisfy the need
makes the historical situation explosive. To quote Ollman:

> Each power is coupled in man with a distinctive need for the
> objects necessary for its realization, to make itself known and
> allow for its development as a power. Likewise, a power is
> whatever is used that "fulfills" a need. To know any power is
> therefore to know its corresponding need and vice versa.[42]

The following brief account is much less detailed than Ollman's exposition (see Part II of his book).

Among the needs that are basic and blend well are
those whose fulfillment is essential for survival. They must
be the foundation of all other needs because life itself depends upon them:

> We must begin by stating the first premise of all human exis-
> tence and therefore, of all history, the premise, namely, that
> man must be in a position to live in order to be able to "make
> history." But life involves before everything else eating and
> drinking, housing, clothing and various other things. The first
> historical act is thus the production of the means to satisfy
> these needs, the production of material life itself. And indeed
> this is an historical act, a fundamental condition of all history,
> which today, as thousands of years ago, must daily and hourly
> be fulfilled merely in order to sustain human life.[43]

The "natural needs" are the permanent and general conditions of life itself, and beyond bare survival, of effective
human living. Fundamental biological values, such as nu-
tritious food, decent shelter, warm clothing, enough rest
and exercise, and health care, cannot be neglected without
undermining all other values. But we would mistake

---

[42]Bertell Ollman, *Alienation: Marx's Conception of Man in Capitalist Society* (Cambridge at the University Press, 1971), p. 78.
[43]*The German Ideology*, in Marx/Engels, *Collected Works* (New York: International Publishers, 1976), Vol. 5, pp. 41–42.

Marx's intent if we were to suppose that he wanted to scale life down to these necessities. The more "ideal values," such as beauty, knowledge, love and cooperation, and creative work, are, if less basal, no less indispensable to the healthy human organism. They are necessary elements in the total organic fulfillment that is Marx's norm of a good life and a good society.

Natural needs are rooted in a core of human nature that is relatively immune to historical change. Looking forward to the future communist society Marx observes:

> Communist organization has a twofold effect on the desires produced in the individual by present-day relations—*namely desires which exist under all relations, and only change their form and direction under different social relations*—[which] are merely altered by the communist social system, for they are given the opportunity to develop normally; but *others— namely those originating solely in a particular society, under particular conditions of production and intercourse*—are totally deprived of their conditions of existence. Which of the desires will be merely changed and which eliminated in a communist society can only be determined in a practical way, by changing the real, actual "desires," and not by making comparisons with earlier historical conditions.[44] (My italics.)

Marx declares that the rifts and conflicts in capitalist society prevent even the relatively fixed desires from developing normally. The fact is

> that one desire of an individual in modern society can be satisfied at the expense of all others, and that this "ought not to be" and that this is more or less the case with all individuals in the world today and that thereby the free development of the individual as a whole is impossible. . . . The communists have no intension of abolishing the fixedness of their desires and needs . . . ; they only strive to achieve an organ-

---

[44]*Ibid.*, pp. 255–256. In Marx's manuscript this passage, including my next quotation, has been crossed out, but the same distinction between permanent and impermanent traits is expressed in *Capital*, I, p. 668.

ization of production and intercourse which will make possible the normal satisfaction of all needs.[45]

"Normal satisfaction" changes the need but not to the point of eradicating it.

Hunger is hunger, but hunger gratified by cooked meat eaten with a knife and fork is a different hunger from that which bolts down raw meat with the aid of hand, nail and tooth.[46]

The refinement and elaboration of animal needs make them human. This fact is evident not only in the case of hunger but of the sex-drive.

The relation of man to woman is the *most natural* relation of human being to human being. It indicates, therefore, how far man's *natural* behaviour has become *human,* and how far his *human* essence has become a *natural* essence for him, how far his *human nature* has become *nature* for him. It also shows how far man's needs have become *human* needs, and consequently how far the other person, as a person, has become one of his needs, and to what extent he is in his individual existence at the same time a social being. . . . From this relationship man's whole level of development can be assessed.[47]

Their modes of satisfaction may be refined and humanized, but hunger and sex and the other "natural needs" remain permanent drives of human nature.

In Chapter 3, I said that among the deep-rooted powers and potentialities discussed by Marx are sociality, productivity, universality, freedom, and wholeness. Corresponding to these are needs that involve more than the simple maintenance of human life; but like the "natural needs," they are among the relatively permanent drives of human nature. The "man rich in needs" cultivates and fulfills these basic propensities.

[45]*Ibid.,* p. 256.
[46]*Grundrisse,* trans. by Martin Nicolaus (Harmondsworth: Penguin Books, 1973), p. 92.
[47]*Economic and Philosophical Manuscripts,* in Marx, *Early Writings,* trans. by T. B. Bottomore (London: C. A. Watts & Co., 1963), p. 154.

7. The Economic System in the Light of Human Needs

In the *Economic and Philosophical Manuscripts* Marx describes the ideal working man from the standpoint of pro-capitalist "political economy." Wages must be held down and work intensified to maximize profits. The workers must save to provide funds for capital investment.

> Political economy, the science of *wealth,* is, therefore, at the same time, the science of renunciation, of privation and of saving. . . . Its moral ideal is the *worker* who takes part of his wages to the savings bank. . . . Its principal thesis is the renunciation of life and of human needs. The less you eat, drink, buy books, go to the theatre or to balls, or to the public house, and the less you think, love, theorize, sing, paint, fence, etc. the more you will be able to save and the *greater* will become your treasure which neither moth nor rust will corrupt—your *capital.* The less you *are,* the less you express your life, the more you *have,* the greater is your alienated life, and the greater is the saving of your alienated being.[48]

The values of a truly human life are the exact opposite of the poverty and wealth of pro-capitalist political economy.

> The fully constituted society produces man in all the plenitude of his being, the wealthy man endowed with all the senses, as an enduring reality. . . . In place of the *wealth* and *poverty* of political economy, we have the *wealthy* man and the plentitude of *human* need. The wealthy man is at the same time one who *needs* a complex of human manifestations of life, and whose own self-realization exists as an inner necessity, a need. Not only the wealth but also the *poverty* of man acquires, in a socialist perspective, a *human* and thus a social meaning. Poverty is the passive bond which leads man to experience a need for the greatest wealth, the *other* person.[49]

In prizing the industrious and frugal worker, the employer is viewing industry from the perspective of the cost and volume of production. When his focus instead is on

[48]*Ibid.,* p. 171.
[49]*Ibid.,* pp. 162, 164–165.

selling the products, his emphasis shifts to extracting money from the consumer by any method that boosts sales:

> No eunuch flatters his tyrant more shamefully or seeks by more infamous means to stimulate his jaded appetite, in order to gain some favour, than does the eunuch of industry, the entrepreneur, in order to acquire a few silver coins or to charm the gold from the purse of his dearly beloved neighbor. . . . Every real or potential need is a weakness which will draw the bird into the lime. . . . The entrepreneur accedes to the most depraved fancies of his neighbour, plays the role of pander between him and his needs, awakens unhealthy appetites in him, and watches every weakness so that later on he may claim remuneration for this labour of love.[50]

In the attempt to increase the margin of profit, the business man manipulates needs by salesmanship and advertising, but the effect is more often to spark pseudo-needs than genuine needs. Long before Herbert Marcuse wrote *One-Dimensional Man*, Marx caustically described the manipulation of needs and its effect in the cheapening of life.

The attempt to substitute pseudo-needs in place of real and genuine needs cannot succeed ultimately. The drives of human nature are too strong: "self-realization exists as an inner necessity." In the Introduction to the *Contribution to the Critique of Hegel's Philosophy of Right*, the youthful Marx speaks of "radical needs" that spring from the deepest levels of human nature and that cannot be satisfied within the existing social structure:

> To be radical is to grasp things by the root. But for man the root is man himself. . . . The *categorical imperative* is to overthrow all those conditions in which man is an abased, enslaved, abandoned, contemptible being. . . . A radical revolution can only be a revolution of radical needs.[51]

Marx asks, Who are the bearers of these radical needs? Who are the revolutionists?

[50]*Ibid.*, p. 169.
[51]*Contribution to the Critique of Hegel's Philosophy of Right: Introduction,* in Marx, *Early Writings,* pp. 52, 54.

This is our reply. A class must be formed which has *radical chains,* a class in civil society, a class which is the dissolution of all classes, a sphere of society which has a universal character because its sufferings are universal, and which does not claim a *particular redress* because the wrong which is done to it is not a *particular wrong* but *wrong in general.* There must be formed a sphere of society which claims no traditional status but only a human status . . . ; a sphere, finally, which cannot emancipate itself without emancipating itself from all the other spheres of society, without, therefore, emancipating all these other spheres; which is, in short, a *total loss* of humanity and which can only redeem itself by a *total redemption of humanity.* This dissolution of society, as a particular class, is the *proletariat.*[52]

The dialectic in the individual psyche and the dialectic in the world of institutions cannot be sundered. Marx speaks of the "forces of production and social relations" as "two different sides of the development of the social individual."[53] Without the spur of radical needs this development cannot occur. The needs are too imperative, too deeply based. They cannot be brushed aside; but to germinate they must be expressed in ideas grasped by the same masses.

> Material force can only be overthrown by material force; but theory itself becomes a material force when it is seized by the masses. Theory is capable of seizing the masses . . . as soon as it becomes radical.[54]

The radical needs embodied in radical ideas are the seeds of revolution.

Agnes Heller, in her penetrating study of Marx's theory of need, points out the consequences:

---

[52]*Ibid.,* p. 58.

[53]*Grundrisse,* trans. Nicolaus, p. 706.

[54]*Early Writings,* p. 52. For Marx's contention that human conditions must get worse before they get better, see *Economic and Philosophical Manuscripts,* trans. Bottomore, pp. 119, 160, 163, 202–203, 208.

Thus only the radical needs enable man, in the interests of satisfying them, to bring about a social formation which is radically, "from the root," different from the previous one, a society in which the radically new system of needs will be different from all earlier ones.[55]

The new system will be different not in the sense that it will deny deeply based needs but that it will liberate the old needs and create new ones. The climax of the inner dialectic, like the climax of the outer dialectic, is revolution. They are the double aspects of the same movement.

8. The Future as History: Revolution and Reconstruction

The word "revolution" has various meanings. It sometimes means the overthrow of an established government, for example, in English history, the expelling of James II and the conferring of sovereignty on William and Mary. Marx would call this change, which did not involve a transfer of power from one ruling class to another, a "coup" rather than a revolution. More truly revolutionary was the destruction of feudal prerogatives and the elevation of the bourgeoisie in the French Revolution. Marx believed that the forthcoming communist revolution will be far more radical than even the French Revolution in penetrating to the root of things. It will not merely shift power from the bourgeoisie to the proletariat but will eventually abolish the political state and economic classes altogether. If we are to use "revolution" in this extended sense, it means a profound change in almost all aspects of life. Revolution of this kind is a long and difficult process—more so than perhaps Marx realized.

In *The German Ideology* Marx indicates that the revolutionary transformation must be twofold, inner and outer. On the one hand "the power of the earlier mode of production and intercourse and social organization is over-

[55]Agnes Heller, *The Theory of Need in Marx*, p. 98. See Heller's book for a detailed interpretation of Marx's theory of need.

213

thrown." On the other hand "there develops the universal character and the energy of the proletariat, without which the revolution cannot be accomplished; and in which, further, the proletariat rids itself of everything that still clings to it from its previous position in society."[56] A new "communist consciousness" must be created:

> Both for the production on a mass scale of this communist consciousness, and for the success of the cause itself, the alteration of men on a mass scale is necessary, an alteration which can only take place in a practical movement, a *revolution*; the revolution is necessary, therefore, not only because the *ruling* class cannot be overthrown in any other way, but also because the class *overthrowing* it can only in a revolution succeed in ridding itself of all the muck of ages and become fitted to found society anew.[57]

In insisting on the interdependence of institutional and psychological transformation Marx is being true to the principle that he stated in his third "Thesis on Feuerbach" that self-changing and the changing of circumstances go hand in hand. The same principle is expressed in *Capital*:

> By thus acting on the external world and changing it, [man] at the same time changes his own nature. He develops his slumbering powers and compels them to act in obedience to his sway.[58]

The thought of these passages is that life is a unity in which the inner and the outer develop interdependently.

If outer change is unaccompanied by inner transformation the result, even though labelled "communism," will be retrogression. In a passage in the Paris *Manuscripts* referring to some communist theories then extant, Marx condemns a form of "crude communism" in which the avarice characteristic of capitalism would persist. He had earlier explained that bourgeois society is dominated by "the sense of having" rather than "the sense of being." "All

[56]*The German Ideology* in *Collected Works*, Vol. 5, p. 88.
[57]*Ibid.*, pp. 52–53.
[58]*Capital*, Vol. I. p. 198.

passions and activities" are "submerged in avarice." Even
the wage earner, although he receives very little of the
goods of life, has little else to live for. "The worker must
have just what is necessary for him to want to live, and he
must want to live only in order to have this."[59] In crude
communism the avarice would remain. The hatred of private property would be a morbid, although inverted, addic-
tion to acquisitive interests. It would not abolish but uni-
versalize the sense of having.

> This communism, which negates the *personality* of man in
> every sphere, is only the logical expression of private prop-
> erty.... Universal *envy* setting itself up as a power is only a
> camouflaged form of cupidity which re-establishes itself and
> satisfies itself in a different way.... Crude communism is
> only the culmination of ... envy and levelling down on the
> basis of a *preconceived* minimum. How little this abolition of
> private property represents a genuine appropriation is shown
> by the abstract negation of the whole world of culture and
> civilization, and the regression to the unnatural simplicity of
> the poor and wantless individual who has not only not sur-
> passed private property but has not yet even attained to it.[60]

The twofold nature of the revolutionary transformation
is clarified in the *Grundrisse*. The very development of industrial mechanization, which has enslaved the worker to a
dehumanizing routine, is fast making that enslavement an
irrational, unworkable anachronism. As a result of the technological progress that we now call "automation," the basis
of productivity has largely shifted from the exploitation of
labor to the practical application of science.

> Direct labour and its quantity cease to be the determining
> element in production and thus in the creation of use
> value.... The transformation of the process of production
> from the simple labour process into a scientific process ...
> subjects the forces of nature and converts them to the service
> of human needs.... The human factor is restricted to watch-
> ing and supervising the production process.... The surplus

[59]*Economic and Philosophical Manuscripts*, p. 172.
[60]*Ibid.*, pp. 153–154.

labour of the masses has ceased to be a condition for the development of wealth in general; in the same way that the non-labour of the few has ceased to be a condition for the development of the general powers of the human mind. Production based on exchange value therefore falls apart, and the immediate process of material production finds itself stripped of its impoverished, antagonistic form. Individuals are then in a position to develop freely. It is no longer a question of reducing the necessary labour time in order to create surplus labour, but of reducing the necessary labour of society to a minimum. The counterpart of this reduction is that all members of society can develop their education in the arts, sciences, etc., thanks to the free time and means available to all.[61]

Marx predicts that the great increase in human productivity and the replacement of labor power by automation will necessitate the most radical revolution that humankind has ever undergone.

As long ago as the fourth century B.C. Aristotle had some inkling of the changes that "automation" could bring. In a remarkable passage in the *Politics,* he pointed out that "if every instrument could accomplish its work, . . . if the shuttle would weave and the plectrum touch the lyre without a hand to guide them, chief workmen would not want servants, nor masters slaves."[62] By the end of the nineteenth century, Oscar Wilde had reinterpreted Aristotle's premonition as the key to a practicable Utopia:

Civilization requires slaves. . . . Unless there are slaves to do the ugly, horrible, uninteresting work, culture and contemplation become almost impossible. Human slavery is wrong, insecure, and demoralizing. On mechanical slavery, on the slavery of the machine, the future of the world depends. . . . At present machinery competes against man. Under proper conditions machinery will serve man. . . . The machines will be the new slaves.[63]

[61]*The Grundrisse,* trans. by David McLellan (New York: Harper and Row Torchbook, 1972), pp. 136, 142.
[62]Aristotle, *Politics,* 1253b.
[63]Oscar Wilde, *The Soul of Man Under Socialism.*

Several decades before Wilde wrote these words, Marx incorporated the following sentences from Wilhelm Schulz, a German economist, in his Paris *Manuscripts:*

> The important distinction between how far men work *with* machines or *as* machines, has not received attention. . . . But in the future life of mankind, the mindless forces of nature at work in machinery will be our slaves and serfs.[64]

In the years that intervened between the writing of the *Economic and Philosophical Manuscripts* (1844) and the composition of the *Grundrisse* (1857–1858), Marx studied in great detail the technological developments that could convert Schultz' Utopian vision into practical reality.

As the technological basis of human emancipation becomes ever more apparent, the irrationality of the institutional fetters becomes more and more obvious. The tension between essence and existence, potentiality and actuality, need and realization, hope and fulfillment, reaches its height. Marx found in these contradictions the necessity for a rebirth of the humanist ideal:

> Thus the old view, in which the human being appears as the aim of production, regardless of his limited national, religious, political character, seems to be very lofty when contrasted to the modern world, where production appears as the aim of mankind and wealth as the aim of production. In fact, however, when the limited bourgeois form is stripped away, what is wealth other than the universality of individual needs, capacities, pleasures, productive forces, etc., created through universal exchange? The full development of human mastery over the forces of nature, those of so-called nature as well as humanity's own nature? The absolute working-out of his creative potentialities, . . . the development of all human powers as such the end in itself. . .?[65]

In these questions, Marx poses anew the humanist ideal that he had expressed in his early writings.

His notes on James Mill written in the spring and sum-

[64]*Economic and Philosophical Manuscripts,* p. 80.
[65]*Grundrisse,* trans. by Martin Nicolaus, pp. 487–488.

mer of 1844 expound his ideal of productive labor as the free expression of man's communal nature:

> Since the essence of man is the true community of man, men, by activating their own essence, produce, create this human community, this social being which is no abstract, universal power standing over against the solitary individual, but is the essence of every individual, his own activity, his own life, his own spirit, his own wealth. . . . Men, not as abstractions, but as real, living, particular individuals, are this community. As they are, so it is too. . . . [66]

There is a difference in emphasis between the comments of Marx in 1844 and his statements in 1857–1858, when he wrote the *Grundrisse*. In 1844 the emphasis was on making work more humane and communal; in 1857–1858 the emphasis was on freeing humanity from work.

The restatement of the human ideal in the third volume of *Capital* combines the two emphases:

> Just as the savage must wrestle with Nature in order to satisfy his wants, to maintain and reproduce his life, so also must civilized man, and he must do it in all forms of society and under any possible mode of production. With his development the realm of natural necessity expands, because his wants increase, but at the same time the forces of production, by which these wants are satisfied, also increase. Freedom in this field cannot consist of anything else but the fact that socialized mankind, the associated producers, regulate their interchange with Nature rationally, bring it under their common control, instead of being ruled by it as by some blind power, and accomplish their task with the least expenditure of energy and under such conditions as are proper and worthy for human beings. Nevertheless, this always remains a realm of necessity. Beyond it begins that development of human potentiality for its own sake, the true realm of freedom, which however can only flourish upon that realm of

[66]"Excerpts from James Mill's *Elements of Political Economy*," in Marx, *Early Writings*, trans. by Rodney Livingstone and Gregor Benton (New York: Random House, 1975), p. 265.

necessity as its basis. The shortening of the working day is its fundamental prerequisite.[67]

Although Marx looked forward to the time when work would cease to be alien, forced labor, he cherished the hope that working time would be sharply curtailed. There would then be the need to cultivate a way of life in accordance with very different possibilities. The humiliating idea that the human being is a working animal would no longer correspond to the facts of life. There would be far more opportunity for love and play and art, the enjoyment of wild nature, the adventures of the mind, the cultivation of life in its sparkle and diversity.

Without discussing the well-worn themes of the political and economic transition to communism, I shall quote Marx's prophecy that the communist society of the future will overcome the schisms and alienations to which human life has been prey:

> *Communism* is the *positive* abolition of *private property*, of *human self-alienation*, and thus the real *appropriation* of *human* nature through and for man. It is, therefore, the return of man himself as a *social*, i.e. really human, being, a complete and conscious return which assimilates all the wealth of previous development. Communism as a fully developed naturalism is humanism and as a fully developed humanism is naturalism. It is the *definitive* resolution of the antagonism between man and nature, and between man and man. It is the true solution of the conflict between existence and essence, between objectification and self-affirmation, between freedom and necessity, between individual and species. It is the solution of the riddle of history and knows itself to be this solution.[68]

9. *Unsituated and Situated Freedom*

Marx's conception of revolution and its creative aftermath is reflected in his attitude toward Shelley. He is said to

[67]*Capital*, III, as translated in Marx, *Selected Writings in Sociology and Social Philosophy*, ed. by T. B. Bottomore and Maximilien Rubel (London: C. A. Watts & Co., 1956), pp. 254–255.
[68]*Economic and Philosophical Manuscripts*, p. 155.

have expressed "regret . . . that Shelley died at twenty-nine, for he was a revolutionary through and through, and would always have been in the vanguard of socialism."[69] S. S. Prawer, in quoting this statement from Edward Aveling's pamphlet, *Shelley's Socialism*, remarks that Aveling was an unreliable informant. I doubt that he was unreliable in this instance. His wife Eleanor Marx, who collaborated in the preparation of the pamphlet, would not have accepted a statement about her father that had no basis in fact.

The intense admiration of Marx for Aeschylus' *Prometheus Bound* would naturally impel him to read its romantic sequel *Prometheus Unbound*. He must have been moved by Shelley's tribute to Prometheus:

> To suffer woes which Hope thinks infinite;
> To forgive wrongs darker than death or night;
> To defy Power, which seems omnipotent;
> To love, and bear; to hope till Hope creates
> From its own wreck the thing it contemplates:
> Neither to change, nor falter, nor repent:
> This, like thy glory, Titan! is to be
> Good, great and joyous, beautiful and free;
> This is alone Life, Joy, Empire, and Victory.

I doubt that Marx approved the line: "To forgive wrongs darker than death or night." He was an angry man, and forgiveness was scarcely in his nature. But Hope and defiance of Power *were* deeply ingrained.

He may have responded warmly to Shelley's characterization of human liberation:

> And behold, thrones were kingless, and men walked
> One with the other even as spirits do,
> None fawned, none trampled. . . .
> The loathsome mask has fallen, the Man remains.—
> Sceptreless, free, uncircumscribed,—but man:
> Equal, unclassed, tribeless and nationless,
> Exempt from awe, worship, degree, the King
> Over himself. . . .

[69]Quoted by S. S. Prawer, *Karl Marx and World Literature* (Oxford at the Clarendon Press, 1976), p. 396.

This vision of an ideal future has been attacked as too negative. It seemed to H. N. Brailsford that man "unclassed, tribeless, and nationless" and "exempt from awe, worship, degree" is too characterless to excite even a "faint interest." "There is something amiss with an ideal which is constrained to express itself in negatives."[70] Similar reaction is implicit in Matthew Arnold's famous description of Shelley as "a beautiful and ineffectual angel beating in the void his luminous wings in vain."[71]

The same kind of attack has been directed against Marx in the concluding chapter of Charles Taylor's fine book on Hegel. Taylor speaks of Marx's "wildly unrealistic notion of the transition" to communism

> as a leap into untrammeled freedom, which simply sets aside the old restraints. . . . For Marx . . . early and late, held to a terribly unreal notion of freedom in which the opacity, division, indirectness and cross-purposes of social life were quite overcome. . . . All that is done in these negative characterizations is to think away the entire human situation. Small wonder then, that this freedom has no content.[72]

These strictures against Shelley and Marx remind me of C. D. Broad's characterization of the "kite-string fallacy." When the string is played out the kite flies high, but the tension of the downward pull of the string keeps the kite from flying higher. A child might think it would soar higher if the string were released. "Actually, as we all know, it would at once fall to the ground."[73] Similarly a naive person might assume that, since freedom is limited

[70]H. N. Brailsford, *Shelley, Godwin, and Their Circle* (New York: Henry Holt and Company, 1913), pp. 241–242.
[71]"Shelley" in *Poetry and Criticism of Matthew Arnold*, ed. by A. Dwight Culler (Boston: Houghton Mifflin Company, 1961), p. 380.
[72]Charles Taylor, *Hegel* (Cambridge University Press, 1975), pp. 554, 557, 559. For a contrasting interpretation of Marx's "vision" of a "free society," see William Leon McBride, *The Philosophy of Marx* (New York: St. Martin's Press, 1977), Ch. 7.
[73]C. D. Broad, *Examination of McTaggart's Philosophy* (Cambridge University Press, 1938), Vol. II, p. 505.

by concrete situations, it would soar much higher if the limitations were abolished. But a situationless freedom is as much of an illusion as a stringless flying kite. "The over-coming of all alienation and division leaves man without a situation," Taylor remarks, and the result "would be an utterly empty freedom."[74]

The attack upon "situationless freedom" may apply to Shelley's ethereal prophecy but less so to Marx's more earthly forecast. The model of organic totality impelled him to reject unsituated freedom. There is no freedom of the "natural man," inherent in the isolated individual, to be recovered by stripping away the "yoke" of social relations. As a young man Marx was deeply moved by the picture of alienated, unsituated men and women in Engels' *Condition of the Working Class in England:*

> The very turmoil of the streets has something repulsive, something against which human nature rebels. The hundreds of thousands of all classes and ranks crowding past each other, are they not all human beings with the same qualities and powers, and with the same interest in being happy? And still they crowd by one another as though they had nothing in common, nothing to do with another, and their only agree-ment is the tacit one, that each keep to his own side of the pavement . . . while it occurs to no man to honour another with so much as a glance. . . . This isolation of the individual, this narrow self-seeking is the fundamental principle of our society everywhere. . . . The dissolution of mankind into monads, of which each one has a separate principle, the world of atoms, is here carried to its utmost extreme. . . . Everywhere barbarous indifference, hard egotism on the one hand, and nameless misery on the other, everywhere social warfare, every man's house in a state of siege.[75]

All his life Marx protested against the "isolation of the individual, . . . the dissolution of mankind into monads, . . . the world of atoms."

[74]Taylor, *Hegel,* p. 558.
[75]Frederick Engels, *The Condition of the Working Class in England* (London: George Allen & Unwin Ltd., 1936), pp. 23–25. Written September 1844 to March 1845; published in Leipzig 1845; English edition, 1892.

How does Marx "situate" freedom? First, he situates it in human nature, and claims it as a universal right. In combatting press censorship as the young editor of the *Neue Rheinische Zeitung* he wrote:

> Freedom is so much the essence of man that even its opponents implement it while combatting its reality; they want to appropriate for themselves as a most precious ornament what they have rejected as an ornament of human nature. No man combats freedom; at most he combats the freedom of others. Hence every kind of freedom has always existed, only at one time as a special privilege, at another as a universal right.[76]

I have already quoted Marx's statement that "Man is a species-being . . . in the sense that he treats himself . . . as a *universal* and consequently free being."[77] Similarly in the *Communist Manifesto* Marx declares: "The free development of each is the condition for the free development of all." He agrees with Kant's contention that "the germs of human nature" propel mankind toward universal freedom.[78]

Marx contends that freedom can flourish only in a planning (not a pre-planned) society. This is the meaning of the statement in the Preface to his *Critique of Political Economy* that the communist revolution will bring "the prehistory of human society to a close." Our society is still in the stage of "pre-history"—the stage governed mainly by the blind movement of economic forces. Human history will truly begin only when the "associated producers," escaping from the tyranny of unconscious forces, will plan and control their own history. "United cooperative societies" will "regulate the national production under a com-

---

[76]*Rheinsiche Zeitung*, May 12, 1842 in Marx/Engels, *Collected Works* (New York: International Publishers, 1975), Vol. 1, p. 155.

[77]*Economic and Philosophical Manuscripts*, p. 126.

[78]See Immanuel Kant, *On History*, ed. by Lewis White Beck (Indianapolis: Bobbs-Merrill Company, 1963), especially "Idea for a Universal History from a Cosmopolitan Point of View."

mon plan.''[79] Mankind will then be the *agent* rather than the *patient* of historical forces.

To be free, this planning must spring from the grassroots of society. In *The Civil War in France* Marx contends that the cells of the new society should be self-governing communes. Productive establishments should be directed by "the cooperative association of the workers employed in them" because "the political rule of the producer cannot coexist with the perpetuation of his social slavery."[80] Robert C. Tucker has suggested "that Marx, if we can imagine him coming alive in Stalin's Russia (like Jesus Christ in Spain of the Inquisition as depicted by Dostoyevsky in the famous chapter of *The Brothers Karamazov*) would have been horrified to see the reality that his thinking had spawned, to whatever extent it had."[81] Marx cannot be entirely absolved from responsibility for these later developments. Although he was aware that "communism" is a mask for tyranny unless accomplished by the democratization and decentralization of power, he failed to make the dangers explicit except in some few stray remarks.

A society to be free must be based primarily on *qualitative* norms of use-value rather than *quantitative* norms of exchange-value. (The difference between the two kinds of value is explained lucidly in Chapter 7 of *Capital* I.) Emphasis on exchange-value is characteristic of an acquisitive society, whether it takes the form of possessive individualism or "crude communism." During the period of capitalistic expansion the norms have been unashamedly quantitative.

> Accumulate, accumulate! That is Moses and the prophets! . . .
> Accumulation for accumulation's sake, production for production's sake; by this formula classical economy expressed

[79] *The Civil War in France*, in Karl Marx, *Selected Works*, 2 vol. edition (New York: International Publishers, no date), II, p. 504.
[80] *Ibid.*, p. 503. See Raya Dunayevskaya, *Marxism and Freedom* (London: Pluto Press Ltd., 1971), p. 97.
[81] Robert C. Tucker, editor, *Stalinism: Essays in Historical Interpretation* (New York: W. W. Norton & Company, 1977), p. 321.

the historical mission of the bourgeoisie and did not for a single instant deceive itself over the birth-throes of wealth.[82]

No better are the propagators of a "crude communism" that is only "a camouflaged form of cupidity which re-establishes itself and satisfies itself in a different way." (See above, pp. 214–215.) Free human beings are not thus obsessed.

Marx's speculations about freedom were governed by his model of organic totality. The concept of achieving "to-tal" freedom by a "total" revolution haunted him. Not until the fragmentation of life by the excessive division of labor is overcome will human emancipation be achieved. The mere fragment of a man must be replaced "by the fully developed individual, fit for a variety of labors, ready to face any change in production, and to whom the different social functions he performs, are but so many modes of giving scope to his own natural and acquired powers."[83]

Finally, freedom is situated in a world of hard necessi-ties—the necessities both of our earthly habitat and of our human constitution. Human beings must struggle against "natural necessity" even in the most advanced commun-ism. "Just as the savage must wrestle with nature in order to satisfy his want," he wrote in a passage I have already quoted, "so civilized man has to do it, and he must do it in all forms of society and under all possible modes of produc-tion."[84] Although he looked forward to the time when work will cease to be "something repulsive, as external, forced labour," he did not suppose that it ever could become "mere fun, mere amusement." It will be "damned ser-ious . . . the most intensive exertion."[85] "The true realm of freedom," he declared, "can flourish only upon [the] realm of necessity as its basis."[86]

[82]*Capital*, I, p. 652.
[83]*Ibid.*, p. 534.
[84]*Capital*, III, p. 954.
[85]*Grundrisse der Kritik der Politischen Ökonomie* (Berlin: Dietz Verlag, 1953), pp. 504–505.
[86]*Capital*, III, pp. 954–955.

10. The Resurgence of the Dialectical Model

We have been mainly concerned with the base-superstructure and organic totality models, discussing the dialectical model only to the extent that it is incorporated in the other two. When we consider the long and deep revolution necessary to realize Marx's ideals, the dialectical model again comes to the fore.

I noted in the Introduction two root metaphors that are sources of the dialectical model. One metaphor is violent conflict. "War is the father of all and the king of all," said Heraclitus; "All things have their origin in strife." In the Communist movement this metaphor has been uppermost. The movement has emphasized beating down the enemy rather than cooperating with him. "Political power grows out of the barrel of a gun," declared Mao.

There are two reasons why the model of violent dialectic is now limited in its validity. One reason is the enormous increase in destructive potentialities since the death of Marx. As his contemporary, Winwood Reade, wrote in 1872:

> It is not probable that war will ever absolutely cease until science discovers some destroying force so simple in its administration, so horrible in its effects, that all art, all gallantry, will be at an end, and battles will be massacres which the feeling of mankind will be unable to endure.[87]

This peak of destructiveness has now been reached, and it is high time for war to be banished to the limbo of defunct institutions. Even the freelance practice of terrorism is intolerable.

The second reason is that the model of violent dialectic violates the ideals of Marx himself. The hope of ridding mankind of war, class struggle, and the repressive state is indelibly written into his creed. So obvious is this that

[87]Winwood Reade, *The Martyrdom of Man* (London: C. A. Watts & Co., Ltd., 1925), p. 415. (First edition, 1872.)

many interpreters of Marx have said that the dialectical process must cease at the stage of advanced communism.

They overlook the second root metaphor that underlies the dialectical model. This is dialogue. To repeat what I have said in the Preface, a dispute may begin when someone advances an idea as true. Advancing a counter-notion, the opponent tries to show that the original idea is false. The argument may continue until each party is made to see the weak spots in his or her own position and the strength of an opponent's. The disputants may then agree on a synthesis that is more inclusive and well balanced than either idea taken in isolation. I shall call this version the dialogic model to distinguish it from the Heraclitean version.

The natural locus of fruitful dialogue is community—a person-taken-as-person relation based on mutual respect. In Plato's "Socratic dialogues" it is ideally a search for wisdom among friends united in love of the truth and love of each other. When Socrates tries to engage in dialogue with an unfriendly adversary, as in the sharp exchange with Callicles in the *Gorgias*, the result is vituperation. Likewise in the *Republic*, when Socrates confronts the Sophist Thrasymachus, the prerequisites of dialogue are absent, and the dispute ends in angry withdrawal. In the remaining conversation between Socrates and Plato's half-brothers, Glaucon and Adeimantus, the brothers play too passive a role to fit the requirements of dialogue. Plato was too much the aristocrat, too unwilling to accept spiritual equality, too bent on dialectical mastery, to realize the ideal requirements of dialogue. Despite his greatness as a philosopher and literary artist, he never wrote "dialogue" in which the dialogic model is adequately exemplified.

Feuerbach stressed the *communal* basis of dialogue. True dialogue, he insisted, is not the conflict and synthesis of abstract ideas, nor the monologue of a solitary thinker with himself: "It is a dialogue between I and thou."[88] The starting point is the flesh-and-blood human being, not as an

[88]Ludwig Feuerbach, *Principles of the Philosophy of the Future* (Indianapolis: The Bobbs-Merrill Company, 1966), p. 72.

isolated individual but as a social person. "The essence of man" declared Feuerbach, "is contained only in the community and unity of man with man; it is a unity, however, which rests only on the distinction between I and thou."[89] Feuerbach conceived of the authentic self as arising from this social matrix:

> The other is my *thou*—the relation being reciprocal—my *alter ego*, man objective to me, the revelation of my own nature, the eye seeing itself. In another I first have the consciousness of humanity; through him I first learn, I first feel, that I am a man: in my love for him it is first clear to me that he belongs to me and I to him, that we two cannot be without each other, that only community constitutes humanity.[90]

The opposite of the I-Thou relation is the I-It relation—the interaction of a human being with a physical thing or a dehumanized individual—the relation of exploitation.

Among twentieth-century philosophers Martin Buber has explored the duality of I-Thou and I-It relations. The reading of Feuerbach's *Essence of Christianity*, he says, was the decisive influence in shaping his philosophy of dialogue. This influence is reflected in the contrast that he draws between the two types of relation. In the I-It relation, I regard the object, even if it be a He or She, as a thing. I stand apart from it in order to manipulate and exploit it—to bend it to my advantage. In this relation there is no reciprocity: the relation is that of master to instrument. If I treat someone as an *It*, I do not acknowledge *his* right to treat me as an *It* in return. In the I-Thou relation, one's essential being is in direct and sympathetic contact with another essential being. The Thou is cherished not as an *object* but as a *presence*, not as a *type* but as an *individual*, not as a *means* but as an *end*. The relation is reciprocal: I-Thou implies Thou-I. I not only give but receive; I not only speak but listen; I not only respond but invite response. The I is

[89]*Ibid.*, p. 71.
[90]Feuerbach, *The Essence of Christianity* (New York: C. Blanchard, 1855), p. 208.

constituted and remade in this relation of reciprocity: "Through the Thou a man becomes I."[91]

That Marx cherished a similar concept of reciprocity is evident from many passages, some of which I have quoted in Chapter 4. A good example is the following:

> In the individual expression of my own life I would have brought about the immediate expression of your life, and so in my individual activity I would have directly confirmed and realized my authentic nature, my human, communal nature. Our productions would be as many mirrors from which our natures would shine forth. This relation would be mutual: what applies to me would also apply to you. My labour would be the free expression and hence the enjoyment of life.[92]

In this ideal of free mutuality Marx is much closer to the Feuerbachian version of dialectics than to the Heraclitean. His grim recognition that the Heraclitean version is closer to the facts of life in no way invalidates the ideal, although it does underline the paradox of pursuing freedom by the methods of represssion. Until the ideal of free mutuality is realized in human affairs the revolution will be incomplete.

Marx realized far more clearly than Feuerbach that this ideal is unattainable in a class-divided society. Classes of men are driven by incompatibility of interests to endless struggles. The poor are in no condition to renounce strife.

> Black, mutinous discontent devours them; simply the miserablest feeling that can inhabit the heart of man.... This world is for them no home, but a dingy prison-house, of reckless unthrift, rebellion, rancour, indignation against themselves and against all men.[93]

[91]Martin Buber, I and Thou (New York: Charles Scribner's Sons, 1937), p. 3. See Paul E. Pfuetze, The Social Self (New York: Bookman Associates, 1954) for an account not only of Buber but of the similar ideas of George Herbert Mead.

[92]Marx, "Excerpts from James Mill's Elements of Political Science," in Early Writings, trans. Rodney Livingstone and Gregor Benton (New York: Random House, 1975), pp. 277–278.

[93]Engels, The Condition of The Working Class in England, p. 117. Quoting Thomas Carlyle, Chartism (London, 1840).

The dialogic model is the appropriate metaphor to symbolize a classless humanism, but it is the sheerest fantasy if meant to portray a class-rent society. There is no escape from a world of strife, Marx contended, except by the abolition of classes through the common ownership of the means of production. Class struggle alone can end class struggle itself.[94] This is Marx's picture of the real world.

The influence of the dialectical model, in both its bellicose and dialogic versions, accounts in part for Marx's emphasis on process and social interaction. In this respect he is linked with social interactionist theorists, such as Albion W. Small, Charles H. Cooley, and George Herbert Mead in the older generation, and with Walter Buckley and Herbert Blumer in the younger generation.[95] He avoids the overemphasis upon organic unity or homeostasis that characterizes organicists of a conservative or reactionary bent, and he is aware of the points of disanalogy between a society and a biological organism.[96] For example, he is quite free from the literalism with which Oswald Spengler depicts the birth, infancy, youth, maturity, decay, and death of cultures.[97]

---

[94]For a keen analysis of Marx's theory of class and class conflict see Ralph Milliband, *Marxism and Politics* (Oxford University Press, 1977), Chapter II.

[95]See especially Walter Buckley, *Sociology and Modern Systems Theory* (Englewood Cliffs, N.J.: Prentice-Hall, 1967), and Herbert Blumer, *Symbolic Interactionism* (Englewood Cliffs, N.J.: Prentice-Hall, 1969).

[96]For a summary of the main points of disanalogy see Piotr Sztompka, *System and Function: Toward a Theory of Society* (New York: Academic Press, 1974), pp. 48–52. The extravagances of the organic approach can be easily dismissed. What remains in Marx and is not easily dismissed is the holistic versus the atomistic approach. Social theorists are now more wary of using terms such as "social organism" (a term that Marx himself uses only rarely), but as prevalent as ever are holistic interpretations under such rubrics as "functionalism," "system theory," "structuralism," "totality," and "methodological holism." See Bertell Ollman, "Marxism and Political Science: Prolegomenon to a Debate on Marx's Method," with comment by Isaac D. Balbus and Joseph O'Malley in *Politics and Society* (Summer 1973).

[97]For a criticism of Spengler's organicism see Melvin Rader, *No Compromise* (New York: The Macmillan Company, 1939), Chapter IX.

11. A Backward Glance

Marx's interpretation of history is a synthesis of diverse currents of thought. The "expressivist tradition" of Hegelian idealism, with which he began his intellectual career, impressed on his mind the concept of a dynamic totality in which the elements are organically linked. In 1843–1844 he also was strongly influenced by the "materialism" of Feuerbach and the radicals he met in Paris. Under this influence he repudiated Hegel's idealistic metaphysics and embraced naturalistic humanism. He then turned to a study of the "material foundation" of society. From the classics of economic theory—especially the works of Adam Smith and David Ricardo—he derived the idea of a largely autonomous and self-regulating economy that conditions all the other strata of society.

Rejecting some ideas and incorporating others, he drew from these sources the principal ingredients of his unique vision of history. The varied nature of the sources is reflected in the apparent incongruity between his two models of historical explanation—organic totality and base-superstructure. That he adhered to both models is evident from many passages. Nevertheless "orthodox Marxism" has stressed the base-superstructure model to the nearly total exclusion of the organic model, thus doing Marx a great disservice.

He must have sensed that there was danger in focussing on either model to the exclusion of the other. If he were to press the organic model too exclusively, the mode of production would lose its determining role and become virtually indistinguishable from the organic totality. On the other hand, if he were to press the base-superstructure model too far, his holistic orientation would be undermined by a kind of economic determinism. Either alternative would rob his interpretation of much of its richness. The tension in his mind caused by these opposite pulls may account for the equivocation in a number of summary passages including the Preface to *The Critique of Political*

Economy. Marx never managed to state his dilemma in unambiguous language, or to indicate just how the two models could be combined. Interpreted as rival descriptions they are irreconcilable, but interpreted as heuristic tools they can be harmonized.

I have maintained that there is no necessary conflict if we think of them as models rather than as descriptions or social entities. They can be reconciled on the basis of an analogy with a complex organism. Just as there are hierarchical relations in the human mind-body, so there are relations of dominance and subordination in the "social organism." The mode of production is the more efficacious, but all the other structural elements are involved in the "organic" play of forces. The simplistic concept of linear causality is replaced by the idea of dialectical interaction and interdependence within a comprehensive field.[98] This solution accounts for both the holistic character of Marx's thought and the strong emphasis on the mode of production.

The great advantage of this reconciliation is that it enriches our understanding. No longer is it necessary to emasculate Marx's complex vision of modern society as an organic totality. The conflicts within the mode of production are now seen as inseparable from the "inner dialectic" of need, alienation, and "abstract" existence. The combination of the inner and outer dialectic avoids both a methodogical individualism that recognizes only the motivations and activities of individuals, and a methodological gestaltism that

[98]The reader may wish to compare my interpretation of Marx's conception of history with that of William H. Shaw, *Marx's Theory of History* (Stanford University Press, 1978). Focussing on the causal connections between the forces and relations of production, his interpretation is narrower and more reductionist. He confines himself almost entirely to "a technological-determinist reading of Marx." Even though he recognizes that Marx had "a very 'organic' conception of society," he restricts himself to an "infrastructural analysis of historical change." His analysis thus contrasts with my more "organic" and humanist interpretation. He admits that "Marx's complexity and occasional inconsistency" bar him from "having proved" his analysis. Although I am aware of the complexity and inconsistency, I have assembled a good deal of evidence in support of my reading of Marx.

recognizes only structural and collective transformations. Neither the synchronic dimension (structure) nor the dia-chronic dimension (process) is slighted. Given this more balanced and inclusive point of view, the whole theory of history takes on added dimensions. The critic can under-take his or her task without the unnecessary burden of either an incoherent or an over-simplified interpretation. But that task lies beyond the present book.

Index

235